PETER THE GREAT'S DISASTROUS DEFEAT

The Swedish Victory at Narva, 1700

Michael Fredholm von Essen

'This is the Century of the Soldier', Fulvio Testi, Poet, 1641

Helion & Company Limited
Unit 8 Amherst Business Centre
Budbrooke Road
Warwick
CV34 5WE
England
Tel. 01926 499 619
Email: info@helion.co.uk
Website: www.helion.co.uk
Twitter: @helionbooks
Visit our blog http://blog.helion.co.uk/

Published by Helion & Company 2024
Designed and typeset by Mary Woolley, Battlefield Design (www.battlefield-design.co.uk)
Cover designed by Paul Hewitt, Battlefield Design (www.battlefield-design.co.uk)

Text © Michael Fredholm von Essen 2024
Illustrations © as individually credited
Colour artwork by Sergey Shamenkov © Helion and Company 2024
Maps by Anderson Subtil © Helion & Company 2024
Illustrations attributed to Army Museum, Stockholm, are reproduced under the Creative Commons licence and derive from the website https://digitaltmuseum.se, with special thanks to Martin Markelius, curator at the museum, and Rauno Vaara, archivist.
    Illustrations attributed to Royal Armoury, Stockholm, are reproduced under the Creative Commons licence and derive from the website http://emuseumplus.lsh.se.
    Illustrations attributed to History Museum, Stockholm, or Economy Museum – Royal Coin Cabinet/SHM, Stockholm, are reproduced under the Creative Commons licence and derive from the website https://samlingar.shm.se.
    Other illustrations are reproduced under GNU Free Documentation Licence (GNU FDL) coupled with the Creative Commons Attribution Share-Alike Licence, or derive from the author's personal collection.
    Photographs attributed to Medström are reproduced with the permission of this publisher.

Every reasonable effort has been made to trace copyright holders and to obtain their permission for the use of copyright material. The author and publisher apologize for any errors or omissions in this work and would be grateful if notified of any corrections that should be incorporated in future reprints or editions of this book.

ISBN 978-1-804514-43-6

British Library Cataloguing-in-Publication Data.
A catalogue record for this book is available from the British Library.

All rights reserved. No part of this publication may be reproduced, stored in a retrieval system, or transmitted, in any form, or by any means, electronic, mechanical, photocopying, recording or otherwise, without the express written consent of Helion & Company Limited.

For details of other military history titles published by Helion & Company Limited contact the above address or visit our website: http://www.helion.co.uk.

We always welcome receiving book proposals from prospective authors.

Contents

Chronology		iv
Dramatis Personae		ix
Introduction		xvii
Prologue: Monarchs and Generals		xix
1	The Great Northern War	29
2	The Swedish Military Establishment	33
3	The Russian Military Establishment	51
4	Narva and Ivangorod	68
5	Tsar Peter Lays Siege to Narva	73
6	King Charles Sails to the Eastern Front	83
7	Tsar Peter Loses Confidence	87
8	The Night Before Battle	90
9	The Russian Order of Battle	94
10	The Swedish Order of Battle	99
11	The Assault	109
12	Battle Between the Lines	115
13	The Russians Regroup	125
14	Dead and Wounded	132
15	Aftermath	139
Colour Plate Commentaries		146
Further Reading		156
Select Bibliography		161

Chronology

All dates are New Style (N.S.)

1699

25 September	Treaty of Dresden between King Frederick IV of Denmark and Norway and King Augustus II of Saxony and the Polish-Lithuanian Commonwealth against Sweden
21 November	Treaty of Preobrazhenskoye between King Augustus II of Saxony and the Polish-Lithuanian Commonwealth and Tsar Peter I of Russia against Sweden
27 November	Tsar Peter issues a decree about the formation of a new, modern army to be used in the planned war against Sweden

1700

21 February	Swedish garrison in Riga, Swedish Livonia, exposes and detains an undercover Saxon assault unit sent in with orders to carry out a coup in support of the forthcoming invasion
22 February	Saxon and Polish-Lithuanian Commonwealth Army invades Swedish Livonia without declaration of war, lays siege to Riga
16 March	King Charles, in Kungsör in central Sweden for bear hunting, learns of the attack on Riga
21 March	Danish Army marches into the Duchy of Holstein-Gottorp, Sweden's ally, without declaration of war, occupies major parts of the Duchy
22 March	Danish Army lays siege to Tønning, the main fortress in Holstein-Gottorp
30 March	King Charles, in Stockholm, learns of the Danish attack on Holstein-Gottorp
24 April	King Charles leaves Stockholm to join the mobilised field army

CHRONOLOGY

17 May	Swedish army under General Otto Vellingk and Major General Georg Johan Maydell relieves besieged Riga, defeats Saxon and Commonwealth invaders at the Battle of Jungfernhof, and pushes them back towards Commonwealth territory
2 June	Tønning rescued by a Swedish relief army under General Nils Gyllenstierna
14 July	Treaty of Constantinople concludes the war between the Ottoman Empire and Russia
15 July	Saxon and Polish-Lithuanian Commonwealth Army under King Augustus again lays siege to Riga
4 August	King Charles lands the vanguard of the Swedish Army at Humlebæk on the main Danish island of Zealand
18 August	Treaty of Traventhal signifies Denmark-Norway's withdrawal from the war
22 August	Colonel Henning Rudolph Horn, Commandant of Narva, learns that Russia has closed the border with Sweden
26 August	Horn sends an envoy, Ensign Simon Daniel Barohn, to Novgorod to enquire about Russia's intentions; upon arrival, Barohn is detained
29 August	In Moscow, Tsar Peter learns of the conclusion of the Treaty of Constantinople
30 August	Tsar Peter issues a manifesto in which he declares war on Sweden
2 September	Moscow Army deploys to Novgorod; Tsar Peter orders the Governor of Pskov, Vasiliy Lodygin, to have the Pskov siege artillery park assembled at Narva on 26 September
10 September	Delegation of Saxon military officers under the former Imperial Field Marshal Charles Eugène, Duke de Croÿ, meets with Tsar Peter in Novgorod, with orders to act as his military advisers; Tsar Peter takes personal command of the Moscow Army in Novgorod
12 September	Prince Ivan Trubetskoy, Governor of Novgorod, marches out with the Novgorod Army; Russian vanguard invades Swedish Ingria
13 September	First Russian units approach Narva, Swedish Estonia
18 September	King Augustus abandons the second siege of Riga
20 September	Prince Trubetskoy lays siege to Narva
28 September	Prince Trubetskoy writes to Colonel Horn, Commandant of Narva, in an attempt to persuade him to surrender

2 October	King Charles, in southern Sweden, learns of the Russian declaration of war and the arrival of a Russian Army at Narva; Lieutenant General Ludwig Nicolaus von Hallart, a Saxon officer, arrives at Narva to assume command of the Russian siegeworks
3 October	Hallart inspects the Russian countervallation line
4 October	Tsar Peter arrives at Narva accompanied by units of the Moscow Army and the Duke de Croÿ, crossing the temporary bridge at Vepsekylla built for this purpose
7 October	Hallart completes a plan for the siege, as requested by the Tsar on the previous day
8 October	Russians at Narva commence the construction of a circumvallation line
9 October	Tsar Peter orders additions to the circumvallation line on the northern flank, and inspects the entire line together with the Duke de Croÿ and Hallart; a Saxon undercover agent, Cavalry Captain Rudolph Felix Bauer, slips out of Narva to report to the Russians
11 October	King Charles and his headquarters, including Chief of Artillery Johan Siöblad, sail from Karlshamn in Southern Sweden
12 October	Russians dismantle the temporary bridge at Vepsekylla and move it to Kamperholm Island to connect Tsar Peter's headquarters with the siegeworks; General Adam Weide brings further Russian reinforcements; in the evening, Colonel Horn, the commandant of Narva, sallies out in force with horse and foot
13 October	First contingent of Russian siege artillery reaches Narva
15 October	Hallart deploys the first battery of siege artillery against Narva
16 October	King Charles arrives in Pernau, Western Estonia, with the vanguard of the Swedish Army; Hallart deploys a first battery of siege artillery against Ivangorod; Tsar Peter has letters sent into Narva, advising the burghers to desert or betray Horn
18 October	Battery of long-barrelled cannons deployed against Ivangorod
22 October	Baron Johann Ernst von Langen, King Augustus's envoy, arrives in the Russian camp at Narva
24 October	General Avtonom Golovin's reinforcements and General Boris Sheremetyev's cavalry contingent arrive at Narva

CHRONOLOGY

30 October	All Russian siege artillery in position, in 10 batteries facing Narva and Ivangorod; during the night of 30/31 October they begin the bombardment of both places
4 November	King Charles reaches Reval, while the army marches towards the assembly point in Wesenberg; Tsar Peter sends the Saxon agent Bauer back to King Augustus; the Russians at Narva catch a 'spy' with an enciphered letter (probably a courier trying to get through the lines)
5 November	Vellingk and his men reach Wesenberg; Sheremetyev and his cavalry set out towards Wesenberg to provide advance warning of the approaching Swedish Army
6 November	Wolmar Anton von Schlippenbach captures Russian transports on Lake Peipus (Battle of Ismen)
7 November	Temporary bridge to Kamperholm Island crushed by the thickening ice cover, Russians salvage and return it to original position at Vepsekylla; new temporary bridge built to Kamperholm Island; Battle of Varja between approaching Swedish Army and Sheremetyev
11 November	Swedes captured by Sheremetyev arrive at the Russian camp at Narva
17 November	Running out of munitions, Russians must resort to firing stone shot from their siege artillery; remaining munitions concentrated on Ivangorod
18–19 November	Russians attempt to storm Ivangorod in a night assault, but fail; on 19 November, the Swedes sally out and drive the intruders from their toehold; in response, Hallart orders artillery fire to be directed at the bridge linking Narva and Ivangorod
21 November	Captain Johan Hummert 'defects' from the Russian camp to Narva
22 November	Hummert's absence noted in the Russian camp; King Charles orders Governor General Erik Dahlbergh to gather supplies for a campaign against King Augustus after Tsar Peter has been defeated
23 November	King Charles marches out from Wesenberg; Vellingk's army reaches Haakhof; Sheremetyev withdraws to Pühajõgi Pass; Tsar Peter, fearful of defectors, orders all his officers and under-officers of Swedish origin to be sent to Moscow for service there
24 November	Horn sallies out from Ivangorod, inflicting significant casualties on the Russians and damaging their siegeworks

27 November	Confrontation at Pühajõgi Pass between Sheremetyev's cavalry and the vanguard of the approaching Swedish army under Major General Maydell; during the night to 28 November, Sheremetyev withdraws
28 November	Sheremetyev's intelligence of the approaching Swedish army reaches the Russians at Narva; alarmed, Tsar Peter begins to persuade the reluctant Saxon officer, Charles Eugène Duke de Croÿ, to assume command of his army; King Charles's army reaches Sillamäe
29 November	Early in the morning, Tsar Peter hands over the army to Croÿ and departs; soon afterwards, Sheremetyev and his cavalry reach Narva; in the evening, King Charles and the Swedish army arrives at Lagena, 14km from Narva
30 November	Battle of Narva
1 December	Surrendered Russian Army departs from Estonia; Saxon prisoners of war brought into Narva
2 December	King Charles rides into Narva; Russian prisoners of war brought into Narva

Dramatis Personae

Sweden

Charles XII (1682–1718; r. 1697–1718), King of Sweden.

Appelman, Gustav Gabriel (1656–1721), Major. Experienced artilleryman who had risen through the ranks during the Scanian War and the Nine Years' War, in which he served the Grand Alliance. During 1696–1697, he trained the soon-to-be King Charles in artillery science.

Barohn, Simon Daniel (1672–1732), Ensign. Ingrian officer in the Narva garrison, sent as envoy to Novgorod.

Dahlbergh, Erik Jönsson (1625–1703), Field Marshal. Military engineer, fortification specialist, intelligence officer, quartermaster, cartographer, and accomplished artist with years of experience from every conflict involving Swedish involvement since the Thirty Years' War. Governor General of Livonia.

De la Gardie, Axel Julius (1637–1710), Governor General of Estonia. The youngest son of Field Marshal Jacob de la Gardie who led Sweden's wars in Russia from 1609 onwards, Axel Julius was primarily an administrator although he had fought in the wars under King Charles X in the 1650s.

Cederhielm, Josias (1673–1729). Secretary of the field chancellery, who in the Battle of Narva served as the aide of Colonel Magnus Stenbock.

Cronstedt, Carl (1672–1750), Senior Artilleryman and Artillery Adjutant.

Dücker, Carl Gustav (1663–1732), Adjutant General of the Drabant Corps. Veteran officer from Livonia who had participated in several campaigns in French service between 1690 and 1697.

Ehrenschantz, Gerdt Ernst (1663–1703), Lieutenant Colonel. Quartermaster General Lieutenant and experienced fortification and intelligence officer.

Funcken (or **Funck**), **Carl Philip von** (d.1704), Major. Veteran of campaigns in Hungary in 1685 and Brabant in 1696

Granatenhielm, Magnus (1644–1714), Lieutenant Colonel. Acting head of the Field Artillery Regiment. Rose through the ranks during the wars in the Polish-Lithuanian Commonwealth and Denmark in the 1650s and the Scanian War.

Grundel, Jacob Jacobsson (1657–1737), Lieutenant Colonel. Veteran of the Scanian War and the Nine Years' War who served as battalion commander of the Dalecarlia Regiment. Half-brother of the late Field Marshal Simon Grundel Helmfelt, who was born 50 years earlier and fell in the Scanian War.

Günthersberch, Per von (d. 1701), Trooper (that is, a Captain) of the Drabant Corps. Veteran of the Nine Years' War.

Gyllenstierna, Nils (1648–1720), General of Cavalry. Veteran of Dutch service and the Scanian War who rose through the ranks, until he was appointed overall commander of the Swedish army in Germany.

Hård, Axel Christopher, af Segerstad (d. 1704), Lieutenant (that is a Colonel) of the Drabant Corps, as well as the King's Chamberlain and equerry.

Horn, Arvid Bernhard, af Ekebyholm (1664–1742), Captain Lieutenant (that is, Major General) of the Drabant Corps. Veteran of Imperial service, in which he fought the Ottomans at Mohács in 1687, and Dutch service in the Nine Years' War.

Horn, Henning Rudolph (1651–1730), Colonel. Commandant of Narva. Veteran of the Scanian War who rose from the ranks, beginning in the artillery followed by service as a pikeman.

Lantingshausen, Gotthard Henrik von (1667–1704), Adjutant General of the Drabant Corps.

Leijonhufvud, Knut (1674–1700), Aide of the Drabant Corps, appointed Adjutant General during the battle, in which he fell.

Maydell, Georg Johan (1648–1710), also known as Maidel or Maijdell, Major General of Infantry. An Estonian veteran of, among others, the Scanian War who rose through the ranks.

Numers, Carl von (d. 1701), Major. Veteran of the Nine Years' War.

Örnestedt, Carl Gustav (1669–1742), Captain of the Life Dragoon Regiment. Veteran of the Nine Years' War.

Patkul, Georg Reinhold (1657–1723), Major. Veteran of service in the Imperial Army in the wars against the Ottoman Empire.

Piper, Carl (1647–1716), head of the field chancellery and Sweden's de facto prime minister. Although a civilian, he volunteered to participate in the battle as the commander of a cavalry squadron.

Posse, Carl Magnus Mauritzson, af Säby (d. 1715), Captain. Battalion commander of the Life Guard of Foot. Veteran of French service in the Nine Years' War. At times known under the nickname 'The Unmild' (Swedish: *Hin omilde*).

Posse, Knut Göransson (1640s–1714), Major General. Commander of the Life Guard of Foot.

DRAMATIS PERSONAE

Rehbinder, Bernhard (1639–1705), Colonel of the Åbo and Björneborg County Cavalry Regiment. Soldier who rose through the ranks.

Rehbinder, Carl Magnus (d. 1709), Colonel of the Åbo, Nyland, and Viborg County Temporary Cavalry Regiment. Younger brother of Bernhard and Hans Henrik Rehbinder.

Rehbinder, Hans Henrik (1645–1700), Colonel of the Karelian (Viborg and Nyslott County) Cavalry Regiment. Veteran of the Scanian War, in which he lost a leg. Younger brother of Bernhard Rehbinder.

Rehnskiöld, Carl Gustav (1651–1722), Lieutenant General of Cavalry.

Rehnskiöld, Frans Anton (1676–1702), Lieutenant. Nephew of Carl Gustav Rehnskiöld

Ribbing, Johan (1642–1700), Major General.

Schlippenbach, Wolmar Anton von (1653–1721), Colonel. Veteran of the Scanian War.

Siöblad, Johan (1644–1710), Chief of Artillery (*generalfälttygmästare*) since 1693 who had risen through the ranks. Veteran of the Scanian War during which he participated in operations in Germany. Appointed Chief of Artillery in 1693, succeeding Erik Dahlbergh.

Sparre, Axel Axelsson, af Sundby (1652–1728), Colonel. Veteran of Dutch service and the Scanian War and commander of the Västmanland Regiment, who because of logistical problems did not reach Narva in time to participate in the battle.

Sparre, Carl Eriksson (1651–1700), Captain. Commander of a battalion of the Life Guard of Foot.

Stackelberg, Berndt Otto (1662–1734), Adjutant General of the Drabant Corps. Veteran officer from Estonia who had served in both the Dutch and French armies.

Staël von Holstein, Johan (1636–1703), Lieutenant Colonel. Commander of the artillery in Narva and Ingria.

Stenbock, Magnus (1665–1717), Colonel of the Dalecarlia Regiment. Veteran of the Nine Years' War, during which he fought in the Battles of Fleurus in 1690 and of Steenkerque in 1692, and of Imperial service in 1693–1696, primarily on the western front but also in Hungary, during which he was promoted to colonel.

Stiernhöök, Olof (d. 1703), Captain of the Life Guard of Foot.

Stuart, Carl Magnus (c. 1650–1705), Major General of Infantry. Erik Dahlbergh's disciple and successor as fortification officer and Quartermaster General.

Tiesenhausen, Hans Heinrich von (1654–1724), Colonel of the Estonian Cavalry Regiment.

Tiesenhausen, Magnus Gabriel von (*c.* 1660–1704), Colonel of the Åbo, Björneborg, and Nyland County Temporary Regiment. Veteran of the Nine Years' War. Distant relative of Hans Heinrich von Tiesenhausen.

Vellingk, Otto (1649–1708), General. Veteran of the Scanian War and French service.

Wachtmeister, Bleichard (Bleckert), af Björkö (1644–1701), Lieutenant General of Cavalry. Veteran of French service.

Wrangel, Fabian Reinhold, af Adinal (1673–1700), Corporal (that is, Major) of the Drabant Corps.

Wrangel, Carl Gustav, af Adinal (1667–1707), Lieutenant (that is a Colonel) of the Drabant Corps. Veteran of French service in the Nine Years' War. Cousin of Fabian Reinhold Wrangel.

Russia

Peter I (1672–1725; r. 1682–1725), Tsar of Russia.

Alexander of Imeretia (1674–1711), Prince and General of Artillery (*General-Feldzeugmeister*). A son of ex-King Archil of Imeretia, he grew up in exile in Moscow with Tsar Peter, studied artillery science in the Netherlands, and was appointed head of the Russian artillery. Although trained, Prince Alexander lacked combat experience.

Angler, Ivan (John or **Johann) Ivanovich** (fl. 1700–1704), Colonel. Officer of unknown origin born or naturalised in Russia.

Bakhmetyev, Stepan Petrovich (fl. 1686–1708), courtier. Commander of the Novgorod Division of old style cavalry.

Balck, Fyodor (Friedrich) Nikolayevich (1670–1738), Colonel. Born in Russia to Friedrich von Balcken, a Livonian noble in Russian service.

Balck, Nikolay Nikolayevich (fl. 1699–1704), Colonel. Born in Russia. Possibly the younger brother of Fyodor Balck.

Baturin, Venedikt Mironovich (fl. 1698–1706), Colonel.

Bauer, Rudolph Felix (1667–1717), Cavalry Captain. Undercover agent despatched by King Augustus to gather intelligence for Tsar Peter. Originally from Holstein, he left service in a Swedish dragoon regiment in Livonia to go into Saxon service for undercover work.

Bayishev, Miron Grigor'yevich (fl. 1692–1704), Colonel. Commander of a streltsy regiment from Novgorod.

Bayishev, Fyodor Mironovich (fl. 1700–1704), Lieutenant Colonel. Son of Miron Bayishev.

Berner, Ivan (Johann) Pavlovich (fl. 1699–1709), Colonel. Officer of unknown origin, born or naturalised in Russia.

DRAMATIS PERSONAE

Berner, Pavel (Paul) Pavlovich (d. 1704), Colonel. Possibly a brother of Ivan Berner.

Bieltz, Il'ya (Johann) Yakovlevich (d. 1708), Colonel. Officer of unknown origin, born or naturalised in Russia.

Blomberg, Johann Ernst von (fl. 1697–1700), Colonel. Commander of the Preobrazhenskiy Guard Regiment. Known to speak in Dutch, so possibly of Dutch origin.

Bruce, Roman (Robert) Vilimovich (1668–1720), Major General. Regimental commander from Novgorod. Born in Russia to Major General William Bruce, a Scot.

Bukovin, Pyotr Kornilovich von (fl. 1700–1707), Colonel. Born in Russia to the Dutch officer Cornelius van Bokhoven.

Busch (later **Bushev**), **Johann (Ivan Alfer'yevich)** (fl. 1700–1715), Colonel. Officer of unknown origin naturalised or possibly born in Russia. His son, Yuriy Ivanovich Busch, served as colonel in at least 1702–1704.

Buturlin, Ivan Ivanovich (1661–1739), Major General. A son of a senior noble, he served Tsar Peter when young and played a role in what would become the Preobrazhenskiy Regiment.

Colomb (possibly **Coulomb** or **Colombe**; Russian: **Kulom**), **Ivan (Jacques)** (d. 1700), Colonel. Regimental commander from Novgorod of unknown origin, naturalised or possibly born in Russia.

Croÿ, Charles Eugène de (1651–1702), Field Marshal.

Cunningham, Pavel (Paul) Vasil'yevich (d. 1700), Lieutenant Colonel. Commander of the Semyonovskiy Guard Regiment. Officer born or naturalised in Russia.

Dedyut, Aleksey Mikhaylovich (fl. 1700–1704), Colonel. Officer of unknown origin, born or naturalised in Russia. Surname also given as **Deidyut** and occasionally interpreted as **De Duit** or possibly even derived from the religious term Eidut.

Del'den, Ivan (Johann) Vilimovich von (fl. 1699–1704), Colonel. Born in Russia to a Dutchman in Russian service.

Del'den, Vilim (Wilhelm) Vilimovich von (1662–1735), Colonel. Brother of Ivan von Del'den.

Devson, Carl Peter Andreyevich (d. 1700), Colonel. Officer of unknown origin, born or naturalised in Russia. Surname also given as Devsen or Deveson.

Fliwerk, Matvey Ivanovich (d. 1700), Colonel. Officer of unknown origin, born or naturalised in Russia.

Dolgorukov, Yakov Fyodorovich (1639–1720), Prince. Appointed to the newly-established position of Commissary General in 1700, which made him head of what effectively was a new ministry of defence. Veteran diplomat and soldier, widely known for honesty and integrity.

Golovin, Avtonom Mikhaylovich (1667–1720), General of Infantry. Early member of the Preobrazhenskiy Regiment and friend of Tsar Peter. Veteran of the first and second Azov campaigns of 1695 and 1696.

Golovin, Fyodor Alekseyevich (1650–1706), Field Marshal General and Admiral General. Cousin of Avtonom Golovin. Diplomat and confidant of Tsar Peter who among other accomplishments concluded the 1689 Treaty of Nerchinsk with the powerful Manchu Empire, according to which Russia abandoned its claim to the lands north of the Amur River. He also played a prominent role in the creation of the Russian Navy. Promoted straight to Field Marshal General immediately before the campaign, he had little military experience.

Gordon, Alexander, of Achintoul (1670–1752), Colonel. Veteran of French service who went into Russian service in 1696. He participated in the second Azov campaign of 1696, in 1697 promoted to colonel. In 1698 he married a daughter of Patrick Gordon.

Gordon, Jacob (James) or **Yakov Petrovich** (1668–1722), Colonel. Son of Patrick Gordon born in Russia, who in his father's footsteps served as colonel of the Butyrsk Regiment.

Gordon, Patrick Leopold, of Achleuchries (1635–1699), General and Rear Admiral. Veteran of Swedish and Commonwealth service who went into Russian service in 1661. Among other duties, he commanded the Butyrsk Regiment and later trained the Preobrazhenskiy Regiment. A good friend of Tsar Peter and instrumental in securing his path to power. He also took part in the First Azov campaign of 1695.

Gulitz (Goltz), Joachim or **Yefim Andreyevich** (fl. 1650s–1709), Colonel. Officer of German origin born or naturalised in Russia. Possibly a son of Major General Andrey Andreyevich Gulitz who went to Russia in 1652–1653.

Gulitz (Goltz), Caspar Andreyevich (fl. 1700–1704), Colonel. Officer of German origin born or naturalised in Russia. Possibly a son of the aforementioned Major General Andrey Andreyevich Gulitz.

Hallart, Ludwig Nicolaus von (1659–1727), Lieutenant General. An engineering officer from Schleswig-Holstein of remote Scottish ancestry. When in Saxon service (as Inspector-General of Fortresses), sent by King Augustus to Tsar Peter as technical adviser. A veteran of Imperial service of the wars against France, in the Nine Years' War, and the Ottoman Empire.

Hummert, Johan (d. 1703), Captain. Overambitious spy of undecided loyalty.

Ivanitskiy (or Evanitskiy), Carl Gustav Ivanovich (fl. 1700), Colonel. Officer of unknown origin, born or naturalised in Russia.

Junger, Tomas Bal'tserovich or **Balsirovich** (d. 1700), Colonel. Officer of unknown origin born or naturalised in Russia.

DRAMATIS PERSONAE

Khilkov, Andrey Yakovlevich (1676–1716), Prince. Diplomat and Resident in Stockholm. Sent by Tsar Peter in early 1700 to convince King Charles that the Tsar had only peaceful intentions towards Sweden.

Kokoshkin, Ivan Mikhaylovich (1655–1714), Colonel. Commander of the Novgorod new style Cavalry Regiment.

Korsak, Bogdan Semyonovich (1640–1721), Major General. Commander of the Smolensk Division of old style cavalry.

Kozodavlev, Vasiliy Vasil'yevich (fl. 1700–1712), Colonel. Commander of a streltsy regiment from Pskov.

Krage, Casimir von (d. 1700), Colonel.

Krogh, Zakhariy Yelizarovich (fl. 1698–1702), Colonel. Officer of unknown origin, born or naturalised in Russia.

Langen, Johann Ernst von (fl. 1700), Major General and Baron. King Augustus's envoy to Tsar Peter.

Lefort (or **Le Fort**), **François Jacques** (1656–1699), General and Admiral. Professional soldier of French Huguenot origin from Geneva who after Dutch service went to Russia in 1675 and after numerous complications joined the Russian Army in 1678. A good friend of Tsar Peter who, together with Patrick Gordon (to whom Lefort was related by marriage), was instrumental in securing his path to power. He also took part in the Tsar's Grand Embassy and the first Azov campaign of 1695.

Lefort (or **Le Fort**), **Pierre** (**Peter**; 1676–1754), Colonel. Nephew of François Lefort. Accompanied his uncle during the first Azov campaign, served as Tsar Peter's secretary during the Grand Embassy, and then went into military service as regimental commander.

Lima, Giorgio or **Yuriy Stepanovich** (d. 1702), Lieutenant Colonel of the First Selected Moscow Regiment, also known as Weide's Regiment (formerly Lefort's Regiment). Naturalised Russian naval officer of Venetian origin, who in 1695 acquired the rank of vice admiral in the newly-established Russian Navy. Lima participated in the second Azov campaign, commanded a galley, but then transferred into the army.

Lodygin, Vasiliy Pavlovich (d. 1700). Governor of Pskov.

Mewes, Ivan (John?) Ivanovich (fl. 1700–1706), Colonel. Officer of unknown origin, born or naturalised in Russia.

Obidovskiy, Ivan Pavlovich (1676–1701), Hetman of Ukrainian Cossacks. Nephew and intended heir of Hetman Ivan Mazepa, and veteran of the first and second Azov campaigns of 1695 and 1696.

Pohlmann, Astafiy Martynovich, surname occasionally given as **Bohlmann** (d. 1700), Colonel. Officer of unknown origin, likely born in Russia. Astafiy is the Russian form of Eustathius which also can be rendered Yevstafiy.

Repnin, Anikita Ivanovich (1668–1726), Prince and General of Infantry. Early member of the Preobrazhenskiy Regiment and friend of Tsar Peter.

Veteran of the first and second Azov campaigns of 1695 and 1696. Did not arrive in time to participate in the Battle of Narva.

Schnewentz, Alferiy Alfer'yevich (fl. 1699–1700), Colonel.

Schweiden, Wilhelm (Vilim Ivanovich) von, also known as **Wilhelm von Schweden** and **Wilhelm von Schwenden**. (d. 1708), Colonel. Little is known about this officer, who was either born, or more likely naturalised in Russia.

Sheremetyev, Boris Petrovich (1652–1719), General of Cavalry. Diplomat and soldier, and veteran of several wars against the Ottoman Empire and Crimean Tatars including the first and second Azov campaigns of 1695 and 1696. Beloved by his soldiers, who wrote songs about him, Sheremetyev wore Western European dress since his return from Western Europe in 1699.

Strekalov, Stepan Matveyevich (fl. 1689–1704), Colonel.

Sukharev, Martem'yan Fyodorovich (d. 1700), Colonel.

Treyden, Ivan (Johann) Ivanovich (fl. 1700), Colonel. Officer of German origin naturalised or born in Russia, possibly related to the noble family Trotta genannt Treyden in Courland.

Treyden, Matvey (Matthias) Ivanovich (fl. 1700), Colonel. Possibly a younger brother of Ivan Treyden.

Trubetskoy, Ivan Yur'yevich (1667–1750), Prince. Major General and Governor of Novgorod. Early member of the Preobrazhenskiy Regiment and friend of Tsar Peter. Veteran of the first and second Azov campaigns of 1695 and 1696.

Vestov, Yuriy Yur'yevich (d. 1704), Colonel. Commander of a streltsy regiment from Pskov.

Vestov, Zakhariy Mikhaylovich (fl. 1696–1700), Colonel. Commander of a streltsy regiment from Novgorod.

Weide, Adam Adamovich (1667–1720), General of Infantry. Soldier and sometime naval officer born in Russia to a foreign officer in Russian service. Early member of the Preobrazhenskiy Regiment and friend of Tsar Peter. Veteran of the first and second Azov campaigns of 1695 and 1696. Author of Russia's 1698 military regulations (*Voinskiy ustav*).

Werden, Erich (Irik Grigor'yevich) von (fl. 1695–1700), Colonel. Naturalised Russian officer from Lübeck.

Werden, Nicolaus (Nikolay Grigor'yevich) von (d. 1712), Colonel. Brother of Erich von Werden.

Yelchaninov, Vasiliy Semyonovich (d. 1700), Colonel. Commander of a former Moscow streltsy regiment exiled to Belgorod.

Introduction

This study describes the Battle of Narva of 30 November 1700, in which King Charles XII of Sweden inflicted a decisive defeat on Tsar Peter the Great's significantly larger Russian Army. It was one of the greatest battles that took place during the Great Northern War of 1700–1721.

Swedish military might and regional power expanded immensely during the seventeenth century. A series of successful conquests transformed the little northern Kingdom of Sweden into a regional great power centred on the Baltic Sea. At the end of the century the accession to the Swedish throne of Charles XII, a mere youngster without any known military experience, convinced the neighbouring monarchs that it was finally payback time. In 1699, King Frederick IV of Denmark and Norway, King Augustus II of Saxony and the Polish-Lithuanian Commonwealth, and Tsar Peter I of Russia formed a triple alliance against Sweden. The three monarchs wanted to reconquer lands lost to Sweden during its expansion into a great power. King Frederick wished to regain the lost Scanian provinces and Holstein-Gottorp. King Augustus coveted Swedish Livonia, while Tsar Peter desired the ports on the Eastern Baltic shore. When the triple alliance went to war against Sweden, Tsar Peter invaded Swedish Ingria and Estonia on the Gulf of Finland. A large Russian Army laid siege to the important port of Narva, in modern-day Estonia.

King Charles responded much faster than the allies expected. First he led an army into Denmark where he forced King Frederick to withdraw from the war. Then, King Charles turned his attention to the eastern front and Russia. After a long and arduous march, the Swedish Army arrived on the outskirts of Narva in late November. The Swedish King ordered his men to immediately attack the fortified Russian lines. With the help of a blizzard and with the wind at their back, the Swedes assaulted and broke through the Russian defences. The Russians fled in panic, and ultimately surrendered to the Swedes. It was a crushing defeat. Tsar Peter lost the entire army, including most of his senior commanders who fell into Swedish captivity. The battle had the immediate effect of Russia evacuating all regular units from Estonia and Ingria.

The Battle of Narva was the first major battle of the Great Northern War, but it can also be described as the last great battle of the seventeenth century. Although both Swedes and Russians had adopted a number of new organisational structures, types of armament, and uniforms, both armies still looked quite similar to, and mostly fought the same as, their seventeenth century counterparts. Neither side had fully adopted the military uniform styles that henceforward would characterise the Swedish and Russian armies. Only a few men had been issued bayonets to go with their new flintlock muskets, pikes remained common in the Swedish army, and many infantry still carried matchlock muskets. Russia still fielded old style cavalry of the traditional type that derived from medieval Mongol, and not from modern European practices. Swedish Kings still led their soldiers from the front, exposing themselves to the same, or because of their distinctive dress even higher, risks as their men. The Great Northern War had its roots in the previous century.

At the time of the war, the belligerent powers followed different calendars. The Gregorian calendar, named after the sixteenth century Pope Gregory XIII who introduced it, had been developed as a correction to an observed error in the old Julian calendar. The visible result of the correction was that the date was advanced 10 days, that is, 4 October 1582 was followed by 15 October 1582. The Holy Roman Empire changed its calendar on this date, as did most Catholic nations including the Polish-Lithuanian Commonwealth. However, many Protestant countries initially objected to adopting a Catholic innovation. Prussia was the first Protestant nation to adopt the Gregorian calendar. Denmark and Norway adopted the new calendar only in 1700, when the date (as of 1 March) had to be advanced 11 days, not 10, to correlate the two calendars (since the Julian calendar continued to have leap years every fourth year while the Gregorian added leap days in centenary years, such as 1700, only when these were divisible by 400).

Sweden in November 1699 decided to adopt the Gregorian calendar from 1700, but rather than implementing it outright, the reform would be carried out over a 40-year period. The plan was to skip all leap days in the period 1700 to 1740. Every fourth year, the gap between the Swedish calendar and the Gregorian would accordingly decrease by one day, until the Gregorian and the Swedish calendar finally merged in 1740. In accordance with the plan, 29 February was omitted in 1700. Yet, the changed priorities of the Great Northern War prevented the implementation of further omissions in the following years. In January 1711, King Charles accordingly decided to abandon the Swedish calendar, which was not in use by any other nation, and instead to return to the old Julian calendar in 1712. An extra day was added to February in the leap year of 1712, thus giving the month a unique thirtieth day (30 February) and this year a 367-day length. (Sweden finally introduced the Gregorian calendar in 1753. The leap of 11 days was then accomplished in one step, with 17 February being followed by 1 March.)

Russia delayed further still, retaining the Julian calendar until 1918. Old Style (O.S.), New Style (N.S.), and Swedish Style (S.S.) are terms commonly used with dates to indicate that the calendar convention used at the time described is different from the one in use at present. To complicate matters further, Sweden's territories in Germany often adopted, and continued to use, New Style regardless of the changing Swedish calendar. The dates given in this book follow New Style throughout. The Battle of Narva was fought on 30 November 1700 (N.S.), which corresponds to 19 November 1700 (O.S.) and 20 November 1700 (S.S.). I have yet to see a work on the Great Northern War without the occasional, wrongly calculated date, and no doubt there will be mistakes in the present volume, too.

Prologue: Monarchs and Generals

Charles XII, King of Sweden

Charles XII (1682–1718; r. 1697–1718), of the Palatinate-Zweibrücken-Kleeburg branch of the House of Vasa, was born two years after his father, Charles XI, in 1680 introduced absolutism in Sweden. That young King Charles was born an absolute monarch became evident to all in connection with his coronation, at age 15, in December 1697. No longer was the King crowned by an archbishop; instead, he put on the crown himself, which was followed by the singing of hymns and the firing of cannon.

The young King received a thorough education. We know that he had a good knowledge of Christian theology, mathematics, and physics. He mastered Swedish, German, and Latin, understood French well enough but was reluctant to speak the language, and had some knowledge of Finnish and Italian. Swedish, Finnish, and German were Sweden's official languages. Young Charles received extensive training in military science by Carl Magnus Stuart, an experienced fortification officer and Quartermaster General.[1] Military science also informed his classical schooling, with *The History of Alexander the Great* by Quintus Curtius Rufus his favourite reading material after the Bible. The King invariably took a copy of both books while he was on a military campaign.

King Charles enjoyed military life, and he spent his entire reign on campaign. Yet, in fairness it should be said that King Charles had little choice in the matter. He was King of Sweden at the outbreak of the Great Northern War, which began when an alliance of several powerful enemy states attacked his kingdom. King Charles fought a defensive war, but like his royal predecessors, he invariably followed an offensive strategy, and whenever possible took the war to his enemies. He had no intention of surrendering either Sweden's great power status or its territory.

---

1 Stuart had learnt the trade under Erik Dahlbergh, a military engineer, intelligence officer, quartermaster, cartographer, and accomplished artist with years of experience in every conflict with Swedish involvement since the Thirty Years' War whom we again will meet as the Governor General of Livonia.

King Charles was also, beyond any doubt, a religious believer. This in itself was hardly surprising, not only was Lutheranism enshrined in law, the conversion of the less fortunate to the Lutheran faith was regarded as something between public duty and public spectacle. In 1695, when the future King Charles was 13 years old, he attended, together with his father (who described the event in his diary) and others of the royal family a special church service in the capital, Stockholm, during which first a Jew, and then a Catholic German monk renounced their false beliefs and were baptised into the Lutheran Church.[2] Such services were not uncommon, nor were they necessarily detrimental to the converts, some of whom moved on to important posts.

However, as an absolute monarch, King Charles served directly under God and was not bound by human laws. Perhaps for this reason, the King's beliefs then and later appear more coloured by personal opinion than received theological knowledge. This becomes clear from the documents of the court of law in which King Charles decided upon matters of capital punishment. The King was advised by several high officials of what in modern times would have been the supreme court, yet in matters which he regarded as governed by God's law, essentially the Ten Commandments of the Bible, King Charles was very strict. Cases of adultery, as can be expected, were not infrequent among army personnel. According to the strict letter of the law the punishment for adultery was death; however, lower courts often pleaded clemency because of mitigating circumstances, for instance when a spouse was ill, when the perpetrator turned himself in voluntarily, and when the perpetrator was unaware of the fact that the other had been married. In fact, even the harsh Articles of War of 1683 deemed a substantial fine sufficient as punishment for adultery under certain conditions (but never in serious cases such as rape or bigamy).[3]

Yet in his first year of rule, 1698, the 16-year-old King expressed very strong opinions when it came to the Ten Commandments. Despite the advice of the officials of the supreme court, who cited legal precedent to punish the perpetrators but to spare them from capital punishment, King Charles was adamant that those who broke God's law must not be spared. His officials argued that such harsh punishments did not exist anywhere in the Christian world. They even quoted Bible scripture against the King, noting that not even famous Kings such as David and Solomon had followed this commandment, and had not Jesus Christ himself argued that only he who is without sin should cast the first stone? Nothing deterred King Charles, however, so upon his insistence a recommendation in favour of capital punishment for adultery was sent to the judicial authorities.[4]

The personal piety of King Charles was also obvious in his devotion to prayer. In 1702, the French diplomat Charles-François Caradas, Marquis du Héron, wrote home that when on campaign, King Charles 'never forgets to

---

2 Hans Villius (ed.), *Karl XII: Ögonvittnen* (Stockholm: Wahlström & Widstrand, 1960, 1995), p.14.
3 Articles of War 88–98.
4 Villius, *Karl XII: Ögonvittnen*, pp.40–45.

pray twice per day. When the time of prayer is at hand and when he is on the march, he halts the entire army and prays, then the march continues.'[5] In 1707, an English diplomat, Thomas Wentworth, Lord Raby, noted that the King always had a beautiful, golden Bible at his bed, and that this was the only possession of his that looked suited to a man of rank. This was presumably no exaggeration; King Charles habitually dressed like a young army officer and not a very high-ranking one at that. In the history of King Charles which Jöran Nordberg, a Lutheran clergyman who served the King as court priest, wrote more than a decade after the King's death, the author recollected that the King read the Bible first thing every morning, and sometimes also on Sundays after vespers. And he did not only read familiar verses:

> By autumn 1708 His Majesty had read through the Bible four times while on campaign and with his own hand he had written down the dates when he began and when he ended. But then he removed this page because, as he said: Somebody may perhaps think that I wished to boast thereof.[6]

While the personal religiosity of King Charles clearly was strong and he knew his Bible, the question remains, exactly what did he believe in? We have seen that King Charles as a young man had already disregarded Biblical precedent in legislation, instead opting for a harsher interpretation. He was not close to the clergymen at his headquarters, nor did he confide in them. A young academic, Anders Alstrin, who in 1707 visited the King's camp in Saxony, noted that three priests whom he met in the headquarters, who had years of experience with the King, admitted that it was only recently that they had realised that the King always fasted on four particular days each year: 'These he had himself chosen, so that nobody had known thereof, and so that nobody would learn; on these days he had ridden out in secret and stayed away until evening, and if anybody had noticed and followed him, he went where they could not have found him anything at the time of dinner.'[7] During all the years these clergymen accompanied the King, he never confided in them on the issue. Of the four annual days of fast the King had selected for himself, one was the day on which he in 1700 had won his first major victory, at Narva against the Russians (the battle which is the topic of this book). Another was the day in 1704 on which King Charles accidentally shot his Chamberlain, Axel Hård, with his ramrod, which the King had carelessly left in his pistol. Hård died of his wound three days later, and the King regretted the accident ever after, which Jöran Nordberg also remembered years afterwards. However, the reason for the King's choice of the other two days on which he fasted, he never revealed. Alstrin, himself the son of Lutheran priest but witty rather than pious, admired the King, yet found him hard to

---

5 Villius, *Karl XII: Ögonvittnen*, p.54. Charles-François Caradas, Marquis du Héron (1667–1703) was the French ambassador to the Polish-Lithuanian Commonwealth.
6 Villius, *Karl XII: Ögonvittnen*, pp.119–25. Lieutenant General Thomas Wentworth, Lord Raby (1672–1739), was the ambassador to Prussia.
7 Villius, *Karl XII: Ögonvittnen*, pp.69–74, on p.71. The individual's choice with regard to the time and manner of fasting corresponded to the belief of Martin Luther and hence Lutheranism which encouraged individual fasting as a spiritual exercise.

King Charles, depicted as he appeared in 1700. The King was tall for his time, 1.75m, and looked taller since he was slim. Art historians suggest that the painter softened the King's features to make him appear yet more regal. Nonetheless, this portrait, widely copied and re-copied, came to define the public image of the Swedish King. (David von Krafft, after a 1707 original by Johan David Schwartz; Gripsholm Castle).

make sense of, since he looked less a King than 'a farm-hand who recently became a soldier.'[8]

The conclusion may well be that while the King was very pious, he took his own counsel when it came to the interpretation of the faith. This became obvious during his five-year stay in the Ottoman Empire, an ally in the war against Russia. In 1710, the King sent Major Cornelius Loos to Constantinople to make drawings of the city and its architecture. In 1712, the King's growing fascination with Oriental architecture caused an argument about the use of statues and paintings in churches. Obviously inspired by Islamic architecture and art, which he admired, the King argued against any kind of depictions in the house of God and communicated to his artist and architect, Nicodemus Tessin the Younger, his desire that a church should be free of statues and paintings or it might be taken for a heathen temple.[9] To Tessin, and most other Swedish Lutherans, this conclusion was preposterous and no further notice was taken of the King's instruction.

But most of these spiritual developments lay in the future. At the time of the Battle of Narva, King Charles was 18 years old. While he had recently seen military action against Denmark, this was a stroll in the park compared to the desperate combat that he now would encounter on the eastern front against Russia.

King Charles never married and had no known children. Later historians have attempted to explain this in a multitude of ways, but perhaps it was as simple as King Charles's court priest Nordberg later related that the deeply religious King once told him:

> I will marry when Our Lord gives us peace and then I want to find a wife, not for reasons of state but one whom I really like, and whom I believe that I henceforth can love, so that I do not need to maintain such a woman who is called *maîtresse* in French and whore in our language.[10]

---

8 Villius, *Karl XII: Ögonvittnen*, pp.69–74, on p.72; see also pp.62 & 124.
9 Villius, *Karl XII: Ögonvittnen*, pp.139–42, on p.141. See also Ragnar Josephson, 'Karl XII som estet,' Gustaf Jonasson (ed.), *Historia kring Karl XII* (Stockholm: Wahlström & Widstrand, 1964), pp.101–125.
10 Bengt Liljegren, *Karl XII: En biografi* (Lund: Historiska Media, 2000), p.398 n.63. Perhaps Nordberg made up the King's choice of words, but other eyewitnesses also reported that King Charles said that he would marry when the war was over.

King Charles went on campaign together with his loyal chamberlain and stable master, the stalwart Hård, his four favourite dogs, named Caesar, Pompe, Turk, and Snushane, several horses including the most famous Swedish horse of all times, the pale grey Brandklipparen ('Fire Clipper'), whom a corporal of the Småland Cavalry Regiment had given to his father on the battlefield of Lund in 1676 when his previous horse was shot under him. King Charles rode his father's horse in several battles (but fortunately not, as we shall see, at Narva) until 1718, when the horse finally passed away, more than 40 years old and again back in Lund.

Baron Carl Gustav Rehnskiöld, Lieutenant General of Cavalry

Carl Gustav Rehnskiöld (1651–1722) was a veteran of the Scanian War of 1675–1679, in which he had distinguished himself as a junior officer at the Battle of Lund in 1676 and was promoted more than once, ultimately to lieutenant colonel. He also participated in the Nine Years' War of 1688–1697, in which he served as part of the Swedish contingent with the Allies at the headquarters of the Grand Alliance. Sweden had, as part of the League of Augsburg, promised its ally the Netherlands to send subsidy regiments, and many Swedes saw service in the war. In his letters to Sweden's King Charles XI, Rehnskiöld noted the inefficient collective leadership within the Grand Alliance and the poor discipline of the Alliance soldiers. Back in Sweden, Rehnskiöld played a major role in developing the tactics and organisation of the Swedish Army, in particular with regard to cavalry.

In 1698, the young King Charles XII ennobled Rehnskiöld and promoted him to lieutenant general of cavalry. Henceforth, Rehnskiöld was the young King's primary military adviser. He almost constantly accompanied the King and clearly played a role as military mentor. However, the fact that the two were in almost constant contact and discussed military matters in person, not in writing, means that there are few letters and little written documentation on which to assess Rehnskiöld's influence. Moreover, Rehnskiöld ultimately acquired a reputation for surliness among some of his fellow generals. Fair or not, this posthumous reputation makes his influence even more difficult to determine, although Rehnskiöld certainly got along well enough with King Charles.

Carl Gustav Rehnskiöld. (Gripsholm Castle).

We do know that Rehnskiöld argued the need for more dragoon units in the Swedish Army. As a result, the King allowed Rehnskiöld to enlist, at the expense of the Crown, a regiment of dragoons, which became known as the Life Dragoon Regiment. Rehnskiöld became the head of the new regiment.

When the Great Northern War broke out, Rehnskiöld accompanied King Charles first to Denmark, and then to the eastern front. We know little of Rehnskiöld's personal opinions on strategy. He was probably one of very few men with whom King Charles discussed strategy and he accordingly knew what was in the King's mind. While Rehnskiöld seems to have been a major influence on the young King, he also remained unflinchingly loyal and did not register any personal views with regard to the King's strategic decisions. Which is unfortunate for historians, since King Charles did not publicise or record his own thoughts on strategy.

Rehnskiöld married Elisabeth Funck in 1697. The couple had a daughter, but she died in 1700, the year in which the Great Northern War broke out and Rehnskiöld left Sweden. Although the couple was able to reunite on the Continent in 1707, the war prevented Rehnskiöld's return to Sweden for 18 years.

Peter the Great, Tsar of Russia

Peter I (1672–1725; r. 1682–1725) of the House of Romanov became Tsar of Russia in 1682. He reigned jointly with his half-brother Ivan V until 1696, but from 1696 on, Peter ruled Russia alone and as an absolute monarch.

Peter's childhood was troubled and far from harmonious and secure. He was caught up in disputes and rivalry for power among various close relatives and their favourites which resulted in rebellions and mutinies. Child Peter witnessed several acts of political violence. When Peter, at age 10, was appointed joint ruler with his half-brother Ivan, who was chronically ill and of infirm mind, he found himself compelled to act out the ceremonies as a sham ruler, while those who held real power – Princess Sophia (Russian: Sof'ya) Alekseyevna and members of her entourage – literally sat hidden behind his throne and ordered the child on what to say and to do. The chronic instability and worries may have been the cause of the older Peter's noticeable facial tics in moments of anger and emotional excitement, a strong convulsive twitching that possibly was a form of epilepsy. It may also have caused the few, but regularly occurring, bouts of unbridled cruelty and violence, as sudden as unexpected, that Tsar Peter occasionally succumbed to from adolescence onwards.

Under these conditions, young Peter unsurprisingly preferred to spend his free time away from the palace, in the royal amusement village of Preobrazhenskoye as well as in Moscow's German (that is, 'Foreigners') Quarter, where most non-Russians lived. He was interested in military affairs, and organised a 'toy' or play army of friends and servants in Preobrazhenskoye, with which he engaged in mock battles. This was the origin of the future Preobrazhenskiy Guard Regiment, which would later play an important role in Tsar Peter's military campaigns.¹¹ In 1685, young Peter marched his toy army in regimental formation through Moscow from Preobrazhenskoye to the village of Vorob'yovo to the beat of drums, himself playing the role of a drummer. In 1686, the 14-year-old Peter equipped his toy army with real artillery, grenades, and fireworks. At age 16, he befriended a Dutch carpenter, Frans Timmerman, and other foreign specialists in Russian service. He restored a boat, learnt how to sail, and ultimately studied arithmetic, geometry, and military science. He added a second toy regiment in the royal amusement village of Semyonovskoye, the origin of the future Semyonovskiy Guard Regiment.¹²

To improve his knowledge of military affairs Peter also befriended experienced foreign officers in the Russian Army, among them notably Patrick Gordon and François Lefort. In a less exalted mood, Peter and his friends also began to engage in drunken parties that encompassed every possible vice including sex, violence, blasphemy, and of course, the launching of fireworks without care or consequences. Around 1690, Peter embarked upon an affair with Anna Mons, the Moscow-born daughter of a burgher from Germany who had naturalised as a Russian citizen. Peter met Anna in the company of Lefort. This liaison was not popular with Peter's mother, Natal'ya Kirillovna Naryshkina. To bring her son to reason, she decided to marry him to Eudoxia (Russian: Yevdokiya) Fyodorovna Lopukhina, the daughter of a noble. Eudoxia bore Peter three children, although only one, Aleksey Petrovich, survived past childhood. However, the marriage was a failure in other ways, and 10 years later Peter forced his wife to become a nun and thus freed himself from the union.

Tsar Peter began the construction of a Russian Navy in 1695. The first warships came to good use when in the following year Tsar Peter participated in his first real war, the second Azov campaign against the Ottoman Empire. Peter took part in the Siege of Azov as the captain of one of his galleys. The two Azov campaigns of 1695 and 1696 also saw the first real service of his former toy regiments, now upgraded to Guard Regiments: the Preobrazhenskiy and Semyonovskiy, as well as Russia's two oldest remaining modern infantry regiments, the First and Second Selected Moscow Regiments (by this time commonly known as the Lefortovo – Lefort's – and Butyrsk regiments). Convinced that these units represented a new and more up-to-date military organisation, Tsar Peter decided to build a modern army on their pattern.

Eager to learn more about modern crafts and sciences, in 1697 Tsar Peter travelled 'incognito' to Western Europe on an 18-month journey with a large Russian delegation, the so-called Grand Embassy. This was a combined diplomatic mission and fact-finding tour during which Peter studied Dutch

---

11 The Preobrazhenskiy Guard Regiment remained in service until 1918. The regiment was revived in 2013 as the 154th Preobrazhenskiy Independent Commandant's Regiment, the official Honour Guard Regiment of the Russian Armed Forces. The regiment is again stationed in Moscow.

12 The Semyonovskiy Guard Regiment remained in service until 1918, with Colonel Nikolay Karlovich von Essen as the regiment's last commander. In 1920, part of the regiment joined Wrangel's White army. Ultimately disbanded by the victorious Bolsheviks, the regiment was revived in 2013 as the 1st Independent Semyonovskiy Rifle Regiment.

Tsar Peter of Russia, as depicted in a portrait painted in 1698 by Godfrey Kneller, while the Tsar was in London visiting King William III of England as part of the Grand Embassy. The portrait, which was the Tsar's gift to King William, shows him in obsolete but awe-inspiring armour with an embroidered golden, ermine-lined cloak. On one side of Tsar Peter, the onlooker can admire his imposing crown on a cushion, on the other, a flotilla of modern warships. Collection of HM King Charles II of Great Britain. (Public domain)

and English naval architecture. During the journey, the Tsar used a false name, so that he could escape unwanted social and diplomatic events. However, although not of a strong build Tsar Peter was a remarkably tall man for his time, so he was easy to identify within the delegation. In mid–1698, Tsar Peter had to interrupt the Grand Embassy upon receiving news of a streltsy mutiny in Moscow. Although the mutiny was suppressed even before the Tsar's return in September the same year, he had many of the mutineers executed.

Tsar Peter now began to transform Russian society. An absolute ruler, he first aimed to change the external signs that distinguished the traditional way of life from what he had encountered in Western Europe. On 8 September 1698, Tsar Peter issued a decree 'On the wearing of German dress, the shaving of beards and moustaches, and schismatics appearing in the attire specified for them.' The decree prohibited courtiers, state officials, and military officers from wearing traditional dress and beards from 11 September onwards. Taxes were introduced for those who persisted in the old ways.

Tsar Peter was brought up in the Russian Orthodox faith, but there is nothing to suggest that he was much of a believer. Moreover, he had a low regard for the Church hierarchy and its xenophobic teachings, both of which he strove to keep under tight governmental control. The traditional leader of the Church was the Patriarch of Moscow. Since the beginning of the Romanov dynasty, strong patriarchs had wielded more power than the tsars. In 1700, when the office fell vacant, Peter accordingly refused to name a replacement. Instead, he allowed the patriarch's deputy to discharge the duties of the office.

Tsar Peter was charismatic and friendly under most conditions, had a brilliant mind, but was dangerous to be around when struck by rage. He brought Russia in line with the rest of Europe and made his country the leading great power on its north-eastern flank.

Prince Charles Eugène of Croÿ-Millendonck, Field Marshal

Charles Eugène de Croÿ (1651–1702), Duke of the Croÿ-Rœulx branch of the princely House of Croÿ of the Holy Roman Empire, served as field marshal in three armies: the Imperial, the Saxon, and the Russian.

The Duke de Croÿ first saw military action as a colonel in the Brandenburg army. He fought in the Battle of Fehrbellin against the Swedes in 1675. Then, when Denmark invaded Sweden in the Scanian War of 1675–1679, he went into Danish service. Distinguishing himself on several occasions, in 1677 Croÿ was promoted to major general. His possibly most unabashed feat was when in 1678 he commanded a Danish army to recover the town of Helsingborg. Although Danish troops gained control of the town, the Swedish commandant, Colonel Carl Hård af Segerstad, withdrew into the citadel, where he held out. In a fantastic ruse, Croÿ had two letters forged and delivered to Hård. During the war, Danish guerrillas had repeatedly raided the Swedish communication lines. In the process, they had captured a large number of Swedish letters and documents, including some signed and sealed by Sweden's King Charles XI. Croÿ accordingly arranged for one of the forged letters delivered to Hård to look like a genuine order from the Swedish King, signed and also sealed with King Charles's personal seal. The letter ordered Hård to surrender Helsingborg in order to spare his men. Amazed, but loyal to King Charles, Hård fell for the ruse and surrendered the citadel, not knowing that King Charles was on his way to relieve the hard-pressed garrison. In acknowledgement of his success, the King of Denmark promoted Croÿ to lieutenant general and appointed him commandant in Helsingborg.

Croÿ succeeded to his father's title as Prince of Croÿ-Millendonck in 1681, and in the same year married Countess Wilhelmina Juliana van den Bergh, a widow 13 years his senior. They had no children.

In 1682, Croÿ went into Imperial service to fight the Ottoman Empire. Wounded in the 1683 Siege of Vienna, he also fought in the Siege of Offen (Buda) in 1686, the Battle of Niš in 1689, and the attack on Belgrade in 1693. He was promoted to field marshal in 1688.

After the war against the Ottoman Empire, Croÿ ended up in Amsterdam in 1698, during Tsar Peter's Grand Embassy. The Tsar invited him to join the Russian Army. Croÿ must have been interested, since he sought out the Tsar. However, ultimately, in 1699, he chose instead to go into Saxon service. This produced much the same outcome, because King Augustus of Saxony and the Polish-Lithuanian Commonwealth almost immediately sent him with a delegation of officers to Tsar Peter, who needed help with the planned attack on

Charles Eugène de Croÿ. In the early stages of the campaign, Croÿ wore a striking red coat and rode a white horse. Tsar Peter told him to dress less conspicuously. Taking the hint, Croÿ switched to a blue coat (as related by Hallart, *Tagebuch*, p. 31). There is a tradition that, after the Tsar's departure, Croÿ again put on the red coat, which he wore in the Battle of Narva. (Austrian National Library)

Sweden. Tsar Peter brought the Saxon officers with him, refusing to let them go and, as narrated below, in 1700 Croÿ perhaps to his surprise suddenly found himself not only in Russian service – but also in the position of commander of the Russian Army.

Croÿ was known as a pleasant fellow who enjoyed social events and a lavish lifestyle. He made friends easily, and never lacked money as long as his associates had funds to lend him. While Croÿ comes along as something of an amiable scoundrel, he was honourable and he had genuine military skills.

1

The Great Northern War

A series of successful conquests, from the Thirty Years' War of 1618–1648 to the 1655–1660 campaigns of the militaristic King Charles X, had transformed the little northern Kingdom of Sweden into a regional great power centred on the Baltic Sea. As a result, Swedish military might and regional power had expanded immensely. In 1697, the young Charles XII inherited the Swedish throne. Charles was only 14 years old and had no previous experience of war, and thus the neighbouring monarchs believed that the time finally was ripe to eliminate the latent military threat from Sweden. In 1699, King Frederick IV of Denmark and Norway, King Augustus II of Saxony and the Polish-Lithuanian Commonwealth, and Tsar Peter I of Russia accordingly formed a triple alliance against Sweden. The three monarchs wanted to reconquer lands lost to Sweden during its expansion into a great power. The result of their ambitious plans was the Great Northern War, a conflict that lasted for a generation, devastated Northern Europe, and directly led to the rise of the Russian Empire as the leading great power of Northern and Eastern Europe.

The initiative to form a triple alliance originated with King Frederick, the new King of Denmark and Norway. He contacted King Augustus 'the Strong', King of Poland, Grand Duke of Lithuania, and Elector of Saxony. Within days of Frederick's accession to the throne, the two monarchs entered into a secret alliance, the Treaty of Dresden of 25 September 1699. King Frederick wanted to regain the Scanian lands in southern Sweden which Denmark had ceded in 1658. Augustus of Saxony had in 1679 also become King of the Polish-Lithuanian Commonwealth for which he wanted to regain Livonia on the eastern shore of the Baltic Sea, ceded to Sweden in 1660. Together, they devised a plan according to which King Augustus would attack Livonia early in 1700. After that, Danish armies would go on the offensive against first the Duchy of Holstein-Gottorp, Sweden's ally to the south of Denmark, and having achieved this objective, also the Scanian provinces. On 21 November 1699, King Augustus and Tsar Peter of Russia agreed in the Treaty of Preobrazhenskoye to join into an alliance to attack Sweden. The treaty called for the partition of the Swedish lands and their annexation by Russia, Saxony, the Polish-Lithuanian Commonwealth, and Denmark-Norway. Since Tsar Peter wanted to expand his power to the Baltic Sea and Black Sea, which entailed the conquest of the Swedish Baltic ports, he accordingly agreed to attack Sweden's other eastern lands: Ingria, Estonia, and Finland. The Treaty

PETER THE GREAT'S DISASTROUS DEFEAT

Scandinavia and the Baltic Region

of Preobrazhenskoye was recognised by the Danish King a few weeks later, whereby the triple alliance against Sweden was a fact. The three monarchs began to lay plans for a three-pronged attack on Sweden. All three parties kept the triple alliance secret, going as far as sending emissaries to Sweden to confirm their sincere friendship.

Soon, the three monarchs set their plans in motion. Campaigns tended to focus on fortified positions, since to deny the enemy an important stronghold was a means of wearing him down. On 22 February 1700 a Saxon and Commonwealth Army marched into Swedish Livonia to lay siege to the city of Riga. This marked the beginning of the Great Northern War. King Charles XII of Sweden was then 17 years old.

But this was not everything. Soon after, on 21 March, King Frederick sent a Danish Army into the Duchy of Holstein-Gottorp, which was a Swedish ally and hosted Swedish troops. The Danes occupied major parts of Holstein-Gottorp and on 22 March laid siege to the Duchy's largest fortress, Tønning.[1] Everybody understood that King Frederick's ultimate target was Sweden.

Despite agreements within the triple alliance to strike simultaneously, Tsar Peter did not make his move at the same time as his Allies. The Tsar was preoccupied with his ongoing war with the Ottoman Empire, with which his representatives managed to make peace only with the Treaty of Constantinople on 14 July 1700. As a result, Tsar Peter formally declared war on Sweden as late as 30 August 1700, the day after he learnt of the treaty concluded with the Ottomans. For his formal *casus belli*, the Tsar claimed that he had not received the proper respect due a sovereign ruler when he travelled incognito to Riga with the Grand Embassy. As a formal cause for war, this was a tenuous claim and contemporaries understood this. Yet, it was only Tsar Peter of the rulers of the triple alliance who formally issued a declaration of war,[2] and King Charles respected Peter for this. By comparison, King Charles's cousins (on his mother's side) Augustus and Frederick went to war against him without bothering with such inter-state conventions.

Even so, Tsar Peter had already made the necessary preparations to launch an attack. On 12 September, Russian units from Novgorod and Pskov began to move into Swedish Ingria at the Gulf of Finland. And, on 20 September, a large Russian army opened a siege of the important port-town of Narva in Swedish Estonia.

The failure of the alliance powers to coordinate their efforts gave Sweden the opportunity to strike against each one at a time, in effect pushing the geographically separated enemies out of the war before they managed to unify their forces and strategy.

This was a very real possibility. Sweden's defensive strategy, which had emerged from the wars in the previous century, rested on three capacities. First, the construction of border fortresses that would hold an enemy invasion army until a field army could be directed to fend off the invaders. Riga and

---

1 Gustaf Petri, *Kungl. Första livgrenadjärregementets historia* 3: *Östgöta infanteriregemente under Karl XI och Karl XII* (Stockholm: Norstedt & Söner, 1958), p.130.
2 Tsar Peter had also, through an envoy, previously asked King Charles to return Narva, or another port in the Gulf of Finland, so the Swedes had some ideas of the Tsar's intentions.

Narva were such fortresses. Second, the means to rapidly mobilise this field army. And third, a strong fleet to secure the sea lines of communication and to transport the field army overseas.

Faced with simultaneous invasions in both the east and south, King Charles decided first to deal with the Danish threat. Although King Charles had never been to war, he was already well versed in military tactics and organisation, and his father had taught him much about army life. On 2 June 1700, the fortress of Tønning was rescued by a Swedish relief army under General Nils Gyllenstierna, consisting of Swedish units from the German territories and an allied contingent from the Duchy of Lüneburg. In southern Sweden, an army gathered to invade Denmark. With the help of an Anglo-Dutch naval squadron, the Swedish navy forced the Danish fleet to retreat towards Copenhagen. On 4 August, King Charles landed the vanguard of the Swedish army at Humlebæk south of Helsingør on the main Danish island of Zealand. The Swedes rapidly dispersed the few Danish defenders. The rest of the Swedish army could not be landed until two weeks later because of poor weather. Having finally assembled the entire army, King Charles marched towards the Danish capital Copenhagen.

This offensive, together with pressure from Britain and the Netherlands, the two Western Maritime Powers, forced King Frederick of Denmark-Norway to withdraw from the war on 18 August, when he agreed to the Treaty of Traventhal. Denmark was forced to return Holstein-Gottorp to its Duke, and abandon the triple alliance. Denmark-Norway had been forced out of the war.

However, the war was not yet over in Livonia. In May, a Swedish relief army commanded by General Otto Vellingk and Major General Georg Johan Maydell came to the rescue of besieged Riga. After a battle at Jungfernhof (modern-day Jumprava), the invaders were pushed back towards Commonwealth territory. In July, King Augustus made a new attempt and Riga again came under siege.

Having forced Denmark out of the war, King Charles at first contemplated a direct attack on Saxony to counter King Augustus's invasion of Livonia in the same way as he had checked King Frederick's invasion of Holstein-Gottorp by a Swedish descent on Zealand. However, the unwillingness of the Maritime Powers to risk disturbances that might harm their own interests made such a solution politically impracticable. The Maritime Powers feared that war in Germany would reduce the chances of the Second Partition Treaty of the Spanish Empire of 1699 to impose a diplomatic solution to the issues that, soon afterwards, would lead to the War of the Spanish Succession. A war between Sweden and Saxony would also preclude Swedish and Saxon military support for the emerging Grand Alliance between the Maritime Powers and Vienna in case France and Spain chose to create a dynastic union.

Accepting political realities, King Charles in October 1700 shipped the Swedish army from southern Sweden to Pernau in Estonia, intending to relieve the siege of Riga. He arrived on 16 October. When King Augustus received the news, he abandoned the siege, instead returning south to his possession of Courland because he feared a Swedish attack. With the threat to Riga averted, King Charles turned his army against the Russians laying siege to Narva.

2

The Swedish Military Establishment

King Charles's Swedish army had an almost century-long history of being at the cutting edge of military development. Much of what at the time was regarded as standard in Continental warfare had originated in Swedish practices during the Thirty Years' War. Sweden's army remained superbly trained and led by experienced professionals.

The Swedish Army and Navy were comparatively strong at the outbreak of war. The Swedish armed forces consisted of a combination of national units and units enlisted abroad. Sweden had established a well-performing system of military mobilisation through the *indelningsverk*, the allotment authority. The national army consisted of a total of 11,000 horse and 25,000 foot. The navy had 6,600 sailors. Soldiers were well equipped, and the institution of provincial regiments resulted in high morale and *esprit de corps*. Moreover, government funding was sufficient to also maintain a force of enlisted regiments to garrison the overseas provinces. Altogether, the national and enlisted units achieved a strength of 76,000 men.[1]

However, Sweden had a small population and few sources of state revenue. The wars of the previous century had shown that Sweden had to fight its wars abroad, on enemy territory, since Sweden itself lacked the capacity to supply even its own army when engaged in wartime operations. It remained uncertain how the system would perform during a period of protracted war. The Swedish model of war had been widely copied in the previous century, so the Swedish Army was no longer unique in its use of efficient organisational structures and aggressive tactics. Sweden's effective form of government administration and taxation, introduced in tandem with the Swedish model of war, had also been copied, at least in part, by neighbouring states such as Brandenburg-Prussia but also Russia.

---

1 For further details, see Lars Ericson Wolke, *The Swedish Army in the Great Northern War 1700–21: Organisation, Equipment, Campaigns and Uniforms* (Warwick: Helion & Co., 2018); Sergey Shamenkov, *Charles XII's Karoliners, 1: The Swedish Infantry and Artillery of the Great Northern War, 1700–1721* (Warwick: Helion & Co., 2022); Sergey Shamenkov, *Charles XII's Karoliners, 2: The Swedish Cavalry of the Great Northern War, 1700–1721* (Warwick: Helion & Co., 2023).

Organisation

The basic organisation of the Swedish Army was similar to that of most Continental armies. Most prestigious was the cavalry, which moved and fought on horseback. Cheaper to raise and arm were dragoons, who moved mounted on horseback but fought on foot. They could also, when mounted, handle reconnaissance duties, patrolling, and so on. Then there was the infantry, even cheaper to raise and necessary during set battles and yet more importantly, for siege work. Finally, there was the artillery, which was vital during sieges although Sweden also had an efficient field artillery.

Sweden published its military regulations in the form of instructions for the various arms of service. The main tactical unit in the cavalry and dragoons was the squadron, which typically consisted of two companies each with an establishment strength of 125 horse, which under optimal circumstances produced a squadron 250 strong. In the infantry, the main tactical unit was the battalion, which commonly consisted of four companies each with an establishment strength of 150 men, which under optimal circumstances produced a battalion of 600 men. This was the traditional organisation, which was reconfirmed in the *Instruction* of 1694. The main administrative formation was the regiment, which typically consisted of eight companies.

On the field of battle, armies were customarily formed up in three operational divisions in which the order of the tactical units often was fixed in advance, according to seniority or necessity. The three operational divisions were the two wings, which chiefly or wholly consisted of cavalry and dragoons, and the centre, which consisted of infantry. The artillery was usually deployed between the infantry units. By tradition, the right wing was regarded as the more prestigious one. However, by 1700 this no longer necessarily influenced tactics, and at Narva, the King actually spent most time on the left wing. The operational units were commonly divided into a first and a second line. The second line was often weaker than the first and to some extent functioned as a reserve. In a large army, there might also be a third line, the real reserve.

Tactical Doctrines

The Swedish Army still enjoyed a high reputation on the Continent, although because of a long period at peace, perhaps less so than earlier. Regular units were nonetheless very disciplined.[2]

Tactics remained essentially unchanged since previous wars. By tradition, the Swedish model emphasised the offensive as a tactical doctrine. The combination of firepower and, above all, rapid movement was regarded as decisive for gaining and retaining the initiative. Since rapid movement also reduced the men's exposure to enemy fire, the aggressive tactical behaviour

---

2   As will be seen, however, the newly raised, fresh units did not always live up to the expected discipline.

THE SWEDISH MILITARY ESTABLISHMENT

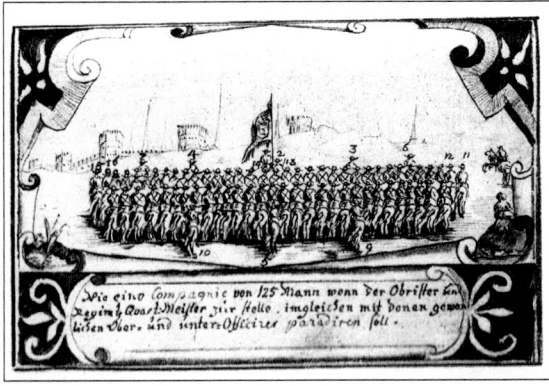 

The deployment of a cavalry company. Left: in preparation for the charge. Right: During the charge itself, with knee behind knee. *Instruction for Cavalry*, 1707. (Public Domain)

actually worked for their protection. Closing rapidly with the enemy was often safer than delaying or defending a fortified position.

The Carolean art of war depended on speed, discipline, and aggressive tactics. Because of past experiences, Swedish Army tactics became known as the *gå på* ('go at them') approach, after the command *Gå på!* which was the order to charge. This applied to both cavalry and infantry. Even the artillery tended to deploy aggressively, and change position when this enabled a better fire solution.

The cavalry operated with the squadron as the key tactical unit. Each squadron typically deployed in two ranks. When a charge was ordered, the men closed ranks so that they rode not only knee to knee, but each man with his knee immediately behind that of his neighbour on the unit standard (inner) side of the formation. The result was a wedge-shaped formation in which the standard, in the middle of the formation, also marked its point. Swedish cavalry was ordered to charge the enemy with sword only. King Charles XI had instructed the cavalry to charge at the trot.[3] In 1700, the cavalry would only increase speed at a distance of 60 paces from the enemy, when it would move into a trot or gallop.[4] It seems that over time, and particularly when under enemy fire, the tendency was for the cavalry to charge at the gallop. At least from 1705 onwards, the charge at the gallop became the norm.

The infantry operated with the battalion as the key tactical unit. On the battlefield, the battalions would form up in a linear formation, each with pikes in the centre (up to one-third of the men carried pikes) and musketeers on each side of them. Grenadiers (12 men per company, or less than one-tenth of the total) marched on the flanks or ahead of the line – not least to avoid accidental deaths if their grenades exploded due to accidents or enemy fire. The basic organisation of pike and shot went back to at least the mid-Thirty Years' war.[5] Grenadiers were permanently attached only in 1700. The infantry battalion typically deployed in four ranks. There was no period of

---

3   *Huru en skvadron skal treffa medh fienden*. Stockholm, 23 April 1694 (O.S.).
4   Heribert Seitz 'Den karolinska värjans taktiska betydelse för kavalleriet,' *Ny Militär Tidskrift* 8 (1944), pp.1–12, on p.2.
5   The organisational model was, for instance, described in Lorentz von Troupitzen's *Kriegs Kunst* of 1633.

preparatory musket fire before the charge began. In 1694, King Charles XI introduced a new instruction for the infantry known as *The New Manner*. The instruction prescribes:

> …when he who commands the battalion orders, Prepare yourself, the pikemen will advance with pikes held high until he reaches a distance to the enemy of 70 paces; then the two rearward lines will be ordered to aim, at which point the two rearward lines will double up with the two forward lines [and fire]; as soon as the two rearward lines have fired, they draw their swords, and as soon as the two forward lines have advanced, the two rearward lines close up behind the forward lines, forming the rear of the battalion files. They will then march in close files and lines towards the enemy, until they reach a distance from the enemy of 30 paces, when the order comes that the two forward lines aim, and as soon as they have fired, they will draw their swords, and then [everybody] charge into the enemy.[6]

After firing the volley, the battalion immediately charged home with pike, bayonet, and sword. The battalion's application of firepower was thus fully integrated with its movement into contact with the enemy. This aggressive doctrine also meant that the pike was retained, despite being regarded as obsolete elsewhere in Europe. The pike frequently played a role in the charge, but experiences from previous wars show that when needed, the pikemen could also play a defensive role, protecting the rest of the army from in particular enemy cavalry. This never became necessary at Narva.

In addition, the infantry by an old tradition that went back at least to the Thirty Years' War advanced in silence against the enemy, which was unusual and may have unnerved some opponents.[7] When a new infantry instruction was issued in 1701, the same general formation and manner of firing remained in use, even though from this point in time the idea was that half the file would fire in a kneeling position instead of standing.

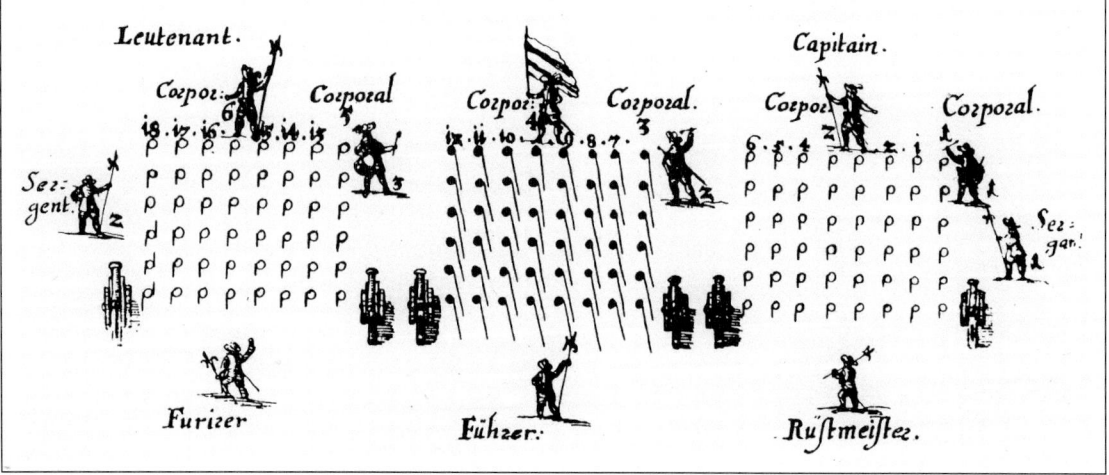

Swedish infantry company deployed in line, as described and illustrated by Lorentz von Troupitzen. (Troupitzen, *Kriegs Kunst*, 1633. Author's Collection)

---

6   Dett Nya Maneret, som A:o 1694 är begynt, att träffa med een Battaillon, Stockholm, 21 April 1694 (O.S.).
7   Michael Fredholm von Essen, *Lion from the North, 1* (Warwick: Helion & Co., 2020), p.216.

THE SWEDISH MILITARY ESTABLISHMENT

Although the instruction specified the charge as maintaining marching speed, possibly in an attempt to maintain cohesion, in reality the infantry would invariably close rapidly with the enemy. They would be under fire at the time, so several eyewitnesses describe how the infantry would run against the enemy after firing their muskets. In fact, there was a tendency for the infantry under King Charles XII to ignore the instruction's planned two volleys and instead, with the full support of the King, only fire one, at a range of 30 paces or preferably even closer.[8]

Based on the aggressive tactics employed by Swedish cavalry and infantry, the traditional interpretation is that the artillery gradually came to adopt a subordinate role. Not even the highly mobile regimental artillery had the necessary mobility to follow such a rapid charge as envisaged above. Although still employed during sieges, artillery was accordingly generally believed comparatively seldom to have played as prominent a role on the battlefield as it had during the latter stage of the Thirty Years' War and the wars of King Charles X.[9] A caveat was ultimately introduced in that the pendulum again swung, and the artillery reacquired its traditional role in the second half of the Great Northern War.[10] Even so, the Swedish artillery had a tradition of rapid movement and redeployment, and it commonly changed firing position several times during a battle. We will see that it upheld this practice at Narva. If anything, the Battle of Narva shows that the Swedish artillery was just as mobile and efficient as in the past, and indeed was central to Swedish Army

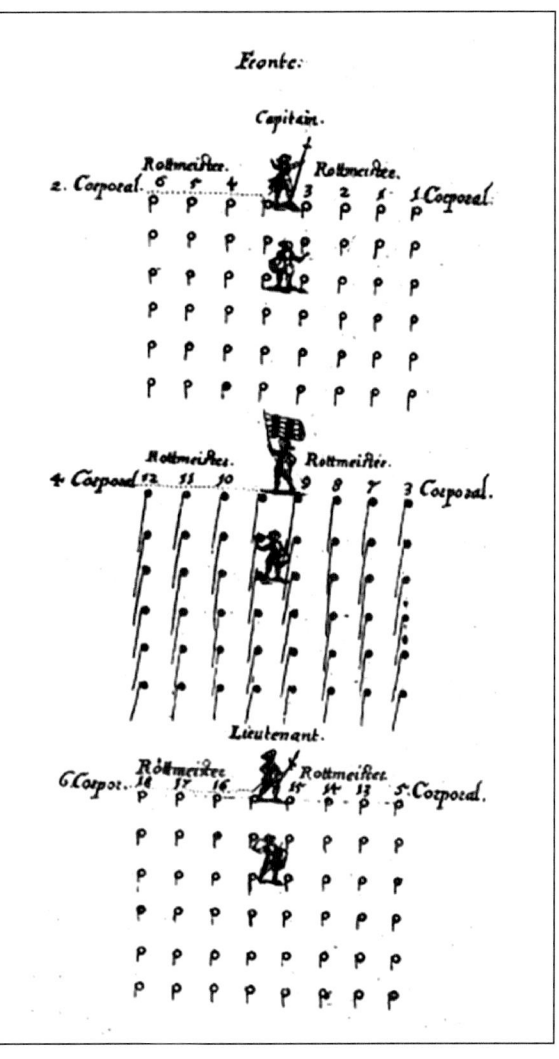

Swedish infantry company deployed in column, again described and illustrated by Lorentz von Troupitzen. (Troupitzen, *Kriegs Kunst*, 1633. Author's Collection)

---

8 According to an observer, 'During all the actions that His Majesty has had with the Russians he has permitted his army only one salvo and then go on with sword in hand.' Anonymous relation, Uppsala University Library (UUB), F 102. A text attributed to Peter Schönström, an infantry captain who served under King Charles in the years after Narva, relates how the King 'wanted the cavalry never to fire their carbines during a charge but attack with swords only. Likewise, he wanted the infantry not to shoot before the enemy's white of the eye was visible, and after firing the first salvo, attack the enemy with pikes, bayonets, and swords.' Carl Hallendorff (ed.), *Karl XII i Ukraina: En karolins berättelse* (Stockholm: Bröderna Lagerström, 1915), pp.40–41.

9 This interpretation seems to rest solely with the text attributed to the aforementioned Peter Schönström. Years later, the text's author reminisced how the King 'argued that for a small army to defeat a large one, it must carry out a rapid and brave charge, during which there is no time to use cannons.' Hallendorff, *Karl XII i Ukraina*, p.40.

10 Hans Ulfhielm (ed.), *Kungl. Artilleriet: Karl XI:s och Karl XII:s tid* (Stockholm: Militärhistoriska förlaget 1993), p.523.

PETER THE GREAT'S DISASTROUS DEFEAT

Swedish infantry company deployed in column outside Gothenburg, *Suecia antiqua et hodierna*, 1709. The organisation remains identical to the one described by Troupitzen. Johan van den Aveelen, based on a late seventeenth century sketch by Erik Dahlbergh in Suecia Antiqua et Hodierna (Stockholm: 1709) (Public Domain)

tactics. We will see that the same lesson can be learnt from the confrontation at Pühajõgi Pass, which took place before the Battle of Narva.

The Chief of Artillery (Swedish: *generalfälttygmästare*) was responsible for all artillery, arsenals, munitions, and everything related thereunto.[11]

Linear Tactics in Battle

The linear tactics exposed the men fighting in the line to exceptional danger as the lines closed with each other, and no man was permitted to take cover when under artillery or musket fire. This took personal bravery or, for most, strict discipline, used to suppress a man's natural instinct, fear. It is likely that most men in the line entrusted their souls to God and merely hoped for the best, since it all too often seemed to be pure chance that decided who lived and died, exposed to artillery fire and enemy volleys fired at short range as they were. Early eighteenth century gunpowder weapons were lethal. Many soldiers loaded their weapons with excessively strong charges of gunpowder, which gave the musket ball a high velocity and produced horrendous wounds. Moreover, it was common to load the musket with multiple and often irregular projectiles, which might explain why during the war so many men and officers suffered from multiple wounds when they were shot. Archaeological evidence from the Scanian War of 1675–1679, fought by King Charles's father, shows that many soldiers cut or otherwise distorted the musket ball so that the projectile would tumble and tear the flesh when it hit. Similar methods were used also during the Great Northern War.[12] But the projectiles were not the only things that resulted in grievous

---

11 The title replaced that of national Chief of Artillery (Swedish: *rikstygmästare*; master of ordnance of the realm), the last of whom was Per Larsson Sparre who held the post until 1682.
12 Battlefield archaeology confirms the use of such projectiles in the Scanian War. Bo Knarrström, *Slagfältet: Om bataljen vid Landskrona 1677 och fynden från den första arkeologiska undersökningen av ett svenskt slagfält* (Saltsjö-Duvnäs: Efron & Dotter, 2006), pp. 60–61, 85–8. The use of shot cut in four parts together with small, irregular pieces is confirmed in a Russian account from 1705. Boris Megorsky, *The Russian Army in the Great Northern War 1700-21:*

wounds and deaths. When projectiles hit gunstocks or pikes, the wooden parts would shatter and fragment, in effect producing shrapnel that burst through men and horses in the vicinity. Perhaps yet more horrifyingly, the same result was produced by sharp bone fragments and, even more so, shattered pieces of teeth. In particular the tooth fragments resulted in vicious wounds, since they produced lethal infections even if the victim survived the immediate impact.

The effect of field artillery fire was even worse. Iron roundshot could be seen while in motion, but due to weight and speed, they could not be stopped or evaded. Yet worse was grape shot, that is, an artillery missile consisting of many musket balls, in effect functioning like a shotgun, and canister shot, artillery missiles consisting of metal fragments in canisters. With such munitions, the field artillery could mow down an entire unit of men. Soldiers knew this and would occasionally take their revenge on artillerymen, by sparing none if they surrendered.

Based on evidence from later, but similar, battles, we can expect that most men in the line would be in a state of psychological shock from seeing friends literally torn to shreds by enemy fire, probably to the extent that quite a few would be physically and psychologically unable to discharge their weapons or draw their sidearms. Which perhaps also indicates their strongest motivation to stay in the line, beside discipline. Almost all Swedish units were raised from a particular geographical area. The soldiers accordingly stood in the line of battle together with family, friends, and neighbours. This provided a strong incentive not to let the others down, or to show oneself inadequate. It is probably fair to say that most men fought for their friends and comrades to a far higher extent than they fought for their country, which in the eyes of many was an abstract and artificial concept. Some might fight for their King, at least in those instances when the King provided an inspiring personal example.

Besides, we should not underestimate the difficulties in exercising command on an early eighteenth century battlefield. First, communications were poor. Despatch riders might or might not reach their destination. Music and signals would not be heard over the gunfire. Geographical factors and indeed weather conditions might prevent visual observation of what was happening anywhere beyond the commander's immediate surroundings. The gunpowder used by firearms and artillery soon created a literal fog of war that was almost impenetrable. Moreover, on a dry day, sparks from the shot would set fire to any dry grass on the field, which produced smoke that reduced visibility even more. At the same time, the thousands of horses that took part in the battle raised dust clouds that mixed with the smoke. As a result, most successful commanders realised that they had to lead from the front, since this was the only way that they could control at least some of their troops. As for what happened elsewhere on the battlefield, there was usually no way of knowing.

Organisation, Materiel, Training and Combat Experience, Uniforms (Warwick: Helion, 2018), pp.83–4.

The Drabant Corps

For later generations, arguably the most famous unit in King Charles's army was the Life Drabant Corps. This was a fighting formation directly under the King who functioned as the unit's captain. In his absence, and for daily activities, the Drabant Corps was commanded by a captain lieutenant (who held the regular army rank of major general) and two lieutenants (both with the regular army rank of colonel). Quartermasters and adjutants were lieutenant colonels, corporals the near equivalent of majors, while troopers were equivalent to captains, or captains of cavalry. The strength of the Drabant Corps was initially set at 200 men. This ideal was never reached. The highest number ever attained was 198 in the summer of 1700. At Narva, the Drabant Corps consisted of 158 men.

In addition to being an elite fighting formation, the Drabant Corps functioned as a training unit for senior commanders. Members of the Corps were frequently handpicked as commanders of other units.

Arms and Armour

Armament had changed but little since previous wars, and there were deficiencies in equipment. It was only from 1696 that the flintlock musket really began to replace the matchlock in the Swedish army, and bayonets were gradually introduced only from 1700 onwards. Far from all Swedish units at Narva had received the new musket. The Life Guard, for instance, only received some of the new flintlock muskets with bayonets in Reval.[13] Most units, including the Life Guard, also retained their pikes.

Officers bought their own arms and, if they desired, armour. Helmets and more extensive armour had already grown obsolete during the Thirty Years' War and at this time were only used when a senior officer posed for a portrait or participated in a parade. However, some would still wear a breastplate and backplate for protection. The armour was not always obvious, however, since most wore a coat over the cuirass. In battle, each would be armed with a sword and two pistols, usually with snaphaunce locks.[14] One particular type of sword developed to mark the position of officer. Known as commander's sword (Swedish: *kommendervärja*), it was used in the Carolean military for all service branches.[15] Infantry and artillery officers would add a half-pike or spontoon, as in the previous century this was supposed to be 5 cubits (2.97 m[16]) in length and in 1698 was mandated for all infantry officers.[17]

---

13   Folke Wernstedt, *Kungl. Svea Livgardes Historia* 4: *1660–1718* (Stockholm: Stiftelsen för Svea livgardes historia, 1954), p.372.
14   Flintlock pistols became standard issue only from model 1699, which was not yet widely distributed. Even wheellock pistols remained in common use.
15   Heribert Seitz, *Svärdet Och Värjan Som Armévapen* (Stockholm: Kungl. Armémuseum, 1955), pp.273–88.
16   One Swedish cubit or ell (Swedish: *aln*) equalled 59.38cm.
17   Anders Larsson, *Karolinska Uniformer och Munderingar åren 1700 till 1721: Samt vissa handgrepp och exercis* (Östersund: Jengel, 2022), p.253.

THE SWEDISH MILITARY ESTABLISHMENT

 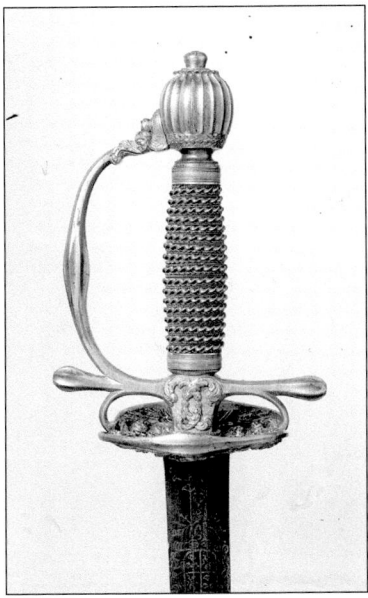 

Commander's sword (Swedish: *kommendervärja*) for infantry officer, manufactured in 1706–1707. Total length: 116.7cm, blade length: 97.8cm, width: 3.1cm, weight: 1.24kg. (Royal Armoury, Stockholm; 9152_LRK).

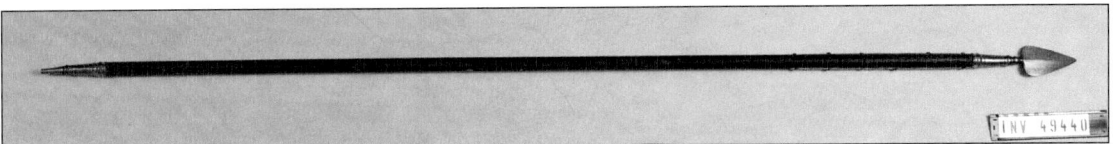

A cavalryman was, according to the instruction of 1695, expected to carry sword, two pistols, and a carbine. The standard cavalry sword was based on model 1675 for the Drabant Corps which in turn developed into the almost identical model 1680 for the Life Regiment of Horse. This sword served as the prototype for what would become known as the famous Carolean cavalry sword model 1708, which greatly influenced future Swedish cavalry sword design.[18]

The standard Swedish firearm calibres were already defined as 20mm muskets, 19mm carbines, and 16mm pistols.[19] It was primarily the calibre that was regulated. Several types of pistols remained in service (even wheelocks such as model 1695[20]), but just before the war the Crown introduced model 1699, a flintlock pistol of modern type.[21] Swedish cavalrymen carried the carbine hooked to a bandolier, and carried their pistols in holsters fixed to the front of the saddle. Swedish cavalrymen were supposed to wear heavy breastplates for protection, but it is uncertain how common they actually were by this time.

Spontoon or half-pike for infantry or artillery officer, first half of the eighteenth century. Total length 2.02 m, weight 1.070kg. (Army Museum, Stockholm; AM.049440).

---

18 Seitz, *Svärdet och värjan*, pp.190–211.
19 Josef Alm, *Eldhandvapen 1: Från deras tidigaste förekomst till slaglåsets allmänna införande*. (Stockholm: Rediviva, 1976), pp.252 & 256.
20 Alm, *Eldhandvapen 1*, p.259.
21 Alm, *Eldhandvapen 1*, p.282.

PETER THE GREAT'S DISASTROUS DEFEAT

Sword for under-officer in the Drabant Corps, commonly known as model 1675 (for the Drabant Corps) or model 1680 (for the Life Regiment of Horse). The sword comes with a thumb ring for further protection. This sword served as the prototype for what would become known as the celebrated Carolean cavalry sword model 1708. Total length 114.0cm, blade length 96.8cm, weight 1.36kg. (Army Museum, Stockholm; AM.030319)

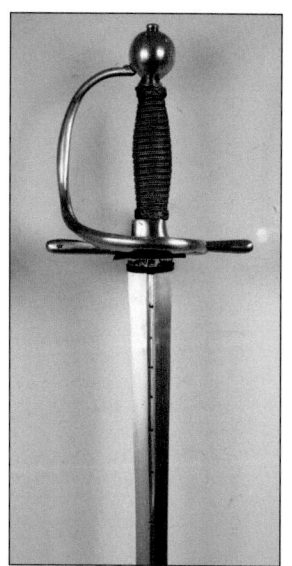
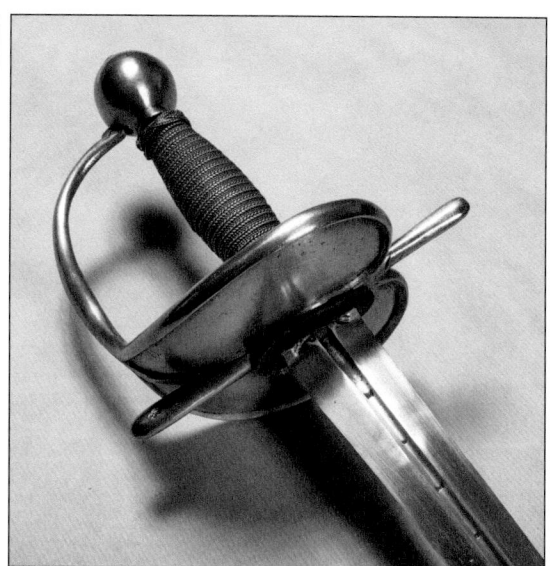
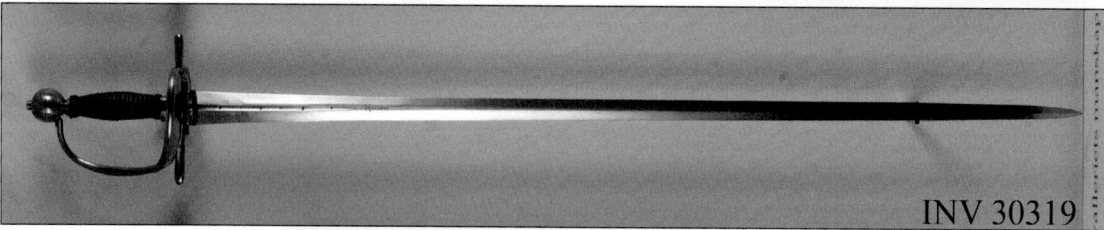

Sword for the Drabant Corps model 1693. The sword comes with a thumb ring for further protection. Blade length 95.1cm. (Army Museum, Stockholm; AM.060061)

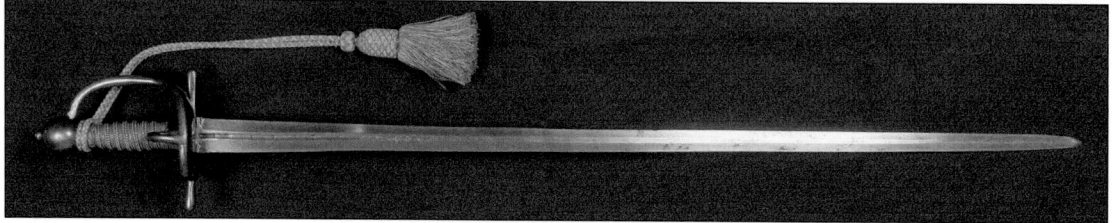

THE SWEDISH MILITARY ESTABLISHMENT

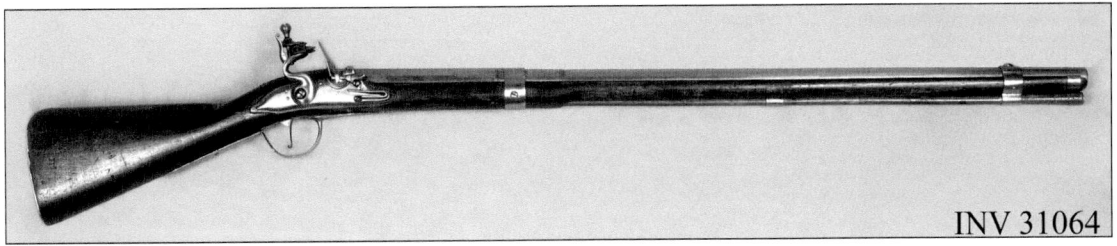

Dragoons were armed with sword, infantry musket, and two cavalry pistols. Previously, dragoons had carried carbines. However, the instruction of 1696 mandated a switch from carbine to musket. Bayonets were introduced in parallel with the infantry, and was from the instruction of 1707 mandatory for dragoons.

Flintlock carbine model 1699 for the Drabant Corps. Barrel length: 86.5cm, total length: 120.5cm, weight: 3.28kg, calibre: 19mm. (Army Museum, Stockholm; AM.031064)

The chief infantry weapon was the musket. At the time of the Battle of Narva, many units still carried matchlock muskets. In 1699 the 150 men of the Life Company of the Dalecarlia Regiment were armed with 48 pikes, 80 matchlock muskets, and 22 flintlock muskets. Of the latter, it was only the 10 flintlock muskets for the grenadiers that came with bayonets. The Dalecarlia Regiment was lucky when war broke out in that the entire regiment, except the pikemen, were rearmed with flintlock muskets with bayonets.[22] Not all were this fortunate. The drill instruction of 1701 presumed that soldiers were mostly still armed with matchlock muskets. Flintlock muskets were being distributed, but not even the entire Life Guard of Foot had yet been issued flintlocks.

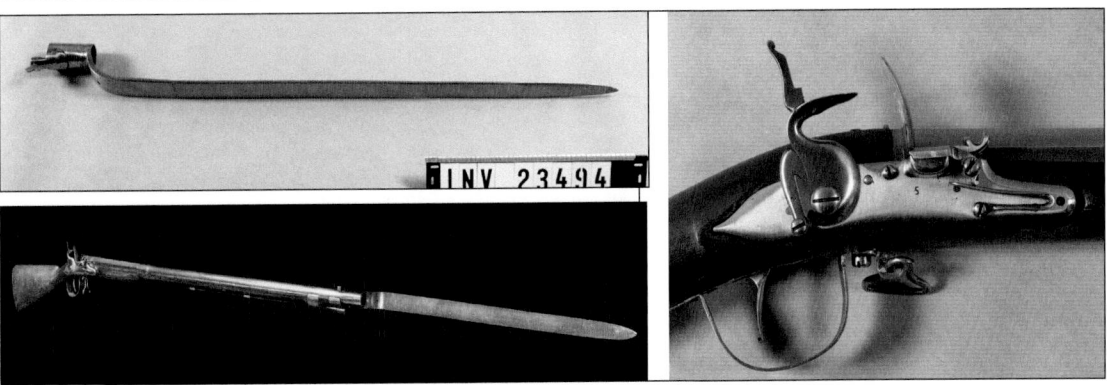

Flintlock musket model 1699 with socket bayonet, of the type distributed to some of the Life Guard of Foot. The bayonet was fastened with a wing screw, a 1693 innovation attributed to Chief of Artillery Johan Siöblad. This prevented the bayonet from falling off, a commonplace problem with socket bayonets across the Continent and in the British Isles. Total length: 148.1cm, barrel length: 108.5cm, weight: 4.4kg, calibre: 20mm. Bayonet length: 67.0cm, weight: 0.67kg. (Army Museum, Stockholm; AM.023493-4)

---

22 Alm, *Eldhandvapen* 1, p.269.

Those infantrymen who did not carry muskets were armed with pikes. Since 1616, the regulation length of a pike was 9 cubits (5.35m). The pike shafts may still have been painted black, since this had previously been a common practice. Generally speaking, the proportion of pikemen in a unit was usually less than a third, and probably closer to a quarter, of the total strength. Most garrison regiments only carried muskets.

A few infantrymen served as grenadiers. Armed with a musket and several grenades, carried in a dedicated container, grenadiers had special tasks including forming the vanguard when storming enemy fortifications.

Each infantryman carried a sword as a sidearm. This was generally the infantry sword model 1685, in Swedish also known as 'service sword' (*kommissvärja*).[23] The soldier wore his sword, and the bayonet if he had one, suspended from a waist belt.

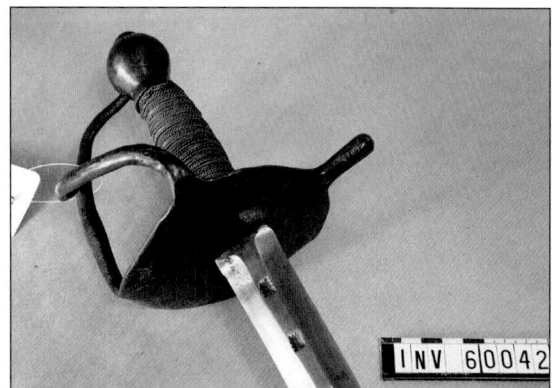
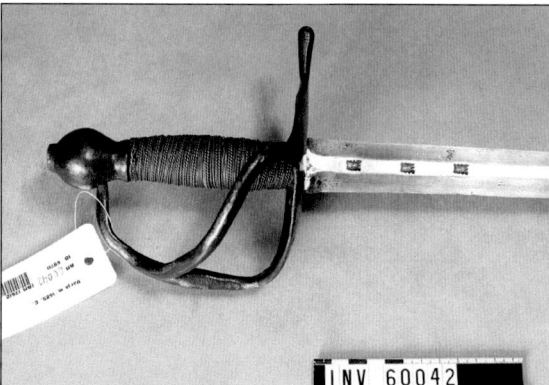
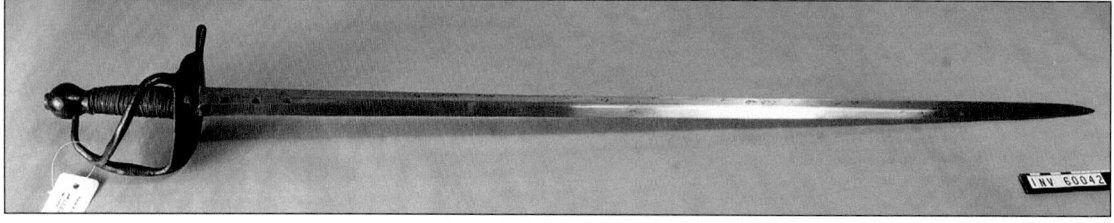

Infantry sword model 1685, in service with the army until the late eighteenth century, with a total production of more than 350,000 over more than 50 years. The model 1685 came with a thumb ring for further protection (not visible in these photos). Blade length: 90.3cm, total length: 105.0cm, blade width: 3.0cm, weight: 1.09kg. Possibly the most successful Swedish weapon of all time. When the army after over a century of service discarded the model 1685, the navy took over remaining stock. Deprived of a thumb ring, shortened for naval use, and distributed as cutlass model 1832, the sidearm remained in service until at least the late nineteenth century. (Army Museum, Stockholm; AM.060042)

Artillerymen were by this time issued special sidearms, more suited to their work with cannon than those used by the infantry. The customary sidearm for the artillery was the artillery hanger or hunting sword (Swedish: *hirschfängare*; from German: *hirschfänger*, 'deer hunter'), introduced in 1675 for both officers and common artillerymen.[24]

---

23 Seitz, *Svärdet och Värjan*, pp.257–72.
24 Seitz, *Svärdet och värjan*, pp.179–83.

THE SWEDISH MILITARY ESTABLISHMENT

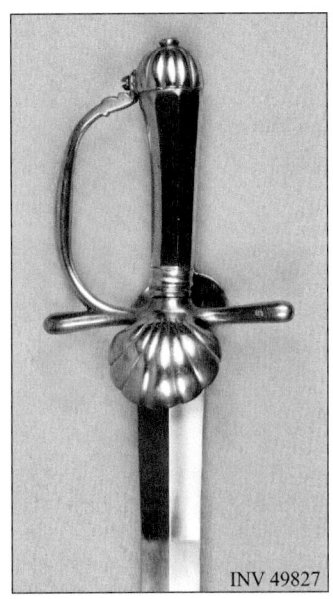

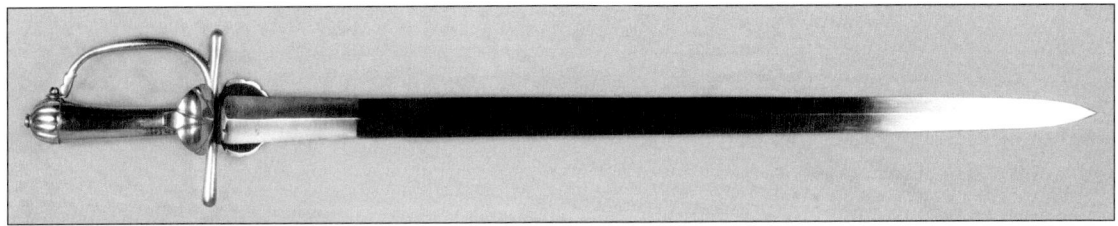

Hanger or hunting sword (Swedish: *hirschfängare*; from German: *hirschfänger*, 'deer hunter') of artillery model 1675. Total length 81.8cm, blade length 68.0cm, weight 0.91kg. This example dates to the early eighteenth century. (Army Museum, Stockholm; AM.049827)

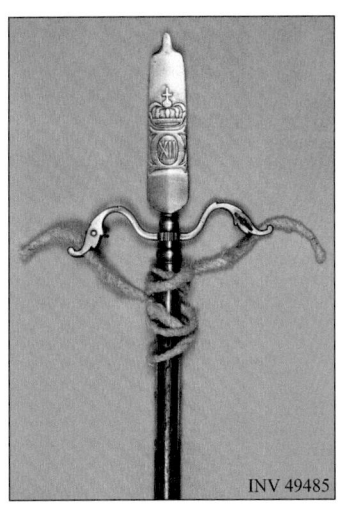

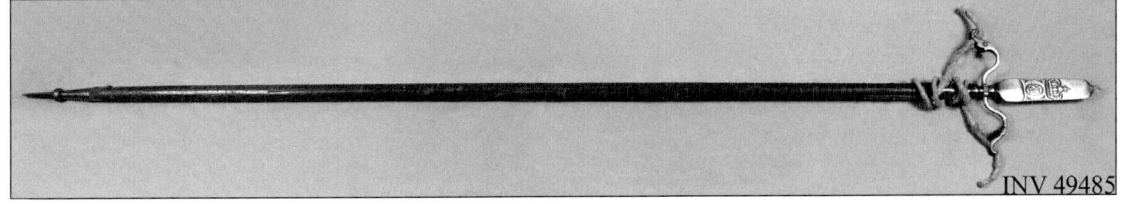

Artillery linstock (Swedish: *luntbardisan*, 'slow match partisan') with the Royal Cypher of King Charles XII, employed by artillery officers when firing cannon or, as in this specimen, when on parade. The fork consists of two branches split to form the clips for the match, with wing screws on the sides to close them. Original length 2.31 m. (Army Museum, Stockholm; AM.049485)

Infantry coat model 1687. This particular coat was supposedly brought to Sweden from France (or Prussia) as a pattern for new uniforms. (Army Museum, Stockholm; AM.015470)

INV 15470

Uniforms

By the late seventeenth century, male civilian dress was strongly influenced by French fashion. The dominant garment was a long, tightly fitting coat with long cuffs and numerous buttons and pleats. Known as *justaucorps*, this long coat served as the model for the regimental uniforms that from then on became standard in European armies. The coat, often with lining and cuffs of a contrasting colour that enabled easier recognition of units at a distance, was worn with narrow breeches, long woollen stockings, and square-toed, often buckled, shoes. A neckcloth and either a brimmed felt hat or a *karpus* cap, a round woollen cap with flaps that could be turned down to protect the eyes, ears, and neck, completed the uniform.

The Swedish Army had for a considerable time aimed for uniform dress. The various regiments had all been issued proper uniforms, although there was no national uniform as such. There was, however, a good understanding of what a uniform should look like. In 1687, King Charles XI decreed that all regiments would wear blue coats. The lining and other details could vary between different regiments. For details about the uniforms of the units that fought at Narva, see Table 1 below. Officers provided their own uniforms. They were expected to conform to regulations but generally used better cloth and materials. New uniforms were only issued when the old ones had worn out, so a given unit might contain uniforms of different types. Furthermore, because of the difficulties in supply, it can be assumed that many of the Swedish units in the field army quickly displayed a rag-tag appearance, for the simple reason of wear and tear. In winter in particular, there was probably a great amount of variation, according to what kind of winter clothing individual soldiers had been able to scrounge. Most would no doubt have acquired at least a grey homespun woollen cloak, cut in a circular shape. There was no formally issued winter uniform.

THE SWEDISH MILITARY ESTABLISHMENT

Table 1. Known Swedish uniforms and colours at Narva, 1700[25]

Unit	Cloak and Coat	Cravat	Breastplate	Breeches	Headgear
Drabant Corps	Light blue with light blue lining	Black taffeta	Yes	Yellow leather	Black hat with gold lace
The Retinue of Nobles in Estonia	Grey cloak with yellow lining, grey coat with yellow lining		Possibly	Yellow leather	Dark grey hat with yellow and blue lace
Life Dragoon Regiment	Blue cloak, blue coat with blue lining	Black taffeta		Yellow leather	Black hat with gold lace
Åbo and Björneborg County Cavalry Regiment	Grey cloak, grey coat with red (or grey) lining		Yes	Yellow leather	
Nyland and Tavastehus County Cavalry Regiment	Grey with red (or grey) lining		Yes	Yellow leather	
Åbo, Nyland, and Viborg County Temporary Cavalry Regiment	Probably grey with yellow lining			Yellow leather	Hat
Karelian Territorial Dragoon Battalion	Grey, described as several years old and in need of replacement				
Life Guard of Foot	Blue cloak with yellow lining, blue coat with yellow lining			Blue, yellow stockings	Hat
Dalecarlia Regiment	Blue with yellow lining			Yellow leather, yellow stockings	Blue karpus with yellow lining
Hälsinge Regiment	Blue with yellow lining			Yellow stockings	Blue karpus
Västmanland Regiment	Blue cloak with blue lining, blue coat with yellow lining			Yellow leather, red stockings	Blue karpus with yellow lining
Närke-Värmland Regiment	Blue cloak with red lining, blue coat with red lining			Yellow leather, blue stockings	Blue karpus with red lining
Ingrian Garrison Regiment (Narva garrison)	Blue with red lining	White		Yellow leather, red stockings	Blue karpus with red lining or hat with blue lace
Artillery	Grey with blue lining			Yellow leather, blue stockings	Black hat

---

25 Primarily Lars-Eric Höglund and Åke Sallnäs, *Stora Nordiska Kriget 1700–1721: Fanor och uniformer* (Karlstad: Acedia Press, 2000), passim.

King Charles's Field Army

The Swedish field army under King Charles which reached Narva consisted of a total of 10,627 combat capable soldiers. Of these, 5,889 were foot soldiers who mostly came from Sweden, 4,314 horse who mainly came from Finland, and 424 artillerymen (Table 2). Notably, the army included a field artillery contingent from Narva consisting of some 90 men: about 36 artillerymen and 54 wagon drivers and similar support personnel. This contingent had previously been detached to the army of Livonia, but now returned home with King Charles's army.[26] Unlike most previous field armies, King Charles's field army mostly consisted of national soldiers. Beside Tiesenhausen's Enlisted Estonian Cavalry Regiment, it was primarily the Life Guard of Foot and the Life Dragoon Regiment that remained raised by enlistment. Even these units were primarily enlisted on Swedish territory, not on the rest of the Continent.

Table 2. The Swedish Army at Lagena, 29 November 1700.[27]

Horse			
Unit	Commander	Coy	Men
His Royal Majesty's Life Drabant Corps	Captain Lieutenant Arvid Bernhard Horn	2	158
The Retinue of Nobles in Estonia	Lieutenant Colonel Reinhold von Liewen	3	400
His Royal Majesty's Life Dragoon Regiment	Lieutenant Colonel Hugo Johan Hamilton	8	514
Åbo and Björneborg County Cavalry Regiment	Colonel Bernhard Rehbinder	7	750
Nyland and Tavastehus County Cavalry Regiment	Lieutenant Colonel Adolph Magnus Klingspor	9	650
Karelian (Viborg and Nyslott County) Cavalry Regiment	Colonel Hans Henrik Rehbinder	7	700
Tiesenhausen's Enlisted Estonian Cavalry Regiment	Colonel Hans Heinrich von Tiesenhausen	3	500

---

26   Ulfhielm, *Kungl. artilleriet: Karl XI:s och Karl XII:s tid*, 49, 326.
27   Generalstaben, *Karl XII på slagfältet 2: Karolinsk slagledning sedd mot bakgrunden av taktikens utveckling från äldsta tider* (Stockholm: P. A. Norstedt & Söner, 1918), 318; Ulfhielm, *Kungl. artilleriet: Karl XI:s och Karl XII:s tid*, 325–7. The army was certainly not stronger than indicated, and possibly weaker. The Life Guard consisted of 1,718 men when it departed from Pernau, leaving some sick men behind. More soldiers fell ill during the march, resulting in a total of 1,580 fit men at Wesenberg. Some may have recovered in time for the battle, but the suggested figure of 1,700 should be regarded as a maximum. The real figure was likely lower. Wernstedt, *Kungl. Svea livgardes historia* 4, pp.371–2.

Unit	Commander	Bat	Men
Åbo, Nyland, and Viborg County Temporary (*tremänning*) Cavalry Regiment	Colonel Carl Magnus Rehbinder	4	340
Karelian Territorial Dragoon (*lantdragon*) Battalion	Major Niklas de Molin	4	302
Total		**47**	**4,314**

Foot			
Unit	**Commander**	**Bat**	**Men**
His Majesty's Life Guard of Foot	Major General Knut Posse	6	1,700
Dalecarlia Regiment	Colonel Magnus Stenbock	2	661
Hälsinge Regiment	Colonel Göran Johan von Knorring	2	568
Västmanland Regiment	Major Mattias Fredrik von Feilitzen	3	556
Närke-Värmland Regiment	Lieutenant Colonel Carl Gustav Roos	2	732
Combined Finnish Regiment with contingents from Åbo County, Björneborg, Tavastehus, Viborg, Savolax, and Nyland Regiments	Major General Georg Johan Maydell	4	933
Åbo, Björneborg, and Nyland County Temporary (*tremänning*) Regiment	Colonel Magnus Gabriel von Tiesenhausen	1	360
Tavastehus, Viborg, and Nyslott County Temporary (*tremänning*) Regiment	Lieutenant Colonel Göran Hastfehr	1	379
Total		**21**	**5,889**

Artillery	Chief of Artillery Johan Siöblad	21? Guns	424
Total			**10,627**

Johan Siöblad. (Portrait by David Klöcker Ehrenstrahl in the collection at Gripsholm Castle)

3

The Russian Military Establishment

Russia had entered the seventeenth century with a traditional military establishment which derived from the medieval Mongol military model, but the country moved into the eighteenth century with a modern European army.

Even before Tsar Peter assumed the throne, Russia had gone to great lengths to transform its traditional military establishment. While the Tsar's army still included traditional cavalry, in the form of men from families defined by hereditary military service, and highly mobile horse archers, in the form of Tatars and some Cossacks, these were primarily used as raiders and played only a minor role in Tsar Peter's modern army. More importantly, Russia also fielded soldiers with up-to-date training and armament.[1] The first of their kind were trained during the Thirty Years' War by officers from Swedish service and according to Swedish standards.

During the Thirty Years' War, Russia had been one of the few foreign powers which supported the Swedish cause. In return, Sweden's King Gustavus Adolphus had assisted Tsar Michael Romanov in modernising the Russian Army by sending officers for the Tsar's new European-style regiments which were first set up in 1630. The new units had been trained in the Continental or, to be more specific, Swedish model of warfare.[2]

In the seven decades since, the Russian Army had fought several wars, made significant achievements on their own, and gained much experience in modern warfare. However, funding was never sufficient to maintain all units on a standing basis. At the beginning of 1700, Tsar Peter regarded only

---

1   For further details on the traditional Russian military system, see Michael Fredholm von Essen, *Muscovy's Soldiers: The Emergence of the Russian Army 1462–1689* (Warwick: Helion & Co., 2018), and on Tsar Peter's modern army, Boris Megorsky, *The Russian Army in the Great Northern War 1700–21: Organisation, Materiel, Training and Combat Experience, Uniforms* (Warwick: Helion & Co., 2018).
2   B. F. Porshnev, *Muscovy and Sweden in the Thirty Years' War, 1630–1635* (Cambridge: Cambridge University Press, 1995), pp.82–83 & p.162; Fredholm von Essen, *Muscovy's Soldiers*, pp.82 & 88–94; Fredholm von Essen, *Lion from the North 1*, pp.59 & 222; Michael Fredholm von Essen, *Lion from the North* 2 (Warwick: Helion & Co., 2020), p.225.

his two guard infantry regiments (the Preobrazhenskiy and Semyonovskiy Guard Regiments, although they were not yet known under these names[3]) as completely up to modern standards, although even their weaponry, equipment, and uniforms left much to be desired. The Preobrazhenskiy Regiment was technically established in 1683 but neither formation was turned into a real military unit before 1691.

Two other infantry regiments, the late François Lefort's Regiment (Lefortovo; officially, First Selected Moscow Regiment) and the Butyrsk Regiment (Second Selected Moscow Regiment), were regarded as in part up to standards. These two regiments were first raised in 1656–1657.[4]

This should not be interpreted as the other regiments being obsolete. When the Narva campaign was underway, Lieutenant General Ludwig Nicolaus von Hallart, an engineering officer in Saxon service, noted that 'all regiments [of the Moscow Army that arrived with the Tsar] were not only well-dressed, they were also particularly well-trained, and well-armed, every regiment in its particular uniform colour, and each battalion consisting of four colours [that is, four companies]'. The Preobrazhenskiy Guard Regiment was dressed in green uniforms, Hallart noted.[5] Most regiments of Tsar Peter's army were issued with new uniforms in 1700, and had a new and up-to-date organisation and a fresh set of regimental colours.

In addition, the Russian military system still included traditional infantry musketeer units known as streltsy ('shooters'; *strelets*, pl. *strel'tsy*). The streltsy lived in separate neighbourhoods within the towns, and at regular intervals, they engaged in unit training of sorts (usually shooting contests). The streltsy were uniformly armed and clothed, since they received their arms and equipment from the state. Tsar Peter strongly disliked the streltsy, in part because they had occasionally rebelled against the central power and against him (in 1689 and 1698), and in part because he considered them old-fashioned. He ordered the disbanding of the mutinous streltsy regiments in 1698. The remaining Moscow streltsy regiments were reformed, with the soldiers and their families exiled from Moscow.

Russia had early on developed a strong artillery, and had all the usual types of cannon that could also be found in other European armies. The period from the mid-seventeenth century onwards saw further improvements. The new infantry regiments received modern regimental artillery in the Swedish manner. From the end of the 1650s to the early 1660s, attempts were made to unify and standardise different calibres and types of cannon.

---

3 In early 1700, the two regiments were still known as the First and Second 'Thousands' of the Third Selected Moscow Regiment under Avtonom Golovin. Vladimir S. Velikanov, 'K voprosu ob organizatsii i chislennosti Russkoy Armii v Narvskom pokhode 1700 goda,' *Voyna i oruzhiye 2:1: Novyye issledovaniya i materialy* (St Petersburg: VIMAIViVS, 2011), p.130–43 on p.136.

4 The First Selected Moscow Regiment was the oldest new style regiment still in service. It remained until disbanded in 1918, and was then known as the 8th Moscow Grenadier Regiment. The Second Selected Moscow Regiment, or Butyrsk Regiment, was the second oldest new style regiment still in service. It, too, was disbanded in 1918, and was then known as the 13th Erivan' Grenadier Regiment (named after Erivan', today Yerevan, the capital of Armenia).

5 Ludwig Nicolaus von Hallart. *Das Tagebuch des Generals von Hallart über die Belagerung und Schlacht von Narva 1700* (Reval: Franz Kluge, 1894), p.25.

THE RUSSIAN MILITARY ESTABLISHMENT

Moreover, Russia was known to carry out a number of innovations in artillery.

The Russian Army was also proficient in modern military engineering. In 1696, the Imperial military engineer Ernst Friedrich von Borgsdorf joined the Russian Army at Azov. He introduced a number of new methods and tactics in combat engineering and also wrote two treatises on the subject, which were translated into Russian and disseminated within the army. There was thus no shortage of knowledge of up-to-date methods in siege warfare.

Tsar Peter's army still relied on the services and expertise of quite a number of foreign military officers. This occasionally caused problems because of the language barrier. Moreover, many members of the Orthodox Church preached religious hatred to all foreigners. As a result, some Russian soldiers found it difficult to trust their foreign officers. However, over time many of the foreign officers naturalised as Russian subjects. The Swedish intelligence officer Erik Palmquist (c. 1650–1676?), who in 1673–1674 participated in an embassy to Moscow with the task to prepare a military intelligence report on the Russian Army and military geography, noted that many of the officers with foreign names in the Russian Army were actually born in Russia.[6] At the time of the Battle of Narva, yet another generation had passed. Suddenly most officers of (ultimately) foreign origin in the Russian Army in reality were second or even third generation immigrants, born in Russia, such as the sons of Tsar Peter's confidants Patrick Gordon, and François Lefort. Such young officers certainly spoke Russian and would not necessarily have been regarded as heathen foreigners by their men. As a result, Russia had plenty of native-born officers well versed in the Continental art of war.

The only type of unit that remained sub-standard in the Russian Army, and had been regarded as such since at least the 1650s, if not before, was the old style cavalry. Composed of the descendants of the princely retinues of the Middle Ages, they included the boyars or nobility. However, the majority of the old style cavalry were not boyars. Instead, they belonged to the category of men known as 'hereditary servicemen' (*sluzhilyye lyudi po*

Field Marshal General Fyodor Golovin, portrait by Pieter Schenk, 1706 (Public Domain)

General of Cavalry Boris Sheremetyev. (Public Domain)

---

6   Erik Palmquist, *Några observationer angående Ryssland, sammanfattade av Erik Palmquist år 1674* (Moscow: Lomonosov, 2012), pp.307–9.

Prince Alexander of Imeretia, depicted while in Swedish captivity. He wears what appears to be an elaborate version of the so-called Hungarian uniform style (see text) issued to the new regiments in 1700. Drawing by Elias Brenner, early 1700s (Author's photo)

Lieutenant General Ludwig Nicolaus von Hallart, depicted while in Swedish captivity. Drawing by Elias Brenner, early 1700s (Author's photo)

otechestvu). This category was in itself divided into those of provincial rank, who were in the majority, and those of Moscow rank, who were considered senior in status. All hereditary servicemen served on the basis of land ownership, either an inherited patrimonial freehold or a service land grant which was conditional on lifelong and unlimited military service. The land grant privilege, too, was heritable; however, although a son was entitled to a land grant, it would not necessarily be the same land that his father had held. The hereditary servicemen could be seen as low level nobility or gentry, but in reality, many held limited land and accordingly were no wealthier than taxpaying peasants. Over time, some actually grew poorer than the taxpaying peasants, since they lacked the time to farm or otherwise manage their lands because of military duties. Hereditary servicemen had to provide their own weapons and supplies when on campaign, which was a heavy burden for those who lacked sufficient lands. The old style cavalry participated in the Narva campaign, with contingents from several towns and cities including Moscow. The capital was the home of the Sovereign's Division (*Gosudarev polk*) which in the past had consisted of the Tsar's personal retainers.

The supreme commander of Tsar Peter's army at Narva was Field Marshal General Fyodor Golovin, who also seems to have been in nominal charge of the Moscow Army. Golovin was not only Field Marshal General; he also held the rank of Admiral General. Golovin was a diplomat and confidant of Tsar Peter who among other accomplishments had concluded the 1689 Treaty of Nerchinsk with the powerful Manchu Empire, according to which Russia abandoned its claim to the lands north of the Amur River. He also played a prominent role in the creation of the Russian Navy. Promoted straight to Field Marshal General immediately before the Narva campaign, he had little military experience.

General Boris Sheremetyev served as commander of the cavalry. A diplomat and soldier, Sheremetyev was a veteran of several wars against the Ottoman Empire and Crimean Tatars including the first and second Azov campaigns of 1695 and 1696. Beloved by his soldiers, who wrote songs about him, Sheremetyev consistently wore West European dress since his return from Western Europe in 1699.

Prince Alexander of Imeretia served as General of Artillery (*General-Feldzeugmeister*). He was a son of ex-King Archil of Imeretia, a kingdom in modern-day Georgia. Prince Alexander grew up in exile in Moscow with Tsar Peter who in recognition of his friendship and knowledge of European artillery system ultimately appointed him head of the Russian artillery. Although trained in artillery sciences, Prince Alexander lacked combat experience.

At Narva, the aforementioned Lieutenant General Ludwig Nicolaus von Hallart, an officer in Saxon service sent by King Augustus as chief fortification officer, was responsible for the siegeworks.

Organisation

When Tsar Peter, on 17 November 1699 (O.S.), decreed the formation of a new army of volunteers and conscripts, he accepted men of almost any background. Only former Moscow streltsy and those obligated to pay taxes (*tyaglyye lyudi*) were not allowed to sign up. Tsar Peter distrusted the former and needed the latter as sources of revenue. This meant that the majority of the recruits who henceforth filled up the ranks of the new army were impoverished hereditary servicemen and serfs, whether conscripted or on the run from their owners.

Tsar Peter wanted his new, modern army to have a unified structure. The Tsar put most effort into the infantry; he wanted each infantry and dragoon regiment, except the guard regiments, to consist of 12 companies. Neither regiments nor companies departed from customary Continental and Swedish standards. Four infantry or dragoon companies constituted a battalion, and when available, two cavalry companies might be formed into a squadron.

When the Tsar raised his new, modern army at Moscow, he also made sure that the units would carry colours of the same pattern. Detailed instructions were issued, and the colours were manufactured in 1700 by workshops in the capital under the central control of the Armoury, which by tradition produced military banners. Since each new line regiment was organised into 12 companies, the new colours reflected this: each regiment received one white colour with the image of a double-headed eagle for the colonel's life company, and 11 company colours of identical base colour and composition with, as described in the decree, 'branches and clouds and the knightly crosses of St Andrew and broadswords and chains.'[7] The company colours of a given regiment were in fact identical, and each colour was only identified by the number of stars depicted on the colour: two stars for the 2nd company, three for the 3rd, and so on. The identification of companies

---

7 Marina Golovanova, 'Flags Dating Back to 1700 in the Documents From the Russian State Archive of Ancient Acts,' Karin Tetteris (ed.), *In Hoc Signo Vinces: The Vexillological Seminar, Stockholm 2011 & 2013* (Stockholm: Armémuseum, 2016), pp.15–19, on p.18.

by a number of stars that corresponded to its number was a practice that had emerged in the seventeenth century. The base colours for the regimental colours were selected from among red, reddish-brown, brown, sand, yellow, light green, green, blue-grey, blue-steel, and light raspberry pink.[8] With so many new regiments, it was obvious that many had to share the same base colour. Staves were painted, often red but sometimes green. Finials were made of copper, gilt for the life company colours and tin for the rest. Some regiments carried finials with the St Andrew's cross on them.

Modern cavalry units were raised as regiments and sub-divided into companies in the normal Continental and Swedish manner. The number of companies varied from regiment to regiment. None came from Moscow, but units of modern cavalry joined the Tsar's army from provincial towns.

Russian drum, captured by the Swedish Army at Saladen (modern-day Saločiai in Lithuania) in 1703. Diameter 52cm, height 53cm. By the second half of the seventeenth century, drums seem to have come in fundamentally two sizes (approximately 40cm and 50cm in diameter and height, respectively), depending on their purpose. The larger ones were so-called colonel's and lieutenant colonel's drums, while the smaller were company drums. This drum is painted in yellow and red triangles with red bands. Other drums may have been richly decorated in gold with the double-headed eagle and various plant motifs. Every drum also had a leather sling for carrying and a cloth cover for protection when not in use. For an illustration of the cloth cover, see the colour section. (Army Museum, Stockholm; AM.137006)

Chekhol, captured at Saladen in 1703. Height including pendants 79cm, diameter 39cm, stave length 3.2m. When drums were not in use, they were protected by elaborate cylindrical cloth covers (*chekhol*, pl. *chekhly*) with a diameter of roughly 40cm to 50cm and a height of 65cm to 85cm, each painted with religious or other motifs such as stylised flowers, or occasionally decorated in appliqué in the same style. Some of these cloth covers, including this one, may also have been used as signs for the commander's quarters while in camp, if so, they were hung from a partisan or spear. This at least was the contemporary interpretation of their function in Sweden, which may be based on eyewitness reports. See, e.g., the official battle reports from the Swedish victory at Saladen, 1703 (reprinted in Höglund, Sallnäs, and Bespalow, *Stora Nordiska Kriget 1700–1721*, Vol. 3, pp.47–48 & 71–72). (Army Museum, Stockholm; AM.083579)

---

8   Golovanova, 'Flags,' pp.18–19.

The old style cavalry still followed traditional organisational forms, which meant that a regimental-sized contingent, best called a division, was raised from each town or city. The various contingents varied widely in strength. The regimental formations were divided into units known as 'thousands' (*tysyachi*), 'hundreds' (*sotni*, sing. *sotnya*), 'half-hundreds' (*polusotni*), and 'tens' (*desyatki*).

The streltsy, despite their hereditary background, were no longer that different from the new infantry regiments. A streltsy regiment was divided into companies of about a hundred men each, a company accordingly being known as a *sotnya* (hundred) like the corresponding unit in the old style cavalry. The regiment was commanded by a headman (*golova*), under whom served a deputy (*podgolova*), below whom were commanders of respectively 100 men (*sotniki*), 50 men (*pyatidesyatniki*), and 10 men (*desyatniki*).[9] A streltsy regiment might consist of from 500 to 1,000 streltsy. Each regiment had its integral artillery, consisting of from six to eight guns. The men were armed similarly to other musketeers.

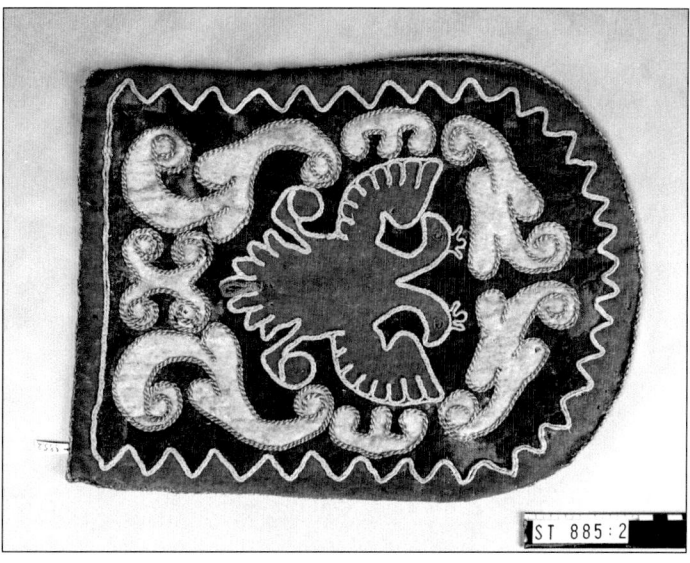

Russian musket lock cover. The Swedish army captured at least 194 items of this type as trophies at Saladen, 1703. The army described them as musket lock covers in the official report of the same year. Although for this reason attributed as lock covers by most Russian historians, there is some doubt about how they actually were used since the shape works poorly as a lock cover. Possibly, they were primarily used for parades. (Army Museum, Stockholm; AM.084839)

Tactical Doctrine

Tactics had begun to change with the introduction of the Swedish style organisational forms and practices. Tsar Peter's new army fundamentally operated like any other Continental army. Compared to Swedes, they can be said to have preferred defensive tactics, preferably from prepared positions behind fieldworks. Yet, the Petrine army was certainly willing and able to charge an approaching enemy. In fact, there were more similarities than differences between the Tsar's new army and its Swedish counterpart.

The first Russian instruction that details military thought on tactics under Tsar Peter was written in 1698 by Adam Weide, then a major of the Preobrazhenskiy Regiment. Weide, who was born in Russia, travelled to the Holy Roman Empire to study the Imperial Army in 1696 and 1697. To gain practical knowledge, he participated in the Battle of Zenta against the

---

9 Grigori Carpofsson Cotossichin [Kotoshikhin], *Beskrifning om muschofsche rijkets staat* (Stockholm: Ljus, 1908, first published in 1669), p.73.

Ottomans in 1697 under Prince Eugène of Savoy. Based on these experiences, he returned to Moscow where he submitted a detailed report to Tsar Peter with a proposal for an infantry instruction. This was the *Voinskiy ustav* ('military regulation') of 1698. The instruction was possibly copied and distributed among Tsar Peter's officers. However, we know it best from the printed edition that finally was issued in 1841 for purposes of documentation. In addition to text, the printed edition contains 56 sketches of infantrymen carrying out various types of drill. While the *Voinskiy ustav* was never adopted in its entirety as a military instruction, abbreviated versions of it were printed as the first Russian official drill manuals in 1699 and 1700.[10]

In comparison, there were no similarities between Continental tactics or doctrine with regard to the old style cavalry, which still fundamentally relied on medieval Mongol tactics. Slow-moving enemy infantry was usually handled by harassment and skirmishes. When confronted with enemy cavalry, the old style cavalry might withdraw in feigned flight until the pursuing enemy could be attacked in the flank by other Russian cavalry or rashly followed all the way into the range of fire of the Russian artillery or infantry, or into an ambush if possible. Raiding and looting were frequently used as a weapon of terror, to reduce the enemy population's will to resist, but also, yet more importantly, as a means to deprive the enemy of supplies in the area of operations.

Arms and Armour

In 1700, most of Tsar Peter's infantry carried flintlock muskets. The new infantry regiments were not issued pikes, but the old Selected Regiments may still have fielded them (and if so, in a ratio between pike and shot similar to the Swedes). Russia produced good flintlock muskets, and in addition, imported significant volumes of them from particularly the Netherlands, but also from Germany. The Russian Army at Narva may well have had a far higher proportion of flintlocks than existed in the Swedish army. Russian infantrymen were issued with plug bayonets, and possibly a few ring or socket bayonets, but swords or similar sidearms were apparently rare in the infantry in 1700.

Although there were no new style cavalry regiments in the army that Tsar Peter raised in Moscow, some such units joined the army from the provinces. New style cavalrymen were generally of hereditary serviceman origin, so could aspire to receiving land grants and were expected to provide for themselves while on campaign duty, including arranging for a horse, food, and fodder. Each soldier of the new style cavalry was also accordingly expected to equip himself, at his own expense, in the same way as the old style cavalry, and was required to muster with a horse, carbine, a pair of pistols, and a sword or sabre. Most probably still wore Russian dress of caftan and traditional boots.

---

10   Megorsky, *Russian Army in the Great Northern War*, p.149.

THE RUSSIAN MILITARY ESTABLISHMENT

Dragoons were issued short muskets. Both dragoon regiments at Narva were also issued 286 polearms each, when established. We do not know whether these were pikes or lances. By tradition, dragoons were infantry, so pikes would seem the more logical choice. However, from 1702 onwards some dragoons certainly carried lances for cavalry missions.

A peculiarity with the two dragoon regiments that fought at Narva is that both primarily consisted of less affluent hereditary servicemen of the type which in times past would have served in the old style cavalry. Technically, these men were, in a similar manner to the cavalry, supposed to provide their own arms and equipment. Since this was unworkable in a modern army, the Tsar distributed money to those who enlisted so that they could purchase cloth for garments in the correct, uniform colour. However, the soldiers themselves had to have the cloth sewn into garments. We accordingly do not know to what degree they actually wore uniform dress. The dragoons were issued weapons from the state, however, so at least they were uniformly armed.

With regard to arms and equipment, the old style cavalry remained much as it had been in the past, armed with sabre, pistols, and the occasional carbine or musket. As before, they were not uniformed but turned out in civilian dress. A limited few may still have worn helmets and perhaps small pieces of armour, although neither seems likely in 1700. The traditional clothes worn by Russians at the time were, like those elsewhere in the region, of Inner Asian origin, ranging from the caftan to the high, soft boots associated with equestrian nomads. Tsar Peter hated these traditional garments, which he believed impaired the modernisation effort, and ultimately was to forbid them.

Uniforms

While organisational forms, tactics, and weapons had adapted to present practices in Continental Europe, Russian soldiers did not yet as a rule wear Continental uniform styles. West European coats for the infantry were introduced only in 1703–1704. Nor did the men in Tsar Peter's new regiments wear traditional Russian garments of the kind that the Tsar loathed and the streltsy still retained. Instead, the soldiers in the new regiments wore a transitional style that looked both to the east and the west: the so-called Hungarian style. Uniforms of the Hungarian style were first issued to the Preobrazhenskiy Regiment in autumn 1698. The new regiments received Hungarian style uniforms in 1700, when they were issued coats of dark green, green, light blue, red, and cherry-coloured (red-

Red caftan, reportedly a war trophy from Narva and hitherto tentatively identified as a Russian officer's coat from Nikolay Balck's Regiment. Unfortunately, there is no certain link between this caftan and the Hungarian style uniforms issued for Tsar Peter's army in 1700. This garment was previously identified as a Polish caftan (Polish: *kontusz*) from the reign of Sweden's Queen Christina (1626–1689: r. 1632–1654). Even if the caftan actually is a war trophy from Narva, there is nothing inherently implausible in a Polish stylistic origin since Polish fashion was common in Western Russia and Moscow. (Royal Armoury, Stockholm; 31483LRK; photo: Helena Bonnevier, Livrustkammaren/SHM)

Blue-green caftan, reportedly a war trophy from Narva and commonly identified as a Russian officer's coat. Again, there is no certain link between this caftan and the uniforms issued for Tsar Peter's army in 1700. While this garment on the surface possibly looks more representative of the so-called Hungarian style uniform, it is significantly longer than the 'garter-length' that Tsar Peter decreed. Moreover, it corresponds to fashion prevalent in Moscow in the 1680s. The garment may accordingly have belonged to a Russian officer at Narva, but if so, it is unlikely ever to have formed part of the uniforms issued in 1700. (Royal Armoury, Stockholm; 19274LRK; photo: Fredrik Andersson, Livrustkammaren/SHM)

brown) cloth (Table 3). We know colour details for some of the new regiments. Unfortunately, there is no conclusive evidence as to what pattern this style of garment employed.

Nonetheless, recent research by Sergey Shamenkov, who has contributed colour plates to the present book, shows that the Hungarian style meant garter-length coats (that is, similar in length to West European coats) split along the front and closed with a set of buttons, with the addition of cords laid along the seams, straight-cut sleeves, and at times, fur trimming.[11] (For modern reconstructions of Tsar Peter's Hungarian style uniforms, see the colour plates.)

Musketeer. Although often identified as a soldier in the new, Hungarian style uniform issued for Tsar Peter's army in 1700, this is merely one of a series of generic soldiers from 1698 that illustrates the exercise of arms. Weide, *Voinskiy ustav*, 1698. (Public Domain)

Grenadier. Although often identified as a soldier in the new, Hungarian style uniform issued for Tsar Peter's army in 1700, this is merely one of a series of generic soldiers that illustrates the exercise of arms. Weide, *Voinskiy ustav*, 1698. (Public Domain)

---

11   Sergey I. Shamenkov, 'Vengerskoye Plat'ye Pekhotnykh Polkov Armii Petra Velikogo,' *Istoriya voyennogo dela: Issledovaniya i istochniki* 1 (2012), 421–63; Sergey I. Shamenkov, 'Vengerskoye Plat'ye Pekhotnykh Polkov Armii Petra Velikogo,' 1699–1703,' *Istoriya voyennogo dela: Issledovaniya i istochniki* 3 (2013), pp.466–90.

THE RUSSIAN MILITARY ESTABLISHMENT

Table 3. Known Russian uniforms and unit colours, 1700. For further details on preserved unit colours, see the colour artwork section.[12]

Unit	Coat	Cap	Boots	Colours
Preobrazhenskiy Guard Regiment	Dark green with red lining	Red	Red	White life company, Black company
Semyonovskiy Guard Regiment	Blue with red lining	Red		White life company, Blue company
Alferiy Schnewentz's 'Preobrazhenskiy' Dragoon Regiment	Dark green			Black
Joachim Gulitz's 'Preobrazhenskiy' Dragoon Regiment	Dark green	Red, red sash		Green
First Selected Moscow Regiment (Lefortovo Regiment)	Dark red			Likely White life company, Yellow company
Second Selected Moscow Regiment (Butyrsk Regiment)	Dark red with yellow lining			White life company with red cross, Red company with white cross or, far more likely in 1700, White life company and Red company similar to those of the First Selected Regiment
Matvey Fliwerk's Regiment	Green with dark green lining			White life company, Green company
Ivan Mewes's Regiment	Blue			
Astafiy Pohlmann's Regiment	Cherry-coloured (red-brown)			
Alexander Gordon of Achintoul's Regiment	Dark green			
Erich von Werden's Regiment	Green			
Nikolay Balck's Regiment	Dark red			
Tomas Junger's Regiment	Green			
Fyodor Balck's Regiment	Dark red			

---

12 Primarily but not exclusively Megorsky, *Russian Army in the Great Northern War*, pp.242–54. Much data is uncertain, and other researchers sometimes suggest differently coloured coats.

Tsar Peter's Field Army

It is difficult to estimate the actual strength and composition of the Russian Army in the Narva campaign, since contemporary sources remain incomplete and some contradict each other. Generally speaking, we have reliable data on Tsar Peter's new, modern army and in particular the units from Moscow. Data on provincial and old style units often remain uncertain and ambiguous. In preparation of the coming war with Sweden, Tsar Peter in November-December 1699 set up three new army divisions (*general'stvo*, pl. *general'stva*; 'generalships'), each of 10 regiments, under Avtonom Golovin, Adam Weide, and Prince Anikita Repnin. By summer 1700, the three divisions each consisted of one new Guard or already-existing Selected Moscow infantry regiment, eight new style infantry regiments, and one dragoon regiment (in two out of three divisions).[13] Each new style infantry regiment had an establishment strength of 1,238 men in 12 companies. The Guard units were larger. Moreover, both Guard units at the time when the divisions were formed were still regarded as one regiment (Third Selected Moscow Regiment), which made Golovin's Division significantly larger than the others. Together, they formed the infantry of the Moscow Army. To this was added the (old style) Sovereign's Division, the traditional noble cavalry from Moscow. Altready largely obsolete before the Great Northern War, the Narva campaign was the last in which the Sovereign's Division participated in the field.[14]

Additionally there was the Novgorod Army, under Governor Prince Ivan Trubetskoy. It consisted of a new division (*general'stvo*), of seven new style regiments. The smallest was a contingent from Ivan Kokoshkin's new style Cavalry Regiment. But the Novgorod Army additionally included the (old style) Novgorod Division, the Novgorod equivalent of the old Sovereign's Division from Moscow.

Tsar Peter also called up the Smolensk Army. It primarily consisted of the (old style) Smolensk Division of traditional noble cavalry. Although the noble cavalry from Smolensk was obsolete, like the old style cavalry from other Russian towns, it was still regarded as a little higher in quality than most others, because it had assimilated some aspects of Polish cavalry tactics and equipment including the use of long lances. Moreover, the Smolensk Army also included a small contingent from Grigoriy Rydvanskiy's new style

---

13 Velikanov, 'K voprosu ob organizatsii i chislennosti Russkoy Armii v Narvskom pokhode,' 136.
14 Contemporary observers estimated that Tsar Peter's army at Narva included as many as 5,000 or 6,000 old style cavalry, of which Hallart claimed 2,000 came from Smolensk. This would seem to mean that 3,000 or 4,000 came from Moscow. Tsar Peter's official history claimed 5,000 old style cavalry from Moscow and Smolensk. Hallart, *Tagebuch*, 38; Tsar Peter's diary, i.e. *Zhurnal ili Podennaya zapiska, blazhennyya i vechnodostoynyya pamyati gosudarya imperatora Petra Velikago s 1698 goda dazhe do zaklyucheniya neyshtatskago mira* 1 (St. Petersburg: Imperatorskaya akademiya nauk, 1770), p.14; Tat'yana S. Maykova (ed.), *Gistoriya Sveyskoy voyny (Podennaya zapiska Petra Velikogo)* 1 (Moscow: Krug, 2004), p.204. However, these figures appear exaggerated. A total of some 4,500 old style cavalry seems more consistent with other data. Velikanov, 'K voprosu ob organizatsii i chislennosti russkoy armii v Narvskom pokhode,' pp.132–3.

THE RUSSIAN MILITARY ESTABLISHMENT

Cavalry Regiment. Although Rydvanskiy's Cavalry Regiment consisted of 1,146 men in 12 companies, only about 200 joined the Narva campaign.

Finally, a number of other units were called up as well. The Tsar had more armies elsewhere, and military units were distributed throughout the vast country.[15] These included three former Moscow streltsy units exiled to Belgorod in the south, the combined artillery parks of Moscow, Novgorod, and Pskov, possibly a few other units from elsewhere that may or not have appeared at Narva, and a division of Ukrainian Cossacks under Hetman Ivan Obidovskiy. It is notoriously difficult to estimate the strength of Ukrainian units, but the division included from seven to nine regiments so numbers were significant. The total number of fighting men raised for the Narva campaign was somewhere between 55,000 and 59,000. However, neither Prince Repnin's nor Obidovskiy's divisions reached Narva in time to take part in the ensuing battle. If we disregard them, Tsar Peter's combined army at Narva and Ivangorod altogether counted an estimated 38,700 men (Table 4).[16] Although most units deployed on the western side of the River Narova, some were on the eastern side, facing Narva's twin fortress Ivangorod. Disease was rampant in the Russian camp, so most of the time a large number, perhaps 2,000 to 3,000 men in Hallart's estimate, were too sick to fight.[17]

The Preobrazhenskiy and Semyonovskiy Guard Regiments, First and Second Selected Moscow Regiments, and the dragoon regiments consisted of professional, trained soldiers, as were the streltsy regiments. The rest were new soldiers. Yet, all were enlisted, many were volunteers, all had received some training, and most were provided with modern flintlock muskets.[18]

Naturally, Tsar Peter's army was also accompanied by a large crowd of non-combatants, of whom we have no information except that they followed the army in the customary manner. They included spouses, servants, and almost certainly levied peasants called up for labour and transportation duties.

---

15   The Swedish intelligence officer Erik Palmquist had reported Russia's mobilisation potential for military purposes as about 300,000 men. However, of this number only about a third, somewhat more than 100,000 men, was on active duty. Most were intended to serve as a defence against the Ottoman Empire and the Tatar Khanate of the Crimea. In hindsight, Palmquist's information seems accurate. Fredholm von Essen, *Muscovy's Soldiers*, p.170.
16   Velikanov, 'K voprosu ob organizatsii i chislennosti russkoy armii v Narvskom pokhode,' 140, suggests 34,000 to 36,000 men. Participants in the battle on the Russian side suggest 35,400, of whom 7,500 horse (Hallart, *Tagebuch*, 24, 25, 33, 38), or 34,000 actually present out of 38,000 (Alexander Gordon of Auchintoul, *History of Peter the Great* 1, pp150 &151).
17   Hallart, *Tagebuch*, p.66.
18   For example, Ivanitskiy's and Ivan von Del'den's regiments were formed from volunteers, while Bieltz's regiment was raised from conscripts. All were raised in Moscow in 1700. Caspar Gultz's Regiment was formed from volunteers in Kazan' in the same year. Most of Prince Repnin's units were raised in the Volga region.

Table 4. The Russian Army raised for the Narva campaign, August 1700 [19]

Sovereign's Old Style Division, under Field Marshal General Fyodor Golovin	
Moscow old style cavalry	2,000 men
Avtonom Golovin's Division	
Preobrazhenskiy Guard Regiment, under Johann Ernst von Blomberg	
	2,204 men in 16 companies
Semyonovskiy Guard Regiment, under Pavel Cunningham	1,589 men in 12 companies
Alferiy Schnewentz's 'Preobrazhenskiy' Dragoon Regiment	1,040 men in 12 companies
Matvey Fliwerk's Regiment	1,219 men in 12 companies
Carl Gustav Ivanitskiy's Regiment	1,347 men in 12 companies
Ivan Mewes's Regiment	1,261 men in 12 companies
Il'ya Bieltz's Regiment	992 men in 12 companies
Astafiy Pohlmann's Regiment	1,250 men in 12 companies
Ivan Treyden's Regiment	1,343 men in 12 companies
Matvey Treyden's Regiment	1,361 men in 12 companies
Carl Peter Devson's Regiment	1,325 men in 12 companies
Total	14,931 men
Adam Weide's Division	
First Selected Moscow Regiment, also known as Weide's Regiment (formerly Lefort's Regiment), under Giorgio Lima	1,018 men in 12 companies
Joachim Gulitz's 'Preobrazhenskiy' Dragoon Regiment	833 men in 12 companies
Alexander Gordon of Achintoul's Regiment	1,079 men in 12 companies
Erich von Werden's Regiment	1,181 men in 12 companies

---

19 Velikanov, 'K voprosu ob organizatsii i chislennosti russkoy armii v Narvskom pokhode,' pp.132–8 & 139–40; Vladimir S. Velikanov, 'K voprosu o sostoyanii russkoy armii posle Narvskogo porazheniya, zima 1700–1701 gg', *Voyna i oruzhiye* 7:2 :*Novyye issledovaniya i materialy* (St. Petersburg: VIMAIViVS, 2016), 26–42; Vladimir S. Velikanov and Aleksey N. Lobin, 'Russkaya Artilleriya v Narvskom pokhode, 1700,' *Staryy Zeughaus* 48 (4, 2012), 3–10; Nikolay G. Ustryalov, *Istoriya tsarstvovaniya Petra Velikago* 4: 2(St. Petersburg: Tipografiya II utdeleniya sobstvennoy Ye. I. V. Kantselyarii, 1863), 465–7, 468–9; Generalstaben, *Karl XII på slagfältet* 2, 319–20. Figures for Repnin's Division derive from 1701. Ustryalov, *Istoriya tsarstvovaniya Petra Velikago* 4: 2, 468.

Nikolay Balck's Regiment	1,187 men in 12 companies
Wilhelm von Schweiden's Regiment	1,306 men in 12 companies
Tomas Junger's Regiment	1,185 men in 12 companies
Fyodor Balck's Regiment	1,011 men in 12 companies
Vilim von Del'den's Regiment	1,192 men in 12 companies
Ivan von Del'den's Regiment	1,203 men in 12 companies
Total	11,195 men

Prince Anikita Repnin's Division	
Second Selected Moscow Regiment (Butyrsk Regiment), under Jacob Gordon	
	est. 1,400 men in 12 companies
Caspar Gulitz's Regiment	est. 1,100 men in 12 companies
Johann Busch's Regiment	est. 1,100 men in 12 companies
Nicolaus von Werden's Regiment	est. 1,100 men in 12 companies
Zakhariy Krog's Regiment	est. 1,100 men in 12 companies
Aleksey Dedyut's Regiment	est. 1,000 men in 12 companies
Pyotr von Bukovin's Regiment	est. 1,000 men in 12 companies
Ivan Berner's Regiment	est. 1,000 men in 12 companies
Pavel Berner's Regiment	est. 1,000 men in 12 companies
Ivan Angler's Regiment	est. 1,000 men in 12 companies
Total	10,800 men

Novgorod Division, under Governor Prince Ivan Trubetskoy	
Ivan Kokoshkin's new style Cavalry Regiment (in part only)	250 men
Total cavalry	250 men
Roman Bruce's Regiment	800 men
Ivan Colomb's Regiment	800 men
Total infantry	1,600 men

Zakhariy Vestov's Novgorod Streltsy Regiment	1,012 men[20]
Miron Bayishev's Novgorod Streltsy Regiment	1,012 men[21]
Yuriy Vestov's Pskov Streltsy Regiment	607 men
Vasiliy Kozodavlev's Pskov Streltsy Regiment	1,012 men
Total streltsy infantry	3,643 men

Novgorod Old Style Division, under Stepan Bakhmetyev	
Novgorod old style cavalry	1,500 men

Smolensk Division, under Major General Bogdan Korsak	
Smolensk old style Division, under Bogdan Korsak	898 men in 7 companies
Smolensk new style Cavalry Regiment (in part only), under Grigoriy Rydvanskiy	1,146 men in 12 companies, of whom 200 only at Narva

Belgorod Contingent	
Martem'yan Sukharev's (ex-Moscow) Streltsy Regiment	659 men
Vasiliy Yelchaninov's (ex-Moscow) Streltsy Regiment	718 men
Stepan Strekalov's (ex-Moscow) Streltsy Regiment	380 men
Venedikt Baturin's (ex-Moscow) Streltsy Regiment	est. 500 men
Total streltsy infantry	2,257 men

Ukrainian Cossack Division, under Hetman Ivan Obidovskiy	
Kiev Regiment	
Nezhin Regiment	
Chernigov Regiment	
Poltava Regiment	
Mirgorod Regiment	
Priluki Regiment	
Starodub Regiment	

---

20 Formerly the First Moscow Streltsy Regiment.
21 Formerly the Second Moscow Streltsy Regiment.

Enlisted Serdyuk infantry	
Enlisted Kompaneyskiye cavalry	
Total	est. 8,000–12,000 mostly infantry
Artillery	
64 siege cannons, 79 regimental cannons, 4 howitzers, 26 mortars, possibly under Colonel Casimir von Krage	230–250 men
Grand Total eventually at Narva (excluding Prince Repnin's and Obidovskiy's divisions):	
	est. **38,724**

Comment. Some uncertainty remains with a number of units raised for the campaign and supposedly present at Narva, not least because Tsar Peter frequently rotated his colonels among the large number of newly formed units. Any reference in sources to Tikhon Khristoforovich Gundertmark's Regiment is likely a mistake for Matvey Treyden's Regiment. Likewise, any reference to Denis Petrovich Rydder's Novgorod Streltsy Regiment probably means the streltsy regiment commanded by Zakhariy Vestov. In the same way, any reference to Danila Zagoskin's Pskov Streltsy Regiment likely means Vasiliy Kozodavlev's regiment. There are references to a regiment under an officer named Ivan von Belt or Jean van Belt. This unit, if it existed, otherwise remains unknown. Finally, Hallart and others suggest that a unit called Amirov's Novgorod Streltsy Regiment was deployed in Prince Trubetskoy's camp, but there is no other information about this unit. Possibly, he meant Venedikt Baturin's regiment, if indeed this regiment was present at Narva. Available Russian records seem not to show any trace of the unit. On the other hand, most modern research has focused on the army from Moscow. More research will be needed to clarify the presence of Baturin's regiment or indeed yet other regiments from the provinces.

4

Narva and Ivangorod

Estonia was brought under the Swedish Crown in 1561 when what was then Northern Livonia asked for Sweden's protection against Muscovy (Russia's predecessor) and the Kingdom of Poland and the Grand Duchy of Lithuania, both of which claimed the territory. Moscow acknowledged Sweden's acquisition of Estonia in the 1595 Treaty of Teusina which concluded decades of war.[1] Poland only accepted the situation in the 1660 Treaty of Oliva. Estonia, with Reval as its capital, was a territory with an estimated population of between 350,000 and 400,000 people in 1695.[2]

The fortified port-town of Narva commanded Ingria further to the east, and had long functioned as a centre of commerce for the trade with Russia. Narva, with 3,000 inhabitants, was Estonia's second largest town after Reval.[3] However, unlike Reval, whose population primarily spoke German, Narva's official language was Swedish. The town was defended by two medieval castles: Hermannsborg (Hermann Castle) and Ivangorod (Ivan Castle), which were separated by the River Narova. Narva and Ivangorod were collectively known as Rugodiv in Russia. By 1700, medieval Hermannsborg formed only a minor part of Narva's modern fortifications, while Ivangorod, technically in Ingria, largely remained as it was built by Italian architects in Muscovite Russian employ in 1492, opposite the then Livonian fortress of Narva. Moscow had intended Ivangorod as a trading port with access to the Baltic Sea rivalling those used by Livonia and the Hanseatic League. Taken by Swedish units in 1612, Ivangorod was formally ceded to Sweden with the rest of Ingria in the 1617 Treaty of Stolbovo.[4] On the surface, Ivangorod looked the more impressive fortress, however, the medieval castle was obsolete and unprepared for modern siege methods.

---

1 The Treaty of Teusina was the first formal revision of the mutual border between Sweden and Russia since the 1323 Treaty of Nöteborg.
2 Data from Estonian Demographic Association, Tallinn, 2024. https://www.popest.ee/theme-b/, accessed on 20 March 2024.
3 Margus Laidre, *Segern vid Narva: Början till en stormakts fall* (Stockholm: Natur och Kultur, 1996), p.36.
4 Sweden's acquisition of Ingria was reconfirmed in the 1661 Treaty of Kardis which ended the war between Sweden and Russia and in which Moscow agreed to return to the situation as determined by the 1617 Treaty of Stolbovo.

NARVA AND IVANGOROD

The Russian siege of Narva, 1700, as seen from the west. This shows the town of Narva in the forefront, with the old castle of Ivangorod on the other side of the River Narova, on the right. Detail of a contemporary print (Author's collection)

Ivangorod. (Photo: Ad Meskens)

Despite the mercantile and strategic importance of Narva, the regency government during the minority of King Charles XI in the 1660s neglected the town's defences. Then, the desperate situation during the Scanian War meant that the Crown lacked funds to improve defences on the eastern border. It was only with the appointment of Erik Dahlbergh as Governor-General of Livonia in 1696, at the very end of the reign of King Charles XI, that improvements began to take place. Dahlberg was an experienced intelligence and fortification officer, whose work would prove vital for the Swedish capability to hold hostile invasion armies at the border fortresses. He had Narva's defences enlarged, with new lines of bastions added beyond the existing, older ones. From 1696 to the beginning of 1700, Narva was reinforced with seven, of nine planned, bastions, and an additional 227 cannon. However, work proceeded slowly, and in 1699 Dahlbergh wrote to Stockholm, arguing the urgency of the completion of the defensive works, only half of which were in a state of readiness. Even so, at the outbreak of war he had only managed to remedy the worst deficiencies. In particular the bastions *Triumph* and *Fortuna* and the defensive lines that joined them were in poor condition.

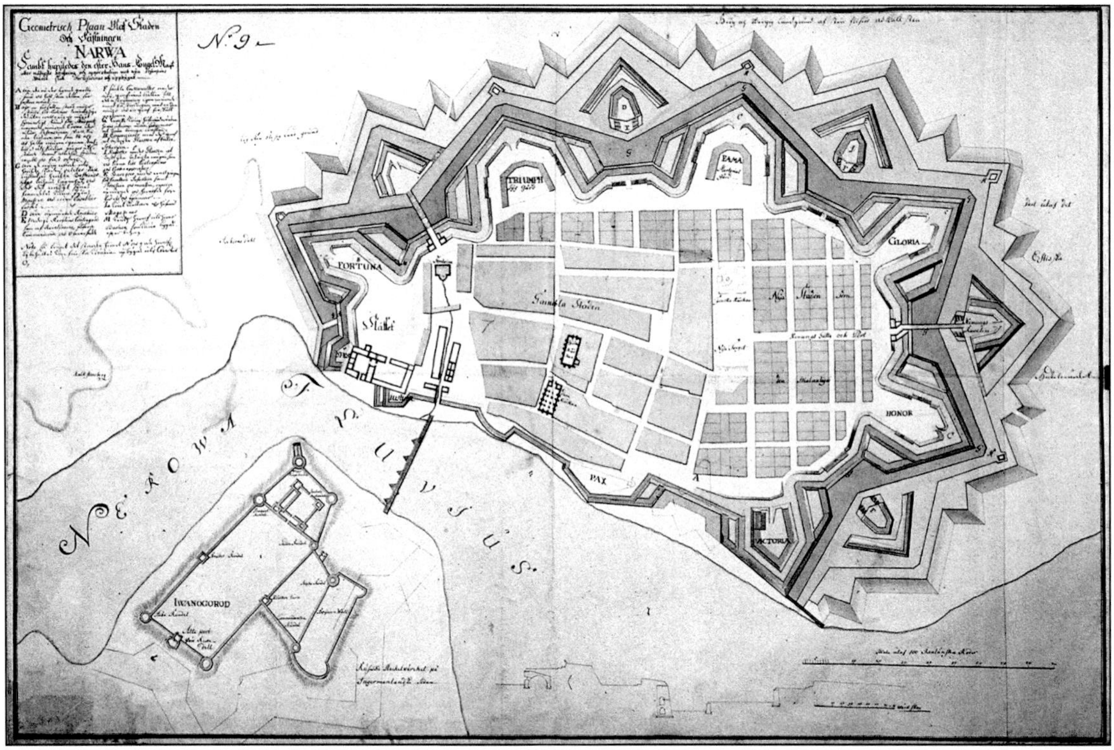

PETER THE GREAT'S DISASTROUS DEFEAT

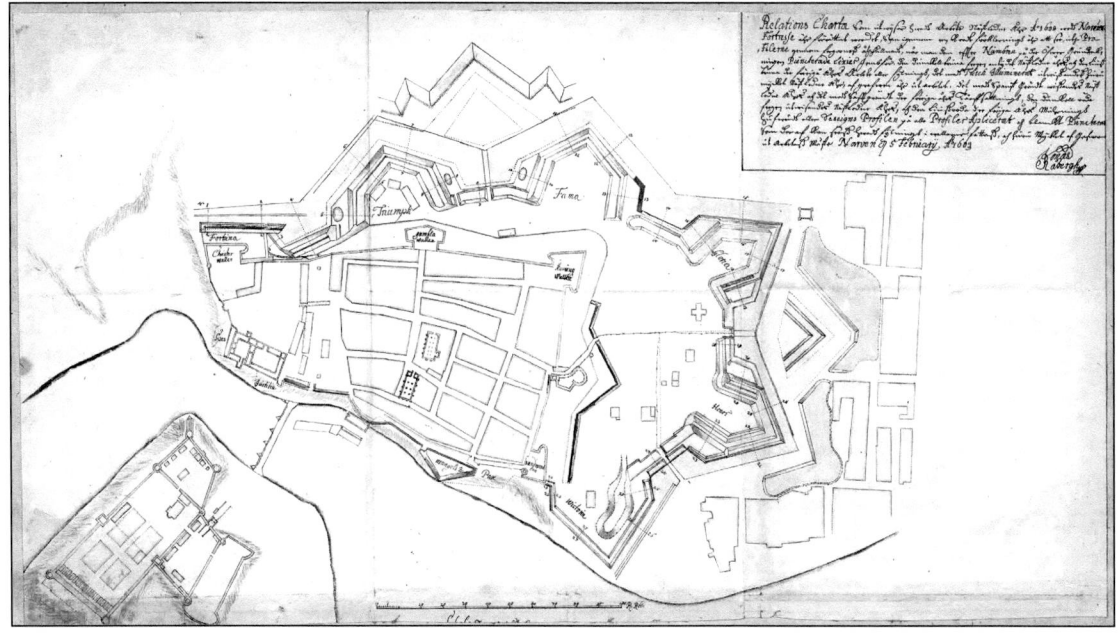

Plan from 1685 of the projected fortifications of Narva, with old Ivangorod in the lower left (south-east) corner. Counter-clockwise from north to south, the bastions were named *Victoria*, *Honor*, *Gloria*, *Fama*, *Triumph*, *Fortuna*, and *Spes*. These bastions were in place in 1700, but most outer defences remained uncompleted. Likewise, the two projected bastions east of Ivangorod were never completed. Only the main gate, known as *Kungsporten* ('King's Gate'), located between *Honor* and *Gloria*, was completed, together with its ravelin, the triangular detached outwork visible on the map. National Archives, SE/KrA/0406/28/031/021 (Photo: Medström)

The actual state of Narva's fortifications a year before the outbreak of war. The map is dated February 1699. (National Archives, SE/KrA/0406/28/031/040)

The joint garrison of Narva and Ivangorod was under Narva's commandant, Colonel Henning Rudolph Horn. The backbone of the garrison consisted of Horn's Enlisted Ingrian Garrison Regiment. According to the June 1699 muster roll of this regiment, it consisted of 1,460 men. It was dominated by Finns (592 men), Ingrians (416 men), and Scanians (216 men), but others included 84 Swedes, 74 Livonians, and 53 Estonians, as well as a sprinkling of Germans, Courlanders, Danes, a Norwegian, a Prussian, and a Pole. Garrison regiments often contained men too old to serve in the field army and Horn's regiment was no exception, with the 85-year-old Thomas Mårtensson, a Finn, the oldest. Slightly younger was the 80-year-old Börge Eriksson from Ystad, Scania, who had already enlisted in 1639, during the Thirty Years' War and well before Scania became Swedish.[5]

Erik Dahlbergh (Author's collection)

Narva had a strong artillery park, but precious few artillerymen. Narva had 290 cannons of various calibres, ranging from twenty-four-pounders down to three-pounders, and an assortment of mortars and howitzers.[6] Narva's field artillery of 16 regimental cannons, four three-pounders, and possibly four howitzers were sent to the Livonian army earlier in the year (and returned with the King's army to take part in the Battle of Narva).[7] Howitzers, like mortars, were primarily fired against area targets during siege operations. Unlike a mortar however, the howitzer could be fired from its wheeled carriage, which made it significantly more mobile. As a result, during the siege Narva had a remaining artillery park of 270 cannon, 28 mortars, and possibly the four howitzers, unless these had been detached for service with the Livonian army.[8] Ivangorod had an artillery park of 103 fully functional cannon, eight obsolete cannon suitable only for firing clusters of multiple small shot or stones, and five mortars.[9] The ordnance was serviced by 81 artillerymen under Lieutenant Colonel Johan Staël von Holstein, commander of artillery in Narva and Ingria. This was too few; another 88 would have been needed to man them all properly.[10]

---

5   Laidre, *Segern vid Narva*, pp.97–98.
6   Narva's artillery park consisted of 61 twenty-four-pounders, 95 eighteen-pounders, 70 twelve-pounders, 5 eight-pounders, 16 six-pounders, 8 four-pounders, and 35 three-pounders. Ulfhielm, *Kungl. artilleriet: Karl XI:s och Karl XII:s tid*, p.105.
7   Ulfhielm, *Kungl. artilleriet: Karl XI:s och Karl XII:s tid*, p.534.
8   Ulfhielm, *Kungl. artilleriet: Karl XI:s och Karl XII:s tid*, p.320.
9   Ivangorod's artillery park consisted of 23 twenty-four-pounders, 30 eighteen-pounders, 6 twelve-pounders, 8 eight-pounders, 16 six-pounders, and 28 three-pounders. Ulfhielm, *Kungl. artilleriet: Karl XI:s och Karl XII:s tid*, pp.105 & 320.
10 Laidre, *Segern vid Narva*, 96. Ulfhielm, *Kungl. artilleriet: Karl XI:s och Karl XII:s tid*, p.320, suggests some 75 artillerymen.

Henning Rudolph Horn, Commandant of Narva (Author's collection)

At the time of the siege, the garrison regiment was supported by small infantry contingents of the Savolax and Viborg Regiments from Finland and Vellingk's Enlisted Ingrian Regiment.

There was also some cavalry: two weak companies of Tiesenhausen's Enlisted Estonian Cavalry Regiment and contingents from the Ingrian Retinue of Nobles and possibly Vellingk's Enlisted Ingrian Dragoon Regiment (altogether 150 horse under cavalry captains Nieroth and Marquard).[11]

Altogether, the garrison consisted of an estimated 1,800 to 1,900 men, this was far too few; Narva was built for a defensive garrison of 3,100 soldiers and 169 artillerymen.[12]

Narva also boasted a 400 strong burgher militia of well-armed and reasonably trained men. Finally, Horn had a contingent of 400 non-combatant levied peasants from Viborg County under Lieutenant Colonel Donnerstedt which he could use for labour duty.[13]

The Governor General of Estonia, Axel Julius De la Gardie, had issued orders to levy the population in northern Estonia to increase the number of combatants, however, the order was issued too late to have the desired effect. Although Horn's garrison was regarded as too small to defend the town, he had plenty of artillery and was well-supplied with munitions and food, including caltrops to make an assault yet more difficult for the assailant.

With the help of Swedish commercial agents in Russia, and Swedish and foreign merchants, Horn had organised an intelligence service, from which he received continuous reports on Russian troop movements – information that he later forwarded to King Charles. As the first Russian units approached the town on 13 September, Horn sent a final report to King Charles. He then ordered the burning of the suburbs of Narva and Ivangorod and put all food and grain stores under central control.

---

11   Generalstaben, *Karl XII på slagfältet* 2, pp.300–301; citing data from 10 October 1700 (N.S). Nieroth and Marquard are otherwise largely unknown.
12   Laidre, *Segern vid Narva*, p.97.
13   Donnerstedt is otherwise largely unknown.

5

Tsar Peter Lays Siege to Narva

Tsar Peter made careful preparations before, on 30 August 1700, he issued the manifesto that declared war on Sweden. He had already closed the border with Sweden in mid-August, so that news about the preparations would not reach Narva. The Tsar concentrated his artillery, both field and siege guns, close to the Swedish border. Most important were the three siege artillery parks in Moscow, Novgorod, and Pskov. On 2 September, Tsar Peter ordered the Moscow artillery park to redeploy to Novgorod together with the Moscow Army. Only mortars, howitzers, and regimental cannon were brought from Moscow, since transportation difficulties would otherwise make the journey too time-consuming. All heavy siege artillery came from Novgorod and Pskov. The Moscow siege artillery park merged with its Novgorod counterpart when the Moscow Army reached Novgorod.

Meanwhile, the Tsar ordered the Pskov siege artillery park to be moved towards Narva by river and across Lake Peipus. On 2 September, the Tsar issued an order to the Governor of Pskov, Vasiliy Lodygin, to have his siege artillery assembled at Narva on 26 September.[1]

Tsar Peter also took the trouble to interrogate and torture an unfortunate Swedish envoy, Ensign Simon Barohn, who had been despatched from Narva before war was declared to ask why the Russians had closed the border.[2]

The Novgorod Army, under Novgorod's Governor, Prince Ivan Trubetskoy, reached the outskirts of Narva on 20 September. Trubetskoy had hoped to take the town in a surprise attack. However, the diligent Horn had despatched his two companies of Tiesenhausen's Estonian Cavalry Regiment to shadow the Russian march, so they had no means to reach Narva without Horn hearing of it.

---

1   Yuriy Yevgen'yevich Manoylenko, '"V nachale slavnykh del": Podgotovitel'nyy etap petrovskikh reform artillerii,' *Russkiy 'bog voyny': Issledovaniya i istochniki po istorii otechestvennoy artillerii* (St Petersburg: Istoriya voyennogo dela, 2017), pp.398–417, on pp.407–8.
2   Barohn was an Ingrian from Narva who spoke Russian. He relates his misadventures in *Karolinska Krigares Dagböcker Jämte Andra Samtida Skrifter* 12 (Lund: Gleerup, 1918), pp.371–8. An English translation is available in Sergei A. Chirkin, 'Military Actions at Narva in 1700 According to the Memoirs of Swedish Warriors,' *RUDN Journal of Russian History* 21: 3 (August 2022), pp.384–393, on p.386.

PETER THE GREAT'S DISASTROUS DEFEAT

Livonia, Estonia, Ingria, and North-Western Russia.

Having installed himself and his men, on 28 September Prince Trubetskoy sent a letter to Horn in an attempt to convince the Swede to surrender. Unsurprisingly, Horn refused. The Russians accordingly had to lay siege to Narva. Fortunately for them, technical expertise was available. On 2 October, the expert engineer, Lieutenant General Hallart, actually in Saxon service, arrived to assume command of the siegeworks. Hallart had been sent by King Augustus to assist the Tsar. And Hallart did not come alone; he brought several experienced siege engineers with him.[3]

On 4 October, Tsar Peter arrived accompanied by units of the Moscow Army. The Tsar was dressed in the green uniform of a captain in the Preobrazhenskiy Guard Regiment. With the Tsar came the Duke de Croÿ and his suite. The artillery train moved slower, but was at least on its way.

Hallart surveyed the Swedish defences, and on 7 October delivered a plan for the siege and a detailed list of all siege artillery, munitions, supplies, and equipment needed. Hallart was a professional, and there is little doubt that he knew what was needed for a successful siege; however, the plan may have disillusioned Tsar Peter. Hallart envisaged the employment of no less than 40 mortars, 60 siege guns ranging from 24pdrs to 48pdrs for close range work, and 20 long-barrelled 12pdrs for fire from greater distances. He also required, as an average, 2,000 cannonballs per gun, 15,000 hand grenades for the infantry, and much else. Tsar Peter had plenty of artillery and munitions, but not quite these numbers. He may also have gasped when he realised the huge volumes of munitions that Hallart said was required to take a fortified town such as Narva. There was another problem as well: Hallart wrote the plan in German, so Tsar Peter had to find somebody to translate the entire document into Russian before the plan could be implemented.[4]

On 9 October, a cavalry captain named Rudolph Felix Bauer slipped out of Narva together with an enterprising English merchant named Samuel Meux. Meux returned to Narva, but Bauer quickly entered the Russian camp, where he told the Russians that he was an undercover agent despatched by King Augustus to gather intelligence on behalf of Tsar Peter.[5] Originally from

Prince Ivan Trubetskoy. Tretyakov Gallery (Public domain)

---

3   Hallart left the siege of Riga on 16 September 1700 with a suite of 20 engineers, officers, and servants. Hallart, *Tagebuch*, pp.15–16.
4   Hallart, *Tagebuch*, pp.27–9.
5   Facing a treason charge, Samuel Meux on the following day had to defend his actions in court. Meux explained that he had ridden out with Bauer in search of celery, and that he

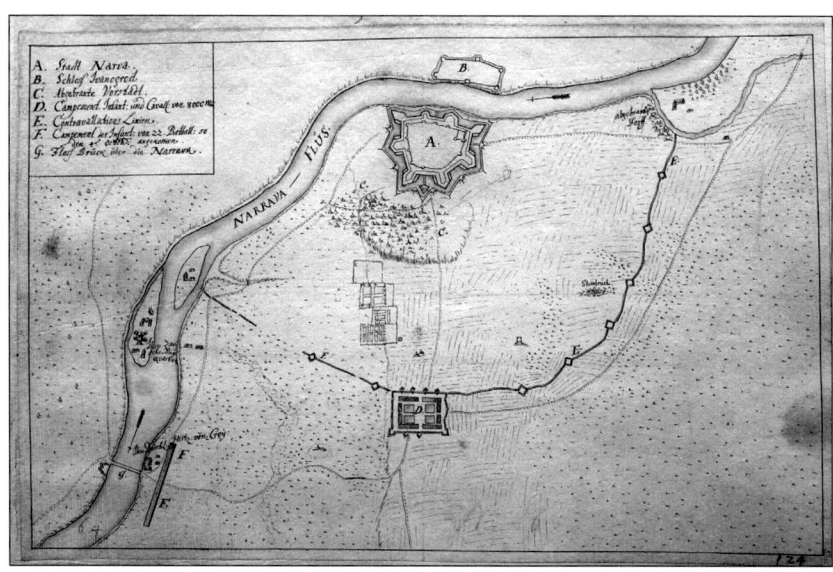

The situation at Narva on 4 October 1700, showing the Russian countervallation line built by Prince Trubetskoy before Tsar Peter's arrival. The defenders have burnt Narva's suburbs and Joala. The Novgorod units are based in Prince Trubetskoy's camp. The newly-arrived units of the Moscow Army have just crossed the bridge at Vepsekylla. Tsar Peter has established a headquarters on Kamperholm Island, while the Duke de Croÿ has found quarters in Vepsekylla. Within four days of the Tsar's arrival, his men commenced the construction of a circumvallation line that would shield the army that laid siege to Narva from any Swedish relief expedition. With thanks to Boris Megorsky who first brought this map to my attention in *Peter the Great's Revenge* (Warwick: Helion & Co., 2018). (Collection of Russian Academy of Sciences Library)

Holstein, Bauer had left service in a Swedish dragoon regiment in Livonia to work undercover for King Augustus.

Possibly somewhat perplexed by this sudden revelation of Saxon undercover activities on his behalf, the Tsar asked Hallart to question Bauer. The Saxon agent revealed the names of the commanders of Narva as well as the number of their men.[6] He also told the Russians that there was no shortage of food supplies in Narva. In addition, Bauer revealed a Swedish ruse: not having enough soldiers to man all of Narva's defences, Horn had ordered his men to put up a show of strength by massing soldiers in those locations which he knew that the Russians could observe. He had

---

was so surprised when Bauer rode into the Russian camp, waving his hat, that the thought of preventing his defection simply never occurred to him. Jully Ramsay, 'Narvas Rådsturätts Protokoll för d. 1 okt. 1700 Angående Generalen R. F. Bauer (Meddel. d. 26 .November 1917)', *Historiallinen Arkisto* 28:7 (1920), pp.12–14. Although little else is known about Samuel Meux, the Englishman may not have been quite as gullible as he implied. We do know of a certain Thomas Meux, described as a 'citizen and mercer of London, merchant in Narva and London, who also traded with the West Indies and the mainland of North America (Virginia, New England), 1698–1711' in the Preston Family Papers, 1637, Virginia Colonial Records Project, An Inventory of Records for the Virtual Jamestown Project (web site, www.virtualjamestown.org/masterDW4.html, accessed on 30 April 2024). The chief English import to Narva, and by extension Russia, was Virginia tobacco, a highly sought-after commodity.

6   Hallart, *Tagebuch*, p.31.

also arranged nightly patrols by men who while patrolling pulled long strings to each of which were affixed several burning slow-matches. Since burning slow match was easily visible at night, this produced the impression that what in reality was one man consisted of a squad of musketeers ready for action.[7] Bauer stayed with the Russians until 4 November, when the Tsar sent him back to King Augustus.[8]

On 12 October, General Adam Weide brought his division to the Tsar's army. The following day, the first contingent of the overdue Russian artillery reached Narva. Over the coming days, the Russians brought a total of 79 regimental cannon (mostly but not exclusively 2pdrs and 3pdrs, although smaller-calibre cannon were used as well) and a siege artillery park of 64 cannon, 4 howitzers, and 26 mortars into camp. Following Hallart's advice, the Russians divided the siege artillery into 10 batteries facing Narva and Ivangorod.

General Avtonom Golovin's Division and General Sheremetyev's cavalry contingent arrived on 25 October, which completed the Russian build-up.

The siege artillery was in position and commenced firing on the night of 30/31 October. Tsar Peter, eager for action, personally fired several cannons. The bombardment continued for about two weeks until the Russians began to run out of ammunition – the bombardment was answered by the Swedish garrison with its own artillery. The Russian cannon did great damage to the town, but not to the extent that Tsar Peter had hoped for. While many Russian cannon were completely new, and in good condition, they were of different calibres and most were still older models, which meant that the available cannonballs did not always fit the cannon.[9] The Russian artillery park was not as homogeneous from a munitions point of view as Hallart had hoped. Moreover, it soon turned out that the gun carriages of the siege artillery suffered

General Adam Weide, depicted while he was in Swedish captivity. Drawing by Elias Brenner, early 1700s (Author's photo)

General Avtonom Golovin, looking somewhat similar to General Weide, as depicted while he was in Swedish captivity. Drawing by Elias Brenner, early 1700s (Author's photo)

---

7   Laidre, *Segern vid Narva*, pp.111–12.
8   Hallart, *Tagebuch*, p.41. Bauer went into Russian service as a major in 1701. Life in the Russian army suited him. Henceforth known as Rodion Khristianovich Bour, the former undercover agent became a successful and widely celebrated commander of dragoons and cavalry.
9   Velikanov and Lobin, 'Russkaya Artilleriya v Narvskom pokhode, 1700,' pp.3–10.

from construction mistakes – when the guns were deployed, many carriages broke.[10]

By 17 November, the Russian artillery was already running out of munitions, so had to resort to firing stone shot from their siege artillery. For this reason, the Tsar decided to concentrate the remaining ammunition on Ivangorod on the eastern side of the River Narova.[11] On the night of 18/19 November, Tsar Peter launched a full-scale assault against Ivangorod. The assault was carried out by the former Moscow streltsy from Belgorod under Colonels Martem'yan Sukharev, Vasiliy Yelchaninov, and Stepan Strekalov. They made three attempts to storm the fortress, but all were repulsed. Although the Russians reached the walls, and managed to create a toehold there, on the following afternoon the defenders sallied out, retook the lost positions, and pushed the Russians out again. In addition, a Swedish cavalry force carried out a successful sortie in which a Russian trench was torn up. Colonels Sukharev and Yelchaninov fought on with a handful of men, 15 to 20 in number. Their bravery was to no avail, and most surviving Russians fled. There is no reason to believe that the streltsy did not do their best; yet, Tsar Peter already distrusted them because of the recent streltsy mutinies, so the failure made him embark upon one of his bouts of rage and violence. He ordered the arrest of the two surviving colonels (Sukharev was killed during the sortie) and the decimation of their men, that is, every tenth man was sentenced to death by hanging.[12] The surviving colonels fared better, both were exculpated in the subsequent court-martial.

Meanwhile, the poor weather conditions brought suffering to the soldiers. An anonymous old style cavalryman of strong religious beliefs who served under Sheremetyev eloquently described the miserable conditions:

> There, because of our sins, it was a time of evil decay. All those days and nights rain fell constantly, and we must continuously sit on horseback, without cover against the rain, while waiting for the arrival of the Germans [Swedes] … In the camp the soldiers endured much hardship because the mud was as deep as a man's knee and a horse's belly; the ground was muddy and the rains heavy, and it flooded and caused great misery for the men.[13]

In a similar vein, a soldier named Larka Stepanovich on 3 October (O.S.) wrote to his parents:

> And we stand under Rugodiv [Narva] for the fourth week and die from cold and hunger. Bread has become expensive; we buy a kopek's worth of bread for two *altyn* [then a copper coin each worth three kopeks]. And may I ask you, father

---

10 Hallart, *Tagebuch*, p.37.
11 Hallart, *Tagebuch*, 46–7; Manoylenko, '"V nachale slavnykh del," p.409.
12 Hallart, *Tagebuch*, p.47. See also Laidre, *Segern vid Narva*, pp.118–19.
13 Anon., 'Letopisets 1700 goda,' *Letopis' zanyatiy Arkheograficheskoy kommissii, 1865-1866*, 4: 3 (St. Petersburg: Arkheograficheskaya kommissiya, 1868), pp.131–57, on p.142.

Stepan Prokof'yevich, if it be possible for you yourself to visit, and bring me a fur coat of some kind, and a shirt and pants, and good boots…[14]

Other soldiers voiced similar requests. In the same month, a soldier named Ul'yan Polyakov wrote to his wife and he too ended the letter with a request for a shirt and pants.[15]

However, it soon became difficult to bring in necessary supplies. The Russians had planned to ship supplies by waterway from Pskov across Lake Peipus, but there the Swedes under Colonel Wolmar Anton von Schlippenbach watched for any opportunity to strike at the Russians. Schlippenbach's men captured numerous Russian transports on the lake in what became known as the Battle of Ismen, the name for the isthmus that divided northern and southern Lake Peipus.

At the same time, the Russians raided Eastern Estonia (a region known as Wierland), where they burnt down farms and villages and captured and murdered civilians. Raiding of this type was a customary feature of northern European warfare, because it prevented any hostile relief army from accessing supplies and horse fodder from the area, thereby preventing it from going on the offensive.

The Russians also cordoned off Narva from the rest of Estonia. As soon as he arrived, Prince Trubetskoy established a fortified camp on the eastern side of the Hermannsberg Hill, which cut the main road from Narva towards the west. Hermannsberg was an open plateau, without forest cover. The Russians soon commenced work on erecting a countervallation line (that is, facing the fortress) to protect the army from sorties while they laid siege to the town. They cut down any trees and bushes near the line. Otherwise, some woodland remained in the hollows between the hills, while near Narva itself, there were cultivated areas and woods of deciduous trees.

The countervallation line consisted of a ditch and a rampart that ran from the burnt village of Joala in the south to Vepsekylla in the north and surrounded the town at an average distance of 1,800 metres. Redoubts were built to support the line wherever a road passed through it. Having completed these defences, the Russians dug angled approach trenches from the countervallation line which came closer to the walls of Narva by the day.

After the arrival of Tsar Peter, work also commenced on a circumvallation line (that is, a line facing the country and away from the town). It was designed to support the countervallation line, so its southern section was drawn next to the countervallation line. The northern section was laid out to safeguard the temporary raft bridge that the Russians were building to the Tsar's headquarters, which he had set up on Kamperholm Island (adjacent and very close, to the eastern shore of the River Narova). Rathshof Hill was included in the defensive line, which established another strongpoint. This strongpoint, too, protected the Russian communication line across

---

14 Sergey A. Kozlov, 'Okopnyye pis'ma russkikh soldat 1700 g', *Istoriya Rossii do XX veka: Novyye podkhody k izucheniyu*. St Petersburg: Istoricheskaya illyustratsiya, 2008), pp.201–13, on pp.201–2.
15 Kozlov, 'Okopnyye pis'ma russkikh soldat,' p.209.

the bridge to Kamperholm Island. A first bridge had been built on rafts at Vepsekylla, where the river was narrow, but since this location was outside the circumvallation line the Russians erected a new bridge to Kamperholm Island inside the defensive perimeter.[16] To protect the Tsar's headquarters, a defensive line was also built on the right bank of the River Narova.

The terrain within the Russian defensive lines in this sector north of Narva was difficult, with broken ground that included two or three lines of muddy ravines that ran in parallel with the river and impeded movement.

The circumvallation line was about 7,200m long, and covered the entire Russian bridgehead west of the River Narova. A series of redoubts was built along the line, on average one per 200m. The Russians could accordingly cover the entire outer line with flanking musketry fire from the redoubts as well as with frontal fire from the circumvallation line itself. The redoubts also included battery places for regimental artillery – about two to three cannon in each. Prince Trubetskoy's camp reportedly had 17 guns, and the Rathshof Redoubt 10 guns.[17] The only exits from the defensive line were those through the redoubts. The layout of the circumvallation line thus shows that its entire purpose was defensive. There were no provisions for, and thus no intention to, a march out in force to confront an enemy force in the open field.

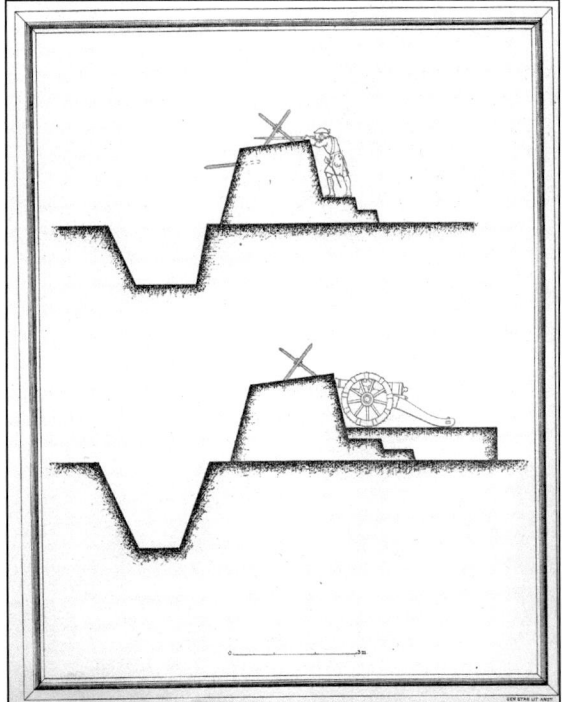

The profile of the Russian defensive line. Generalstaben, *Karl XII på slagfältet* 2 (Author's collection)

The profile of the defensive line allowed four metres from the bottom of the ditch in front to the top of the breastwork on the rampart. The Russians also built a barrier of anti-cavalry obstacles, based on the *cheval-de-frise*, a portable frame with projecting spikes that was positioned in front of the breastworks so as to provide additional protection. Although this provided a reasonable degree of protection for the defenders, significantly stronger profiles were already the norm elsewhere, and indeed had been in common use for decades. Possibly, the length of the circumvallation line prevented the construction of stronger defences within the available timeframe.

The Russian soldiers were housed in barracks, huts, dugouts, and tents built between the circumvallation and countervallation lines. Since the distance between the two lines was often as short as 70m, almost the entire space was occupied by barracks and stores. There

---

16　The Russians dismantled the raft bridge at Vepsekylla on 12 October and moved it to Kamperholm Island, but on 7 November this bridge was crushed by the thickening ice cover. The Russians salvaged the bridge and returned it to the original position. Hallart, *Tagebuch*, p.42. Soon afterwards, the Russians built a second, stronger bridge to Kamperholm Island. The bridge at Vepsekylla was located outside the defensive lines. Near-contemporary maps include both bridges.

17　Ulfhielm, *Kungl. Artilleriet: Karl XI:s och Karl XII:s tid*, p.321.

was accordingly little space for moving units within the camp. This, too, was significantly less than what was the norm elsewhere, where free space between camp and circumvallation line was more commonly around 200m, and that between camp and countervallation line around 400m so as to enable rapid redeployment and movement. There were also no provisions for the rapid movement of cavalry to exposed positions, in case a Swedish relief force broke through. However, there was more room for manoeuvre in the northern sector, with more space between the two lines and their respective anchor points at the river than in the south. Moreover, east of Rathshof the hills safeguarded the deployment. On the other hand, the area was divided by broken ground into two sectors, which meant that units there were cut off from access to the other sectors of the lines.

Prince Trubetskoy's camp was located on the Hermannsberg Hill, which rose westwards to a dominant position, from which the camp was vulnerable to artillery fire. This was possibly overlooked when the defensive lines were laid out, and this omission would play a role in the ensuing battle.

Colonel Horn actively defended Narva. On the evening of 12 October, he carried out a sortie in force with both horse and foot. Four days later, on 16 October, Tsar Peter retaliated by sending proposals, 60 written in German and 20 in what was described as Latvian, into the town by attaching them to arrows shot over the town walls. The letters recommended the defenders to desert or otherwise betray Horn.[18] Nobody took up the offer.

On 21 November, a captain from the Preobrazhenskiy Regiment by the name of Johan Hummert deserted to the Swedes in Narva. Hummert was born in Dorpat (modern-day Tartu, Estonia), so was, or at least had been, a Swedish citizen. He had been close to the Tsar, so he may have been a person of some consequence within Tsar Peter's entourage of 'drinking buddies'. His defection was noted in the Russian camp only on the following day. Hummert brought a daring scheme to Horn; if Horn would give him 600 men, he would capture Tsar Peter and hand him over to the Swedes. While the offer was tempting, Horn knew that if something went wrong, for instance if Hummert led the Swedes into a trap, he would lose a third of his fighting force on a fool's errand. Perhaps this was Hummert's intention all along? Hummert also very likely revealed some information about the Russians to Horn, but the latter was unimpressed, instead reaching the conclusion that the defection was a ruse.[19] Hummert never revealed his true intentions to anybody, and certainly not to Tsar Peter, who was bewildered by the apparent defection. Perhaps Hummert hoped to hog the glory by bringing a *fait accompli* to the Tsar? Hummert's motives have been discussed ever since, without finding any conclusive evidence one way or the other.[20]

---

18 Hallart, *Tagebuch*, p.35.
19 Russian official reports from the time assign much blame to Hummert for the subsequent defeat, arguing that he must have revealed the Russian plans and deployment to Horn. However, even if he did, the besieged Horn had no means to convey this information to King Charles, so in truth any information divulged played no role in the ensuing battle.
20 After the battle, Hummert wrote to the Tsar from his prison, complained that he was suspected of espionage, asked for monetary support, and also pointed out that it was easier to conquer Narva in a surprise attack in winter than to carry out a siege of the type that ultimately failed

When news of the apparent defection reached Tsar Peter, on 23 November in an unexpected move, inspired possibly by sudden panic or conceivably belated precaution, he ordered all his officers and under-officers of Swedish origin to be sent to Moscow for service there. They would retain their rank and salary, but the Tsar did not trust them to participate in a war against Sweden.[21]

On 24 November, Horn ordered another sally, this time of 150 men from Ivangorod. They caused great damage to the Russian siegeworks and inflicted significant casualties. The Swedes also captured the newly-released Colonel Vasiliy Yelchaninov, whose men still manned the Russian siegeworks there.[22]

---

in 1700. It accordingly seems that Hummert continued the attempt to play both sides until the very end. In 1702, a Swedish court sentenced Hummert to death by hanging for treason and suspected espionage. He was executed in the following year. Hummert left a wife in Moscow. Edvard Beckman, 'Några anteckningar om slaget vid Narva,' *Historisk Tidskrift* 21 (1901), pp.317–32, on pp.318–28.

21 Hallart, *Tagebuch*, p.49; Carl J. H. Hallendorff, 'Ryska berättelser om slaget vid Narva.' *Historisk Tidskrift* 20 (1900), pp.288–97, on pp.295–6.
22 Hallart, *Tagebuch*, p.50.

Plate A
The Swedish Life Guard Assaults the Russian Circumvallation Line at Narva
Colour artwork by Steve Noon © Helion & Company
See Colour Plate Commentaries for further information.

Plate B
King Charles at the Battle of Narva
See Colour Plate Commentaries for further information.

Plate C
Swedish Musketeer, Life Guard of Foot
Colour artwork by Sergey Shamenkov © Helion & Company
See Colour Plate Commentaries for further information.

Plate D
Swedish Grenadier, Dalecarlia Regiment
Colour artwork by Sergey Shamenkov © Helion & Company
See Colour Plate Commentaries for further information.

Plate E
Swedish Trooper, Åbo and Björneborg County Cavalry Regiment
Colour artwork by Sergey Shamenkov © Helion & Company
See Colour Plate Commentaries for further information.

Plate F
Swedish Artilleryman
Colour artwork by Sergey Shamenkov © Helion & Company
See Colour Plate Commentaries for further information.

Plate G
Russian Musketeer, Preobrazhenskiy Guard Regiment
Colour artwork by Sergey Shamenkov © Helion & Company
See Colour Plate Commentaries for further information.

Plate H
Russian Musketeer, Semyonovskiy Guard Regiment
Colour artwork by Sergey Shamenkov © Helion & Company
See Colour Plate Commentaries for further information.

Plate I
Russian Musketeer, Yuriy Vestov's Pskov Streltsy regiment
Colour artwork by Sergey Shamenkov © Helion & Company
See Colour Plate Commentaries for further information.

Plate J
Russian Dragoon, Joachim Gulitz's 'Preobrazhenskiy' Dragoon Regiment
Colour artwork by Sergey Shamenkov © Helion & Company
See Colour Plate Commentaries for further information.

Plate K
Russian Old Style Cavalryman, Sovereign's Division
Colour artwork by Sergey Shamenkov © Helion & Company
See Colour Plate Commentaries for further information.

Plate L
Russian Field Marshal Charles Eugène Duke de Croÿ
Colour artwork by Sergey Shamenkov © Helion & Company
See Colour Plate Commentaries for further information.

Plate M
Nyland and Tavastehus County Cavalry Regiment
Colour artwork by Lesley Prince © Helion & Company
See Colour Plate Commentaries for further information.

Plate N
Karelian (Viborg and Nyslott) Cavalry Regiment
Colour artwork by Lesley Prince © Helion & Company
Tiesenhausen's Enlisted Estonian Cavalry Regiment
See Colour Plate Commentaries for further information.

Plate O
Preobrazhenskiy Guard Regiment, 15th Company
Early eighteenth-century painting showing original colour, and photo of the colour in its present condition
See Colour Plate Commentaries for further information.

Plate P
Semyonovskiy Guard Regiment, Colonel's Life Company
Early eighteenth-century painting showing original colour, and photo of the colour in its present condition
See Colour Plate Commentaries for further information.

**Plate Q
Semyonovskiy Guard Regiment, 3rd Company**
Early eighteenth-century painting showing original colour, and photo of the colour in its present condition
See Colour Plate Commentaries for further information.

**Plate R
First Selected Moscow Regiment, also known as Lefortovo Regiment, Colonel's Life Company**
Early eighteenth-century painting showing original colour, and photo of the colour in its present condition
See Colour Plate Commentaries for further information.

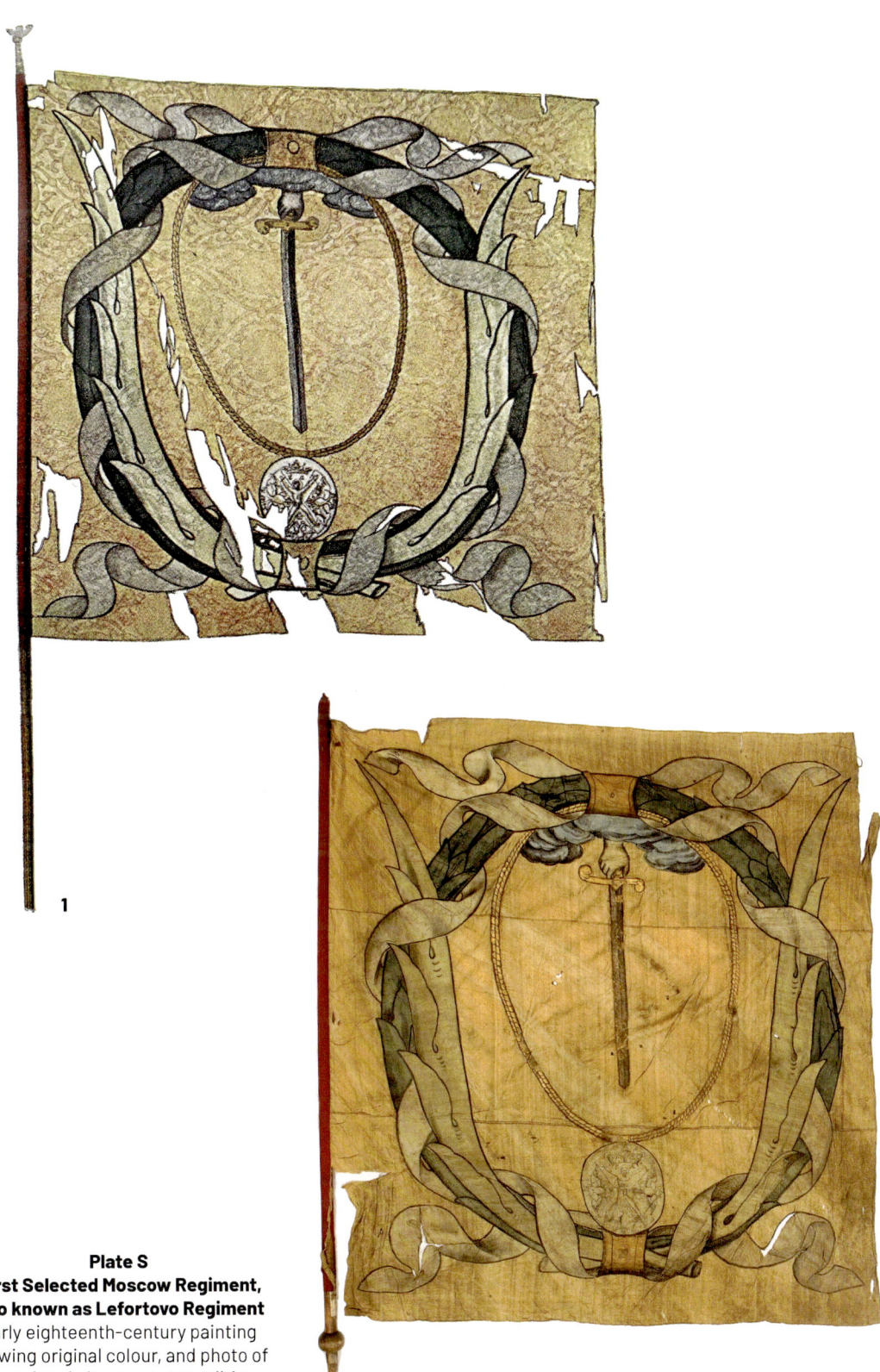

Plate S
First Selected Moscow Regiment, also known as Lefortovo Regiment
Early eighteenth-century painting showing original colour, and photo of the colour in its present condition
See Colour Plate Commentaries for further information.

Plate T
Alferiy Schnewentz's 'Preobrazhenskiy' Dragoon Regiment
Early eighteenth-century painting showing original colour, and photo of the colour in its present condition
See Colour Plate Commentaries for further information.

**Plate U
Joachim Gulitz's 'Preobrazhenskiy' Dragoon Regiment, 8th Company**
Early eighteenth-century painting showing original colour, and photo of the colour in its present condition
See Colour Plate Commentaries for further information.

Plate V
Matvey Fliwerk's Regiment
Early eighteenth-century painting showing original colour,
and photo of the colour in its present condition
See Colour Plate Commentaries for further information.

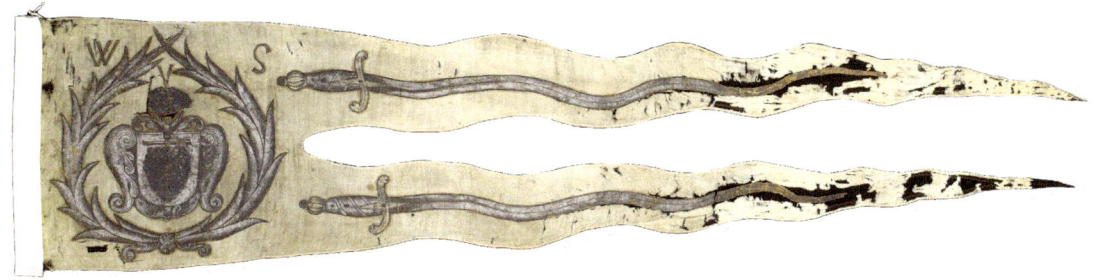

1

Plate W
Wilhelm von Schweiden's Regiment, Colonel's Pennant
Boris Sheremetyev's Old style Cavalry, Company Banner
See Colour Plate Commentaries for further information.

2

Plate X
Ivan Kokoshkin's Pskov Streltsy Regiment, Colonel's Company
Prince Ivan Trubetskoy's Personal Standard
Drum Banner
See Colour Plate Commentaries for further information.

6

King Charles Sails to the Eastern Front

After Denmark's surrender and exit from the triple alliance, the Swedish main army prepared to transfer to the Baltic theatre of war. The redeployment took place in early October when King Charles and his troops were shipped from Karlshamn in Southern Sweden to Estonia. King Charles and the first units of the army landed at Pernau on 16 October. Some troops landed on the island of Ösel (modern-day Saaremaa) and others in Reval. The King sent a letter to Narva's commander, Horn, with a Persian merchant who reluctantly accepted the clandestine mission. However, neither the merchant nor the letter got through to Horn. The Russians did not allow the merchant to enter Narva, and he wisely seems to have discarded the letter before or during the battle. There may have been other attempts to get information across the lines. The Russians at Narva captured a 'spy' with an enciphered letter on 4 November.[1]

King Charles continued to Reval, which he reached on 4 November, and meanwhile, the army marched towards the east. The artillery had left 550 horses in Sweden and it was difficult to find replacements. The assembly point for all units was Wesenberg (modern-day Rakvere) about 112km west of Narva, where General Otto Vellingk and his men arrived on 5 November and the rest of the army somewhat later. Due to a crop failure in Estonia, the main army could not be provided with sufficient provisions and with enough fodder for the horses, and worse still, the Russians had devastated the lands around Wesenberg. There was still another problem as well; the logistical effort to provide winter clothing for the soldiers, who had arrived straight from the summer campaign with the, in respect of the weather, more agreeable Denmark, had failed miserably. The men were not only hungry, they also felt the biting cold of early winter, and being Swedish, they knew that the cold would only get worse.

On 7 November, Major Georg Reinhold Patkul was sent out of Wesenberg with two squadrons (possibly 600 men) of Tiesenhausen's Enlisted Estonian

---
1 Hallart, *Tagebuch*, p.41.

Cavalry Regiment to stop the Russians from ravaging the area. Between the villages of Varja and Haakhof (modern-day Aa), they encountered a dispersed Russian force from Sheremetyev's cavalry contingent who were out foraging.[2] Tsar Peter had sent Sheremetyev with 5,000 cavalry on a reconnaissance mission towards Wesenberg on 5 November to ascertain whether King Charles's army was marching towards Narva, and if so, to determine its strength and route of march.[3] He also had his men devastate the country so as to prevent any approaching Swedes from finding supplies there. Taken by surprise, Sheremetyev's dispersed men took cover in the local settlements and villages. Setting houses on fire, the Swedes drove out and killed some Russians, while the remainder surrendered or were forced to retreat. While the Swedes plundered the Russians' supplies, they were in turn surprised by the arrival of Sheremetyev with his main force. Sheremetyev promptly attacked the Swedes, who dispersed and fled, losing some men in the process. The Russians lost 40 dead and 70 wounded.[4] Swedish casualties are difficult to determine. Some Swedes were captured, including Patkul.[5] From the prisoners, the Russians learnt of King Charles's approaching army, but Patkul lied about its size. The Russians drew the conclusion that 24,000 or 25,000 Swedish soldiers were marching on Narva – a great exaggeration.[6]

On 23 November, King Charles and his army left Wesenberg bound for Narva. Prior to the journey, each man received a four-day ration and was asked to leave behind all excess baggage. Several officers were sceptical of the decision to march, they wanted to wait for reinforcements because Narva's situation was unknown, the army had a shortage of provisions, and there were rumours that the Russian Army numbered upwards of 80,000 men.[7] Approaching Narva, the Swedish army was met by a devastated landscape in Eastern Estonia. Houses and villages had been burnt down, peasants had been murdered, and even the graves in the cemeteries had been opened and looted by marauders in search of gold.

On 27 November, the Swedish vanguard under Major General Maydell arrived at a pass near the River Pühajõgi's exit into the Gulf of Finland. The village at the pass, also named Pühajõgi, was important because both roads from Western Estonia merged here, before a single road continued towards the east. The pass was held by Sheremetyev and his cavalry. When the Swedes arrived at the pass, and rapidly brought up and deployed six regimental cannons, a confused skirmish began.[8] As noted, Sheremetyev thought that

---

2   Although these skirmishes are today known as the Battle of Varja, contemporary Swedish and Russian reports referred to the engagements as the Battle of Purtse or Purtz, which lay somewhat further to the west.
3   Hallart, *Tagebuch*, p.42.
4   Hallart, *Tagebuch*, p.44.
5   On 11 November, Sheremetyev sent 26 captured Swedes to the Russian camp at Narva. Hallart, *Tagebuch*, p.43.
6   Hallart, *Tagebuch*, p.57.
7   Carl Magnus Posse of the Life Guard to his brother Nils Posse, 9 December 1700 (S.S.), Emil Hildebrand, 'Ur frih. Carl Magnus Posses korrespondens,' *Historisk Tidskrift* 2 (1882), pp.81–94, on p.86.
8   Carl Gustav Wrangel, of the Drabant Corps, wrote a report that included a description of the skirmish. 'Några anteckningar om och af generalmajoren och kaptenlöjtnanten vid drabanterna

King Charles's army greatly outnumbered his own. Moreover, he probably did not realise that Maydell's force was only the vanguard, not the entire army. Sheremetyev had orders to observe, not fight to the death, so he correctly withdrew when charged by what he believed to be superior numbers. Sheremetyev retreated with his cavalry during the night of 27/28 November.

The Swedes crossed the Pühajõgi Pass, but during the next two days of marching the soldiers and horses were beset by difficulties. From the outset the limited food supplies were running out. The soldiers had trouble sleeping due to massive rains that turned the ground into mud. When the soldiers on the evening of 28 November made camp at Sillamäe, two days from Narva, they found it arguably the worst

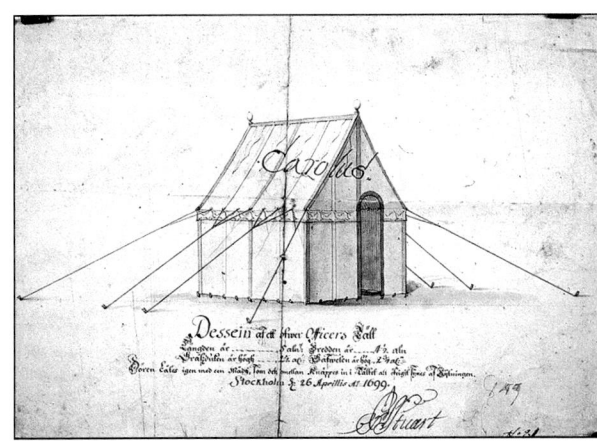

Officer's tent model 1699. Length: 3m, width 2.7m, wall height 1.5m, maximum height under ridge 3m. Designed by Carl Magnus Stuart and approved by King Charles (through the signature Carolus across the drawing). (Army Museum, Stockholm; photo: Medström)

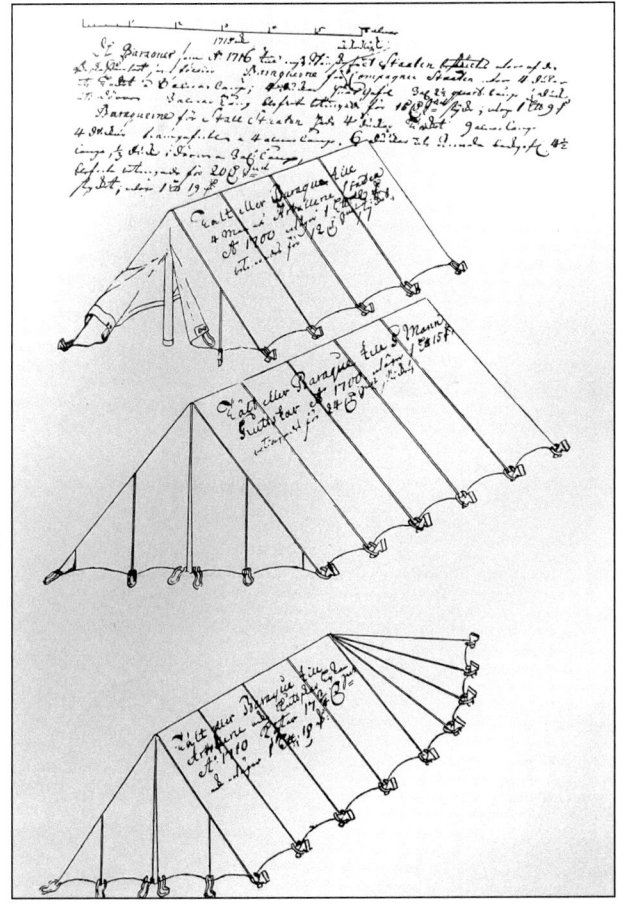

The tents of common soldiers were smaller, lacked side walls, and were far less luxurious. They had the following dimensions: Length: 2.7m, width 2.3m, maximum height under ridge 1.7m. Each tent housed two under-officers or respectively four or five common soldiers (upper and centre). Below: coachman's tent. All according to specifications in 1700 and 1710 for the artillery. Johan Möllerheim, 1720 (Author's collection)

Karl Wrangel.' *Karolinska Förbundets Årsbok* 1910: pp.112–153, on pp.141–143.

Large supply wagon for the artillery, to be pulled by six horses. The infantry used smaller versions of the same model, pulled by four horses. The ribs were normally covered by water-proof canvas. Johan Möllerheim, 1720 (Author's collection)

Kettledrum carriage for the artillery, 1716. Johan Möllerheim, 1720 (Author's collection)

camp during the entire campaign. They called it the 'dirt camp' (Swedish: *lortlägret*; German: *Drecklager*), a scornful term used by Swedish soldiers when they literally had to sleep in the mud and mire as it rained, without any cover, fire, food, or even such limited sanitary facilities as they expected.[9] A scribe, Carsten Pfeif, noted that the dirt camp was the worst he had ever seen, and that it was impossible even to lay down: 'All must stand up without cover with mud up to the knees.'[10]

After a sleepless night, the soldiers continued the march, until on the evening of 29 November they made camp at Lagena (modern-day Laagna), an abandoned village 14km from Narva, near a burnt out manor house known as Wrangelshof. And it was still raining.

---

9 Michael Fredholm von Essen, *Charles XI's War: The Scanian War between Sweden and Denmark, 1675-1679* (Warwick: Helion & Co., 2019), p.124.

10 Anton Pihlström, *Kungl. Dalregementets historia* 3: *Kungl. Dalregementet under karolinska tiden 1682-1721* (Stockholm: P. A. Norstedt & Söner, 1906), p.87. Casten Pfeif (1662–1739) was a scribe of the field chancellery.

7

Tsar Peter Loses Confidence

When Sheremetyev abandoned the Pühajõgi Pass, he sent couriers with his intelligence on the Swedish army to the Tsar's headquarters at Narva. Sheremetyev reported that his interrogation of prisoners suggested a Swedish army of 24,000 or 25,000 men. This was unwelcome news to the Russian headquarters. If correct, the Swedish army was not much smaller than the Russian, at least with regard to the, in a siege, all-important infantry, and Tsar Peter knew that the Swedish army was better trained than his own.

Sheremetyev's retreat also left the road to Narva open. At this point, Tsar Peter lost confidence in his undertaking. Getting cold feet, he decided that it was better for himself and Russia to leave the army in the hands of a professional and then return to Novgorod.

Tsar Peter had such a man in his camp in the person of Charles Eugène de Croÿ, an experienced soldier and former Imperial Field Marshal of the princely House of Croÿ. Although tempted to go into Russian service in 1698, the Duke de Croÿ had instead chosen to serve King Augustus of Saxony and the Polish-Lithuanian Commonwealth. However, King Augustus immediately sent him and several other Saxon officers on a diplomatic mission to the Russian Tsar to act as military advisers (in return, King Augustus asked for a Russian auxiliary corps of 20,000 men with artillery). Croÿ had joined Tsar Peter in Novgorod as late as 10 September. From this moment onwards, Tsar Peter had refused to let the Saxon officers leave, apparently intending to retain them in his service indefinitely despite their diplomatic status.

Having received the reports from Sheremetyev, Tsar Peter on 28 November immediately asked Croÿ to assume command and responsibility for the Tsar's army. The Tsar provided confectionary, wine, and vodka to make Croÿ amenable to his suggestion. Croÿ was known as a *bon viveur*, yet he declined, saying that he did not know the troops and they also did not know him. He did not speak Russian, and few Russians knew German. Besides, Croÿ was a professional; he did not wish to take command of an unknown but likely inexperienced army that was already engaged in combat with an enemy who, Croÿ knew from personal experience, had a well-deserved reputation for military competence. After all, he had himself fought the Swedes in the Scanian War and was familiar with the Carolean art of war.

In the evening, Tsar Peter again sent messengers to Croÿ, inviting him to discuss the situation further. Tsar Peter had to send seven messages within an hour, but the reluctant Croÿ still did not come. Finally, the Tsar, in an angry mood, himself descended upon Croÿ's room at around 04:00 a.m., to insist that he assume command. Croÿ probably felt that in his situation, he had little choice but to humour the unpredictable Tsar. Yet, Croÿ insisted that if he must assume command, he first needed a written instruction in the Tsar's own hand. Croÿ then went to see King Augustus's envoy Baron Johann Ernst von Langen and Hallart, who shared a room in the overcrowded camp, to discuss the situation. They decided to bring a document with a few key bullet points about the commission to Tsar Peter and Field Marshal General Fyodor Golovin, the Tsar's supreme commander, for the Tsar to sign. But when Baron von Langen arrived in the Tsar's quarters with the document early in the morning of 29 November, he learnt that the Tsar and the Field Marshal General had already left the headquarters at about 5:00 a.m. and departed towards Novgorod.[1] Tsar Peter had left a hastily handwritten instruction behind, which was neither dated nor sealed.[2] The instruction, which was written in German, stated only the following:

> In the name of God.
> Since His Majesty the Tsar is departing on urgent business, together with the Field Marshal General, to confer with His Majesty the King of Poland, We hereby deliver our entire army to His Serene Highness [Prince de Croÿ[3]] together with Our Privy Council and Commissary General Prince Yakov Fyodorovich Dolgorukov, with the other Generals, according to the following Articles, namely:
> 1. His Highness shall be in overall command.
> 2. All Generals and Officers down to common soldiers shall be under his command during Our absence, as if under Our own, and under the same Articles.
> 3. His Highness shall, after the receipt of a sufficient quantity of all artillery equipment, in every way, with the help of God, endeavour to take the town of Narva and Ivangorod, which His Majesty the Tsar desires, both for himself and for the King of Poland, since one cannot supply any kind of assistance without conquering this stronghold.
> 4. His Highness shall also carefully gather intelligence on the Swedish relief army, and when he receives certain intelligence on its arrival, and when he conclusively learns that it is on its way, he shall halt the attack on the town, if the enemy is strong, and instead diligently make sure that no enemies enter the town, and with God's help seek with his every ability to carry out the plan [to take the town]; but only, in God's name, when he assuredly can do so before the enemy arrives.
> 5. Food supplies to the soldiers will be delivered by the Quartermaster General, and if orders to deliver more supplies are issued to His Majesty the Tsar's lands, then the Quartermaster General will arrange it. But if the border governors

---

1 When sunrise finally came, at 8:34 a.m., Tsar Peter and Field Marshal General Golovin were already far away.
2 Hallart, *Tagebuch*, pp.50–52.
3 The Tsar addressed Croÿ as *Ihre Hochfurstlige Durchlaucht* ('Your Serene Highness'), the customary term of address for sovereign Princes.

neglect to deliver these supplies, then he shall deal with them as with his own subjects, even if they deserve death, and the same with all other commanders and mayors.

Peter [name written in Cyrillic letters and in Russian style][4]

The instruction definitely gave overall command to Croÿ, yet it offered no advice on what he was expected to do while in command, except maintaining a broadly defensive stance for an indefinite period of time. If a Swedish relief army arrived, the instruction clearly stated that Croÿ should halt the attack on Narva. While that much was clear, was he expected to move out to engage the Swedish relief army in battle, or should he merely remain on the defensive behind the lines of fortifications? The exhortation to 'make sure that no enemies enter the town' suggested the latter. Yet, the instruction could perhaps be interpreted either way, unless the Tsar's apparent anxiety signified his intention to switch to a completely defensive strategy. Additionally, Article 3 was vaguely ominous in its apparent conclusion that Croÿ had received 'a sufficient quantity of all artillery equipment.' No other artillery supplies were expected. What should he do if the supplies turned out to be inadequate? Unfortunately, Croÿ saw no way out of the unwelcome commission.

Although the Russian Army had employed foreign officers for more than a century, many soldiers did not trust them. Moreover, the language barrier made the issuing of orders difficult. Croÿ faced the same problems, but in his case, it was worse. Despite the Tsar's clear instruction, many Russian officers found Croÿ's appointment irregular and refused to follow his orders. Tsar Peter even found it necessary to write to the Russian generals directly: 'I have ordered that the Duke de Croÿ will command the troops and you. Know this, and act according to the Articles written by my hand and left with him, and trust this.'[5] Even this straightforward communication did not seem to make any impact of the Russian generals, who remained unwilling to follow Croÿ's orders. And even worse, Sheremetyev's recent defeat at the Pühajõgi Pass and the Tsar's sudden departure negatively impacted upon the resolution and morale of all of the army.

Hours after the Tsar's and the Field Marshal General's departure, Sheremetyev and his men reached Narva. At the same time, the Swedes were marching towards neighbouring Lagena. It was the morning of 29 November.

---

4   Hallart, *Tagebuch*, pp.53–54. Repetitions and unintended ambiguity as in the original. Tsar Peter wrote the instruction after hours of heavy drinking so his clarity is impressive for the circumstances.
5   Aleksandr V. Petrov, *Gorod Narva, yego proshloye i dostoprimechatel'nosti v svyazi s istoriyey uprocheniya russkago gospodstva na Baltiyskom poberezh'ye, 1223–1900* (St Petersburg: Ministerstvo Vnutrennikh Del (MVD), 1901), p.220.

8

The Night Before Battle

Arriving at the deserted village of Lagena in the evening of 29 November, the Swedes at 7:00 p.m. fired two signal rockets – the traditional Swedish salute but this time as a visual signal – to inform Narva of their approach and that relief had arrived. The salute was answered by Narva, which showed that Horn was aware of the army's approach. King Charles wanted to attack Tsar Peter's army straight away on the next day. All preparations for the coming battle had to be concluded at night. Quartermaster General Lieutenant Gerdt Ehrenschantz, who among other duties was in charge of military intelligence, despatched reconnaissance patrols under Colonel Bernhard Rehbinder of the Åbo and Björneborg County Cavalry Regiment, Captain Carl Gustav Örnestedt of the Life Dragoon Regiment, and a number of fortification officers.[1] There is good reason to believe that several cavalry patrols had already been sent out on 28 November, and if so, these patrols were complemented by yet more. The Swedish Army by this time had a long history of systematic intelligence collection before battle was decided upon. The officers made their way to the Russian lines, surveyed the Russian fortifications and the gun emplacements, and under the cover of darkness measured the depth of the ditches and the height of the rampart. Their work took place in pouring rain, which made it difficult to survey the Russian defences but possibly also reduced the awareness of the Russian sentries.

The cavalry patrols systematically reconnoitred the Russian lines, apparently under the supervision of Ehrenschantz himself. The intelligence and reconnaissance effort that had begun during the night continued on the following day (30 November) while the army marched to the battlefield. Reconnaissance work seems to have been concluded by noon, when Ehrenschantz had a drawing of the enemy camp prepared. The results of the reconnaissance, including the map, were not returned to Lagena, but delivered directly to King Charles and his generals as they approached the battlefield at about 11:00 a.m. on 30 November. The Swedes also had intelligence from deserters and agents. As a result, they had a good idea of the layout and quality of the fortified lines. However, Swedish intelligence

---

1 Örnestedt would ultimately be promoted to field marshal.

greatly overestimated the strength of the Russian army, assessing it as at least 50,000 and probably 80,000 strong.[2] It seems that the Swedes believed that both Prince Repnin's and Obidovskiy's divisions were in fact at Narva, although neither had yet actually reached the town.

The soldiers had not received much rest at Lagena, nor could they rest on the march. The heavy rains did not cease before the morning of 30 November. Roads were muddy and slippery, and eyewitnesses described them as 'unspeakably deep and evil' due to the pervasive mud.[3]

On the Russian side, Croÿ had the Tsar's instruction translated and read to all generals. We do not know how he interpreted the tactical situation. Croÿ may have expected that King Charles would settle down on the western part of the Hermannsberg to make detailed plans for an assault on the Russian defensive line. He may also have expected the Swedes to rest after the difficult march from Wesenberg. What we do know is that he instructed his commanders, orally to those who understood German and in writing to the rest, to be vigilant, send out continuous patrols, and immediately report any alarm directly to him. To diminish the risk for misunderstandings and false alarms, he ordered that anybody who fired a gun in the camp at night would be executed.

Croÿ also issued orders that half of each regiment and battalion must be on alert throughout the night. Officers and under-officers were not allowed to undress during the night but must remain in uniform. In the morning, gunpowder and shot would be issued so that each musketeer received powder and bullet for 24 shots (incidentally, the same amount as in the Swedish army). All old munitions should then be removed or discharged, so that every gun was ready for use.

In case of alarm, whether by night or day, three cannon shot in rapid succession should be fired. This was the old Imperial salute, also used by Denmark and the Polish-Lithuanian Commonwealth and very familiar to Croÿ from his previous wars. Henceforth, the firing of three shot also became the Russian salute. Hearing this signal, all soldiers must form up in units in their appointed places. Croÿ also ordered all artillery crews to be mixed, with both Russians and Germans and foreign specialists. When the enemy attacked, nobody was allowed, on the pain of death, to fire before the enemy had a reached a distance of from 20 to 30 paces. Finally, Croÿ ordered all units to move out and take up their positions in the defensive lines at dawn on 30 November, so that he could inspect the troops and remedy any deficiencies then detected.[4]

These were sensible instructions, and we can be certain that Croÿ also had them translated into Russian and distributed. Croÿ was possibly unsure about the army he had been ordered to command. It was clear from the

---

[2] Magnus Stenbock reported an estimated 50,000 Russians. *Magnus Stenbock och Eva Oxenstierna*1: *En Brefväxling* (Stockholm: P. A. Norstedt& Söner, 1913), p.147. Hallart related that his Swedish counterparts said that they had estimated 80,000 Russians. Hallart, *Tagebuch*, p.66.

[3] Liljegren, *Karl XII: En Biografi*, p.88.

[4] Hallart, *Tagebuch*, pp.54–55.

instructions that Croÿ, at least at first, intended to stay on the defensive, this was also what Tsar Peter had instructed him to. Yet, there were differences in opinion among the Russian commanders as to whether it was better to stand still behind the defensive lines, or march out to face the Swedes in open battle. Sheremetyev who was the only Russian commander who actually had engaged King Charles's Swedes, argued for an offensive strategy. He noted, accurately, that if the army remained behind the defensive line, less than 10 percent would be able to fight in the ensuing battle. But if the army marched out, its full strength could be brought to bear on the Swedes.

Soon before sunset at 3:17 p.m. on 29 November, Swedish cavalry patrols under Rehbinder and Örnestedt approached. The sentries raised the alarm, and all Russians manned their positions. Despite the heavy rain, Rehbinder and Örnestedt accordingly got a good view of how the Russians planned to conduct the defence. Croÿ ordered a cavalry patrol of 100 horse to patrol in front of the circumvallation line, all the way from Vepsekylla to Joala. Sheremetyev and Prince Dolgorukov confirmed the order but for some reason did not carry it out.[5] The Tsar's sudden and unexpected appointment of Croÿ, an outsider who had not even been in Russian service, as overall commander must have caused resentment among the Russian generals, and the Tsar's and Field Marshal General Golovin's equally sudden departure had shaken them.

Portrait of Prince Yakov Dolgorukov, Commissary General and thereby in charge of Russia's new de facto ministry of defence, as depicted while he was in Swedish captivity. Drawing by Elias Brenner, early 1700s (Author's photo)

By 7:00 p.m., the Russians observed the two signal rockets launched from the Swedish camp, and then in response, two more from Narva.[6] Croÿ ordered an increased state of alert for all units. He did not expect a night attack, so accepted that the units on the defensive line could step down.

Croÿ's assessment was correct. On 30 November, the Swedish army broke up from Lagena at 6:00 a.m., firing a double Swedish salute with their cannons. Again, Narva responded in the same manner.[7] It was still dark, since sunrise only came at 8:36 a.m. While the terrain permitted a march in order of battle, this was unnecessary, since the Russian positions now were well known. The army marched out divided into three columns, to be redeployed into a left wing, a centre, and a right wing during the march, with the left wing leading the way along the only road that led to Hermannsberg, the aforementioned hill that offered a good view

---

5 Hallart, *Tagebuch*, p.54.
6 Hallart, *Tagebuch*, p.55.
7 Hallart, *Tagebuch*, p.55.

of the Russian camp. As already noted, Hermannsberg was open, and free from woodland.

King Charles did not intend to delay the assault. The distance from Lagena to Narva was short, the army was running out of supplies, and there was nothing to be gained by delaying battle. The Swedish army marched out at such a time that most of the battle could be expected to be over before sunset at 3:16 p.m.

The vanguard reached the western slope of Hermannsberg around 10:00 a.m. The few Russian pickets on the hill were quickly overwhelmed or fled. Henceforth, the Swedish approach could continue in the partial cover of the ridge, and in part covered by the woodland south and southeast thereof. From the Russian lines, it was impossible to see the centre and right wing of the approaching army. The Russians could also not estimate the real strength of the Swedish army, so assumed that it still consisted of 24,000 or 25,000 men.[8] The Swedes then deployed the artillery on Hermannsberg, from which it opened fire on both the Russian fortifications and the Russian units that remained outside the defensive line, and as a result, these Russians units soon withdrew into the fortified area.

---

8   Hallart, *Tagebuch*, p.57.

9

The Russian Order of Battle

On the Russian side, the night and morning were calm. They had noted the double Swedish salute from King Charles's army, and Narva's response. It has been noted that Croÿ had already, on the previous day, ordered an inspection of the army, so early in the morning he and his generals mounted their horses to carry out the inspection and remedy any deficiencies or defects. They began on the right wing, but then, when Croÿ and his staff had reached the large bastion two kilometres south of Vepsekylla, they could already observe the approaching Swedish vanguard – first the cavalry, but soon also the infantry.

Since the Tsar had ordered a defensive posture, indeed proscribed offensive action unless success was certain, Croÿ decided merely to observe the Swedish approach to learn what King Charles planned to do. We do not know how Croÿ intended to respond to an assault, whether he planned to regroup to meet it or whether he actually planned to retain the dispersed defensive deployment already in place. Croÿ was an experienced officer who would have realised the advantage in meeting the Swedish army in force, but he was unfamiliar with his army and possibly felt obliged to follow the Tsar's instructions. He ordered all commanders to their posts, and this time, they followed orders. The Russian music sounded the alarm, and the units moved into position, planting their flags on the wall. With the defensive deployment completed, Croÿ and his staff continued their inspection tour on the left wing.

Croÿ soon found the already-implemented defensive deployment a sham. The defensive line was so long (7,200 m) that he, in the specialist Hallart's assessment, would have needed from 60,000 to 70,000 men to man the entire line in an adequate manner, but even his establishment strength was less than 29,800 foot – which enabled at most four men per metre of wall while not allowing for any second line, or indeed reserves of any kind. In reality, Croÿ had significantly fewer men at his disposal than this. Some of his infantry, an estimated 4,000, were already engaged in the trenches that faced the town of Narva. Moreover, the soldiers were exhausted by a lack of food, the poor weather, and diseases such as dysentery which plagued the crowded camp. It has already been noted that many men, about 2,000 to 3,000 in Hallart's estimate, were too sick to serve. Hallart estimated an effective 24,000 foot deployed along the line, and he may well have been correct.[1] No space remained within the lines to redeploy units against a concentrated Swedish assault.

At approximately 10:00 a.m., both the Swedish and Russian artillery went into action at the centre of the defensive line, at a distance of about 900 to 1,100 metres from each other. Croÿ was then at Joala, on the left wing, where he discussed the situation with Generals Sheremetyev and Weide. Apparently, he then rode to the exposed centre of the defensive line, because there is a tradition that a Swedish cannonball almost hit him at that point but Croÿ escaped harm, although the cannonball tore away a part of his spectacular red coat.[2] The Swedish artillery then advanced across the Hermannsberg, until one battery was as close as 400m from Prince Trubetskoy's camp.[3] Croÿ immediately rode to Trubetskoy's camp, which was at the most exposed section of the line. Croÿ at first concluded that the Swedish artillery fire in itself did not necessarily suggest an imminent assault. However, soon he and the other Russian generals could observe, through their spyglasses as well as with their naked eyes, that the Swedes were deployed in battle formation. While the cavalry at first had been closer to the Russian line, at this point the units advanced in a mixed formation of both infantry and cavalry. Then, having advanced further, the Swedish infantry deployed in the centre, while the cavalry units took up positions on the wings. The Swedish deployment was completed around 1:00 p.m. Meanwhile, the Russians remained in their original defensive positions, distributed along the entire circumvallation line. The Russian order of battle is described in Table 5 below.

Croÿ wondered whether what he saw was the entire Swedish army, or merely its vanguard. Trusting that what he observed was only the vanguard, he concluded that the Swedes were unlikely to begin an immediate assault.[4] Russian cavalry had captured a Swedish dragoon. When interrogated, he claimed that the Swedish army consisted of 10 cavalry regiments, six dragoon regiments, 16 infantry regiments, and 32 cannon. Either the captured dragoon lacked knowledge of the army's real strength, or he exaggerated, as had the Swedish officer, Patkul, previously captured by Sheremetyev. Either way, the information seemed to confirm the Russian headquarters' estimate that the Swedish army had a strength of at least 24,000 to 25,000 men, based on Sheremetyev's interrogations of captured soldiers.[5] If the Swedish units

---

1 Hallart, *Tagebuch*, p.56, which states the depth of the defensive line as two to three men. Hallart, *Tagebuch*, p.66 on the number of sick.
2 Ludwig Wisocki-Hochmuth, *Karolinska Krigares Dagböcker Jämte Andra Samtida Skrifter* 2 (Lund: Gleerup, 1903), pp.101–214, on pp.124–5. For some reason, said to be caused by haste, Croÿ on this day wore an odd pair of boots, one of French, the other of Russian manufacture.
3 This may have been the time when the Swedish artillery divided into two batteries, a northern one under Granatenhielm and a slightly weaker southern one, in a forward deployment, under Appelman. By plan or coincidence, Appelman's battery was in a position to provide supporting fire, if needed, on Granatenhielm's target, but Granatenhielm's battery could not, because of the terrain, engage Appelman's immediate target.
4 After the battle, he said as much to the French Ambassador, Count Louis de Guiscard (1651–1720). Gustavus Adlerfeld, *The Military History of Charles XII, King of Sweden* 1 (London: J. and P. Knapton, 1740), p.57.
5 Hallart, *Tagebuch*, pp.56–57.

lined up against the fortified line only constituted the vanguard, the Swedes were unlikely to carry out an assault before the rest of the army arrived.

Around 2:00 p.m., the Russians observed how Swedish infantry carrying fascines and assault ladders were advancing on both sides of the Hermannsberg. This surely marked the beginning of an assault, and there was no longer any time for Croÿ to redeploy his units, even if he wanted to. Instead, Croÿ had to trust his men.

Table 5. The Russian Order of Battle at Narva and Ivangorod, 30 November 1700[6]

Supreme commander: Field Marshal Charles Eugène Duke de Croÿ

Headquarters
Commissary General of War Prince Yakov Dolgorukov
General of Artillery Prince Alexander of Imeretia

Right Wing
(Golovin's Division, except Ivan Treyden's and Carl Peter Devson's Regiments)
Commander: General of Infantry Avtonom Golovin
Deputy: Major General Ivan Buturlin

Infantry and Dragoons:
Preobrazhenskiy Guard Regiment, under Johann Ernst von Blomberg
Semyonovskiy Guard Regiment, under Pavel Cunningham
Matvey Fliwerk's Regiment
Alferiy Schnewentz's 'Preobrazhenskiy' Dragoon Regiment (dismounted)
Carl Gustav Ivanitskiy's Regiment
Ivan Mewes's Regiment
Il'ya Bieltz's Regiment
Astafiy Pohlmann's Regiment
Matvey Treyden's Regiment

Infantry and Dragoons **total: 12,263 men**

Artillery:
Approximately 34 regimental guns, crewed by regimental artillerymen

Right wing total: 12,263 men

Centre
(Novgorod Division, except cavalry but reinforced with Carl Peter Devson's Regiment)

---

6   Velikanov, 'K voprosu ob organizatsii i chislennosti russkoy armii v Narvskom pokhode,' pp.132–138 & pp.139–40; Velikanov, 'K voprosu o sostoyanii russkoy armii posle Narvskogo porazheniya,' pp.26–42; Generalstaben, *Karl XII på slagfältet* 2, 329–30. The actual deployment of some units, in particular the streltsy regiments, remains uncertain.

Commander: Major General Prince Ivan Trubetskoy

Infantry:
Ivan Colomb's Regiment
Carl Peter Devson's Regiment
Roman Bruce's Regiment (Novgorod)
Miron Bayishev's Novgorod Streltsy Regiment
Zakhariy Vestov's Novgorod Streltsy Regiment[7]
Yuriy Vestov's Pskov Streltsy Regiment
Vasiliy Kozodavlev's Pskov Streltsy Regiment

Infantry **total: 6,567 men**

Artillery:
Approximately 17 regimental cannons, crewed by regimental artillerymen

Centre **total: 6,567 men**

Left wing
(Weide's Division, reinforced with Ivan Treyden's Regiment)
Commander: General of Infantry Adam Weide

Infantry and dragoons:
First Selected Moscow Regiment, also known as Weide's Regiment (formerly Lefort's Regiment)
Alexander Gordon of Achintoul's Regiment
Joachim Gulitz's 'Preobrazhenskiy' Dragoon Regiment (dismounted)
Ivan Treyden's Regiment
Erich von Werden's Regiment
Nikolay Balck's Regiment
Wilhelm von Schweiden's Regiment
Tomas Junger's Regiment
Fyodor Balck's Regiment
Vilim von Del'den's Regiment
Ivan von Del'den's Regiment

Infantry and dragoons **total: 12,538 men**

Artillery:
Approximately 28 regimental cannons, crewed by regimental artillerymen

Left wing total: **12,538 men**

Cavalry Group
Commander: General of Cavalry Boris Sheremetyev

---

[7] Lieutenant Colonel Fyodor Bayishev, the son of Colonel Miron Bayishev, assumed command of Zakhariy Vestov's Regiment after the latter's death in the ensuing battle.

Sovereign's Old Style Division, under Boris Sheremetyev: 2,000 men
Smolensk Old Style Division, under Bogdan Korsak: 898 men
Novgorod new style Cavalry Regiment, under Ivan Kokoshkin: 250 men
Smolensk new style Cavalry Regiment, under Grigoriy Rydvanskiy: 200 men

Total: at most **3,348 men**, and probably less because of previous battle losses

Grand total facing the Swedish relief army:
At most **33,151 men** including cavalry, less units engaged in the trenches that faced the town of Narva and those too sick to serve

Siege artillery
64 siege cannons, 4 howitzers, 26 mortars,
divided into 10 batteries facing Narva and Ivangorod
Crews: **230–250 men**, assisted by an unknown number of detached infantrymen

Containment force on the eastern side of the River Narova, facing Ivangorod
(while some uncertainty remains, at least the following units seem to have formed part of this contingent)

Cavalry:
Novgorod Old Style Division, under Stepan Bakhmetyev

Cavalry total: at most **1,500 men**, and probably less because of previous battle losses

Infantry:
Stepan Strekalov's Belgorod (ex-Moscow) Streltsy Regiment
Vasiliy Yelchaninov's Belgorod (ex-Moscow) Streltsy Regiment[8]
Martem'yan Sukharev's Belgorod (ex-Moscow) Streltsy Regiment[9]
Venedikt Baturin's (ex-Moscow) Streltsy Regiment

Infantry total: at most about **1,800 to 2,000 men**, and probably less because of previous battle losses

---

8   Yelchaninov was wounded and captured at Ivangorod.
9   Sukharev fell already during the attempted storm of Ivangorod.

10

The Swedish Order of Battle

The Swedes knew that a surprise attack, in the normal sense of the word, was out of the question. The Russians were well aware that the Swedish Army was approaching, and they had already manned the fortifications. Under such circumstances, it was customary to dig in, build an armed camp, and then carefully reconnoitre the terrain before commencing a siege that ultimately would result in an assault. However, the Swedes had good reasons for disregarding the customary practices and instead carry out an immediate assault. Indeed, the Swedes had little choice but to attack – they were out of supplies, so did not have the luxury of the time to prepare for a siege. Furthermore, the few available supplies would not last for a retreat. No additional supplies could be had in the settlements around Wesenberg. Finally, at Lagena the Swedes had already learnt that the Tsar had departed in order to bring reinforcements. It was believed that another Russian army of 30,000 men with artillery already stood at the border; if so, Tsar Peter might return within a few days.[1] We have seen that Prince Repnin and Obidovskiy operated there with their divisions. Perhaps the Swedish commanders also realised that it was unlikely that generals schooled in the Continental model of warfare, such as Croÿ, would expect an immediate assault. Besides, if the Russians understood how few the Swedes actually were, this would raise morale and increase their willingness to resist. If such thoughts were in King Charles's and his commanders' minds, this would have strengthened their resolve to carry out an immediate assault.

As was customary in the Swedish Army, King Charles and his generals decided on the battle plan while in the field. There was never a written plan. In light of the King's youth and inexperience, it was almost certainly Lieutenant General Carl Gustav Rehnskiöld who devised the battle plan together with Quartermaster General Lieutenant Gerdt Ehrenschantz and Chief of Artillery Johan Siöblad. Yet, King Charles rode to Narva with the vanguard and apparently took immediate and personal control of the battle, without previous discussion with any general except Rehnskiöld. There was apparently no council of war immediately before the assault, and some senior

---

1   Generalstaben, *Karl XII på slagfältet* 2, p.332.

commanders found this disconcerting.² Accompanied by Rehnskiöld and General Vellingk, King Charles rode up on the Hermannsberg to personally observe the enemy lines. He then sent his aide of the Drabant Corps, Knut Leijonhufvud, to order the men to assemble the necessary tools, fascines, light assault ladders, and then switch to combat load (that is, remove knapsacks and cloaks if they had them), and prepare for an immediate assault.

While King Charles gave orders and encouraged the men, Rehnskiöld likely exercised overall operational command to the extent that his physical position on the battlefield allowed. This was certainly the opinion of his subordinates, including Colonel Magnus Stenbock who wrote to his father-in-law shortly after the battle that next to God and 'His Majesty's unshakeable resolve,' the victory belongs to 'Lieutenant General Rehnskiöld's mature disposition' of the army.³

The most important component of the Russian defences was Prince Trubetskoy's fortified camp on the eastern side of the Hermannsberg. However, the Swedish artillery, when deployed on the higher ground on the western side of Hermannsberg, found itself in a position to dominate the Russian camp. In short, the Russians had deployed in a strong position, but the defences contained flaws. An infantry attack combined with substantial artillery support would have a good chance of penetrating the Russian line. Moreover, a concentrated assault force, or rather two assault columns, one on each side of the camp, would be numerically superior to the Russian defenders, spread out as they were. By tradition, the Swedish army deployed in assault columns when it faced enemy fortifications, although on an open battlefield, deployment in lines remained the norm. When sufficient space was again available, a column customarily redeployed into line.

Moreover, the Swedes knew that the Russian defensive lines lacked exit points for rapid evacuation. The Russians accordingly had no way out from their carefully prepared fortifications, in the event that circumstances turned against them. The Russian centre and left wing had no retreat route eastwards due to the River Narova, so their only remaining escape route was through the Russian right wing across the river via the Kamperholm Bridge, a raft bridge. The Swedish plan accordingly seems to have been an attack with two columns against the Russian centre. Once that was done, the two columns would veer off in each direction and roll up the Russian flanks so that the Tsar's army was trapped in two pockets against the River Narova. If the Swedes could seize the Kamperholm Bridge, this would prevent the retreat of the entire Russian army.

But there was also a strong Russian bastion on the Rathshof Hill. Located further to the north, the distance was around 1,100m from Hermannsberg, which would make Swedish artillery fire ineffective. It was accordingly

---

2   '[The head of the field chancellery and de facto prime minister Carl] Piper is very distressed to see important issues being decided without discussion; in one word, here things proceed in an odd manner, nobody is consulted anymore'. Magnus Stenbock to Bengt Oxenstierna, 24 December 1700 (S.S.), cited in Generalstaben, *Karl XII på slagfältet* 2, pp.341 & 354.

3   Frans G. Bengtsson, *Karl XII:s levnad: Till uttåget ur Sachsen* (Stockholm: Norstedt/Mån Pocket, 1992), p.120.

important to detach part of the Swedish artillery for a deployment further to the north. The Swedes also detached a separate infantry column under Colonel Stenbock to move against Rathshof Hill. This column would be particularly well equipped with siege tools.

Because of the limited supplies, each infantryman received no more powder before the battle than for 24 shots.[4] Each man attached a whisk of straw to his hat in the customary Swedish manner as a field sign to distinguish friend from foe. This was a practice that derived from the late 1630s. The Swedish battle cry, like the whisks of straw also used to enable easier recognition: 'With God's help' (Swedish: *Med Guds hjälp*).

The Swedish commanders concentrated the infantry into three assault columns, headed by grenadiers whose task it was to suppress the enemy's fire while the infantry climbed across the fortified lines. There was nothing new in this application of tactics, which had been used by the Swedish army for most of the seventeenth century.[5] It was also customary for the Swedes to deploy cavalry behind the infantry during an assault, so as to retain the option rapidly to move into and gain control of the open area behind the fortified lines, after they had penetrated them. The cavalry could also be used to deal with sallies from the defensive lines, if such took place. King Charles, Rehnskiöld, and Siöblad concentrated the artillery in two locations, so as to maximise its potential to support the assault.

Carl Piper. Engraving by Martin Bernigeroth. (Author's collection)

Ultimately, King Charles personally decided upon the order of march of the assault column. Major General Posse, who commanded the infantry on the right wing, wanted to confirm the details of the planned assault with the other generals (this was, after all, the young King's first real battle), but none was available at the time. Presumably, they had gone to join their commands and Posse's messages seem to have gone unanswered, or at least the response did not reach him in time. King Charles then gave Posse orders, in minute detail, on how to form the assault column. He ordered Posse to deploy Grenadier Lieutenant Frans Anton Rehnskiöld with 50 men at the head of the column, followed by the rest of the grenadiers under Captain Jacob Sperling, immediately followed by the Major General himself accompanied by Lieutenant Colonel Carl Gustav Palmquist, with Major Carl von Numers on his right and Captain Edvard Ehrensteen on the left. Captain Carl Magnus Posse's battalion would follow that of Numers,

---

4   Carl Magnus Posse to his brother Nils Posse, 9 December 1700 (S.S.), p.88.
5   While the early twentieth century General Staff historians were keen to portray the tactics employed by King Charles as a departure from previous tactics, there is no evidence to support their interpretation.

Magnus Stenbock, portrait by Georg Engelhard Schröder, 1708. (National Museum, Stockholm)

while Captain Carl Eriksson Sparre's battalion would support Ehrensteen. The King also provided other detailed dispositions (Table 6).[6] When battle commenced, it soon became clear that a number of Swedish civilians joined the fray as well. This was not unusual in the Swedish Army. Most senior among them was Carl Piper, head of the field chancellery and Sweden's de facto Prime Minister, who despite his advanced age stepped in to command a cavalry squadron.[7] When Piper rode into battle, so did his secretary, Josias Cederhielm, who took up a position as aide to Colonel Stenbock.

What Croÿ and the Russian generals had observed was the Swedish redeployment into two wings, with infantry in front and cavalry held back on the side. The right wing under Vellingk consisted of 11 battalions of foot under Major General Knut Posse, and 24 squadrons of horse under Lieutenant General Bleichard Wachtmeister. The right wing received orders to break through the Russian line at 'old Rathshof', that is, just south of Prince Trubetskoy's fortified camp. The strong cavalry contingent, under Wachtmeister, was possibly intended to safeguard the flank against Sheremetyev's mostly old style Russian cavalry which was deployed behind the defences at Joala, at the extreme south of the Russian line.[8]

The left wing was led by Rehnskiöld and was ordered to break through the Russian line 'above Vepsekylla', the wing was divided into two columns. The left of these columns was entrusted to Colonel Stenbock, who was tasked with two battalions of foot to capture the Rathshof Redoubt. Possibly, Stenbock also received orders to seize the bridge to Kamperholm Island, since such a move would prevent the Russian army from retreating. The right column under Major General Maydell consisted of eight battalions of foot, and 10 squadrons of horse under Rehnskiöld himself, who from his position at the head of the Drabant Corps followed the King wherever battle conditions looked most critical. The right column received orders to attack the fortified line between the Rathshof Redoubt and Prince Trubetskoy's fortified camp.

---

6 Carl Magnus Posse to his brother Nils Posse, 9 December 1700 (S.S.), p.87.
7 Josias Cederhielm to his brother Germund Cederhielm, 27 November 1700 (S.S.), *Karolinska Krigares dagböcker* 8, pp.137–257, on pp.162–3.
8 Hallart certainly thought that Sheremetyev's cavalry could have prevented the Swedish victory, had it acted more forcefully. Hallart, *Tagebuch*, p.57.

The Swedish Application of *Auftragstaktik*

Most Continental armies from the sixteenth century onwards based their system of tactical battlefield command on what in the twentieth century became known, in German, as *Befehlstaktik* (command-type tactics). *Befehlstaktik* is a method of command in which the overall commander issues detailed orders to his subordinate commanders, who then are expected to follow orders to the letter and, for this reason, enjoy little or no freedom to take personal initiative.

Befehlstaktik stands in stark contrast to the style of command practised in the Swedish army. At Narva, each Swedish unit received its particular tactical objective. Lieutenant Colonel Roos of the Närke-Värmland Regiment, for instance, was ordered to take 'the second bastion from the big one.' The early twentieth century Swedish General Staff historians regarded the issuance of tactical objectives of this type instead of detailed orders as a Swedish innovation and the essentially first application ever of *Auftragstaktik* (mission-type tactics).

Auftragstaktik is a method of command and delegation in which the overall commander gives each of his subordinate commanders a clearly-defined objective, timeframe, and forces with which to accomplish the objective, but leaves them freedom of planning and executing the mission independently. *Auftragstaktik* enables flexibility in execution, faster decision-making, frees the senior commanders from the need to micro-manage tactical details, and allows them to focus on strategic decisions.

Few regular armies even in the twenty-first century base their style of command on *Auftragstaktik*, since this effectively transfers the battlefield initiative from senior commanders to junior ones – a scary prospect for many higher-ranking officers! Yet, *Auftragstaktik* was a central component of German military tactics from the nineteenth century onwards and is commonly regarded as a key reason for the frequent tactical battlefield successes of German armies in the two world wars. The Swedish army, too, regarded the application of *Auftragstaktik* (which in Swedish is known as *Uppdragstaktik*) as central for battlefield success and still upholds the concept in doctrine and training.

Were the Swedish General Staff historians correct in attributing the introduction of *Auftragstaktik* to King Charles at Narva? No, but there is indeed some evidence that Swedish tactics already displayed the characteristics of *Auftragstaktik* in the seventeenth century, at a time when most of their neighbours insisted on the slower and less flexible *Befehlstaktik*. Does this mean that the Swedish army introduced this concept to the Continent, and that subsequent German armies picked it up from the Swedes, in the same way that they copied much else of the Swedish model of war?

The answer to this question can possibly be found in a never-completed book by King Gustavus Adolphus who led Swedish armies in the Thirty Years' War. In the treatise *On the Duties of Soldiers*, he explains what he expected of his commanders. Gustavus Adolphus listed the characteristics of a good commander as 'virtue, knowledge, caution, authority, and luck.' He wanted leaders who in clear conscience could tell their men that 'I want you to follow not only my instructions and orders but also my example.' To avoid empty words, Gustavus Adolphus succinctly defined what he meant by a commander's virtue: 'I demand of him virtue in the form of honesty in his daily life, vigour and industriousness in his duties, bravery in danger, diligence in his work, and speed in fulfilment.'[9] Since the Swedish King never completed the book, we do not know whether he also considered the question of the benefits of *Auftragstaktik* versus those of *Befehlstaktik*. Yet, it is clear that Gustavus Adolphus wanted his subordinates to display speed, industriousness, and take initiatives by following his example – and not only his instructions.

---

9   Gustavus Adolphus, 'Om Krigsmäns Pligter,' C. G. Styffe (ed.), *Konung Gustaf II Adolfs skrifter* (Stockholm: P. A. Norstedt & Söner, 1861), pp.62–8, on pp.63–64.

Each unit received its tactical objective. Lieutenant Colonel Roos of the Närke-Värmland Regiment, for instance, was ordered to take 'the second bastion from the big one.'[10]

There was also a cavalry reserve consisting of 13 squadrons of horse led by Major General Johan Ribbing. The Swedish artillery was tasked with providing support for the advance of the infantry columns and was divided into two batteries: the battery to the left under Lieutenant Colonel Magnus Granatenhielm, and the battery to the right under Major Gustav Appelman.

During the battle the two cavalry wings began to move further away from the assault columns. Units of the left column of the left wing continued all the way to Vepsekylla, where they seized the bridge.

Table 6. The Swedish order of Battle at Narva and Ivangorod, 30 November 1700 [11]

Notes:
The Finnish infantry battalions consisted of ad hoc contingents from Åbo County, Björneborg, Tavastehus, Viborg, Savolax, and Nyland Regiments.
The total number of cannons in King Charles's army is believed to have been 21.
Data for the garrison is dated June 1699.

Supreme commander: King Charles XII
Aides:
Drabant Lieutenant and Chamberlain Axel Hård
Drabant Corporal Fabian Reinhold Wrangel
Drabant Trooper Per von Günthersberch

Headquarters
De facto Chief of staff: Lieutenant General of Cavalry Carl Gustav Rehnskiöld (also in overall operational command)
Quartermaster General Lieutenant, Lieutenant Colonel Gerdt Ehrenschantz
Aide of the Drabant Corps, Knut Leijonhufvud (promoted to Adjutant General during the battle)
Adjutant General Berndt Otto Stackelberg
Adjutant General Carl Gustav Dücker
Adjutant General Gotthard Henrik von Lantingshausen

Right Wing
(formed in assault column; units from right to left, unless stated otherwise)
Commander: General of Cavalry Otto Vellingk (positioned in the approximate middle of the column)

---

10   Generalstaben, *Karl XII på slagfältet* 2, p.339, citing Roos's service record, National Archives.
11   Generalstaben, *Karl XII på slagfältet* 2, 300–301, 313, 318, 335–8; Ulfhielm, *Kungl. artilleriet: Karl XI:s och Karl XII:s tid*, 325–7; Laidre, *Segern vid Narva*, 96–8.

THE SWEDISH ORDER OF BATTLE

Infantry:
Commander: Major General Knut Posse (positioned immediately after the grenadiers in the vanguard)

Vanguard
Life Guard of Foot, 50 selected grenadiers under Lieutenant Frans Anton Rehnskiöld
Life Guard of Foot, the grenadier battalion under Captain Jacob Sperling

First line
Life Guard of Foot, one battalion under Major Carl von Numers
Life Guard of Foot, the Life Battalion under Lieutenant Colonel Carl Gustav Palmquist
Life Guard of Foot, one battalion under Captain Edvard Ehrensteen

Second line
Life Guard of Foot, one battalion under Captain Carl Magnus Posse
Life Guard of Foot, one battalion under Captain Carl Eriksson Sparre

Third line
Hälsinge Regiment, one battalion under Colonel Göran Johan von Knorring
Västmanland Regiment, one battalion under Captain Casimir Sigismund Wrangel

Fourth line
Åbo, Björneborg, and Nyland County Temporary Regiment, one battalion under Colonel Magnus Gabriel von Tiesenhausen
Hälsinge Regiment, one battalion under Major Gotthard Wilhelm von Wulffen
Västmanland Regiment, one battalion under Captain Knut Kurck

Total: 11 battalions, 2,998 men

Cavalry:
Commander: Lieutenant General of Cavalry Bleichard (Bleckert) Wachtmeister

Right column
Åbo, Nyland, and Viborg County Temporary Cavalry Regiment, two squadrons under Lieutenant Colonel Carl Magnus Rehbinder
Karelian Territorial Dragoon Battalion, two squadrons under Major Niclas de Molin
Karelian Cavalry Regiment, seven squadrons under Colonel Hans Henrik Rehbinder

Left column
Life Dragoon Regiment, four squadrons under Lieutenant Colonel Hugo Johan Hamilton

Nyland and Tavastehus Cavalry Regiment, nine squadrons under Lieutenant Colonel Adolph Magnus Klingspor

Total: 24 squadrons, 1,928 men

Left wing
(formed in assault column; units from right to left, unless stated otherwise)
Commander: Lieutenant General of Cavalry Carl Gustav Rehnskiöld (positioned at the head of the cavalry column)

Infantry (right column):
Commander: Major General of Infantry Georg Johan Maydell (positioned immediately after the grenadiers in the vanguard)

Vanguard
Two grenadier platoons

First line
Närke-Värmland Regiment, one battalion under Lieutenant Colonel Carl Gustav Roos
Dalecarlia Regiment, one battalion under Lieutenant Colonel Jacob Grundel

Second line
Närke-Värmland Regiment, one battalion under Captain Gideon Fock
Finnish Regiment, one battalion under Colonel Gustav Adolph Mellin

Third line
Västmanland Regiment, one battalion under Major Mattias Fredrik von Feilitzen
Finnish Regiment, one battalion under Lieutenant Colonel Ernst Lode

Fourth line
Finnish Regiment, one battalion under Captain Reinhold Sass
Finnish Regiment, one battalion under Major Otto Reinhold Berg

Total: 8 battalions, 2,375 men

Infantry (left column):
Commander: Colonel Magnus Stenbock (positioned immediately after the grenadiers in the vanguard)

Vanguard
One grenadier platoon of the Dalecarlia Regiment, under Captain David Klijssendorff

First line
Dalecarlia Regiment, one battalion under Colonel Magnus Stenbock

Tavastehus, Viborg, and Nyslott County Temporary Regiment, one battalion under Lieutenant Colonel Göran Hastfehr

Total: 2 battalions, 516 men

Cavalry:
Commander: Lieutenant General of Cavalry Carl Gustav Rehnskiöld

Right column
Life Drabant Corps, two squadrons under Captain Lieutenant Arvid Bernhard Horn and Lieutenant Carl Gustav Wrangel
Life Dragoon Regiment, four squadrons under Major Philip Fredrik Rothlieb

Left column
Åbo, Nyland, and Viborg County Temporary Cavalry Regiment, two squadrons
Karelian Territorial Dragoon Battalion, two squadrons

Total: 10 squadrons, 736 men

Artillery
Commander: Chief of Artillery Johan Siöblad

Right battery
Probably 8 guns, under Major Gustav Gabriel Appelman

Left battery
Probably 13 guns, under Lieutenant Colonel Magnus Granatenhielm

Cavalry Reserve
Commander: Major General Johan Ribbing

Right column
Åbo and Björneborg County Cavalry Regiment, seven squadrons under Colonel Bernhard Rehbinder

Left column
Tiesenhausen's Enlisted Estonian Cavalry Regiment, three squadrons under Colonel Hans Heinrich von Tiesenhausen
The Retinue of Nobles in Estonia, three squadrons under Lieutenant Colonel Reinhold von Liewen

Total: 13 squadrons, 1,650 men

Total horse: 4,314
Total foot: 5,889
Total artillerymen: 424
Grand total for field army: 10,627

Garrison of Narva and Ivangorod
Commandant: Colonel Henning Rudolph Horn

Horse:
Tiesenhausen's Enlisted Estonian Cavalry Regiment, two companies
Ingrian Retinue of Nobles
Possibly a contingent of Vellingk's Enlisted Ingrian Dragoon Regiment

Total: 3 companies, 150 men

Foot:
Horn's Enlisted Ingrian Garrison Regiment, under Henning Rudolph Horn
Originally 1,460 men but now significantly less
Possibly contingents of the Savolax and Viborg Regiments and Vellingk's Enlisted Ingrian Regiment
Burgher militia   400 men

Total: 1,570 to 1,670 men

Artillery:
Narva: 270 cannon, 28 mortars, and possibly four howitzers
Ivangorod: 103 ordinary cannon, 8 obsolete cannon suitable only for firing clusters of multiple small shot or stones, and 5 mortars
Artillery crew: 81 artillerymen, under Lieutenant Colonel Johan Staël von Holstein
Contingent of non-combatant levied peasants from Viborg County for labour duty, under Lieutenant Colonel Donnerstedt 400 men

Total for the Garrison   1,800 to 1,900 combatants

11

The Assault

The Swedish assault commenced at approximately 2:00 p.m. This was late in the day, and probably later than they had anticipated; the sun would set at 3:16 p.m, and the sky was probably already overcast. The assault was initiated by the launching of two signal rockets, so that all Swedish units would advance at the same time.[1]

King Charles positioned himself with the artillery on Hermannsberg, since this enabled him the best overview of the battlefield. Meanwhile, the artillery duel between the Swedish and Russian batteries continued.

The approach of the Swedish infantry along the Hermannsberg also marked a change in weather: it grew colder, and a winter storm was rapidly coming up. Dark clouds covered the sky, and it began snowing.

The Swedish columns advanced towards points located near the centre of the Russians' defensive line. They apparently took some casualties from Russian artillery fire, although it seems that the terrain protected them at least during the initial advance. The artilleryman Carl Cronstedt later wrote that the Russian artillery 'at first fired like a devil'.[2] And then, at the critical moment, the snowfall suddenly turned into a blizzard. The Swedes felt the strong wind in their backs, in effect carrying them forwards, while the Russians were hit like a blow straight at them in the face. It was no longer possible to see the approaching Swedes. The Russians only saw their enemies again when they suddenly stormed across the defensive line and pushed into the Russian formations. With snow and strong winds blowing into their eyes, the Russians could not aim their weapons.

Cronstedt later wrote:

> …in the same moment that our men began the assault, the Highest God gave us a strong and dense blizzard which blew against our back and covered us to the extent

---

1   C. H. P. Sperling, *Karolinska Krigares Dagböcker Jämte Andra Samtida Skrifter* 3 (Lund: Gleerup, 1907), pp.1–59, on p.11; Wrangel, 'Några anteckningar,' 146; manuscript from 1720, f. 38 (then in Tsarist General Staff Library); cited in A. Petrov, 'Narvskaya Operatsiya,' *Voyennyy Sbornik* 7 (1872), pp.5–38, on p.30.
2   Carl Cronstedt to Jacob Troilius, 6 December 1700 (S.S.), *Handlingar Rörande Skandinaviens Historia* 19 (Stockholm: A. Wiborg, 1834), pp.401–404, on p.403.

PETER THE GREAT'S DISASTROUS DEFEAT

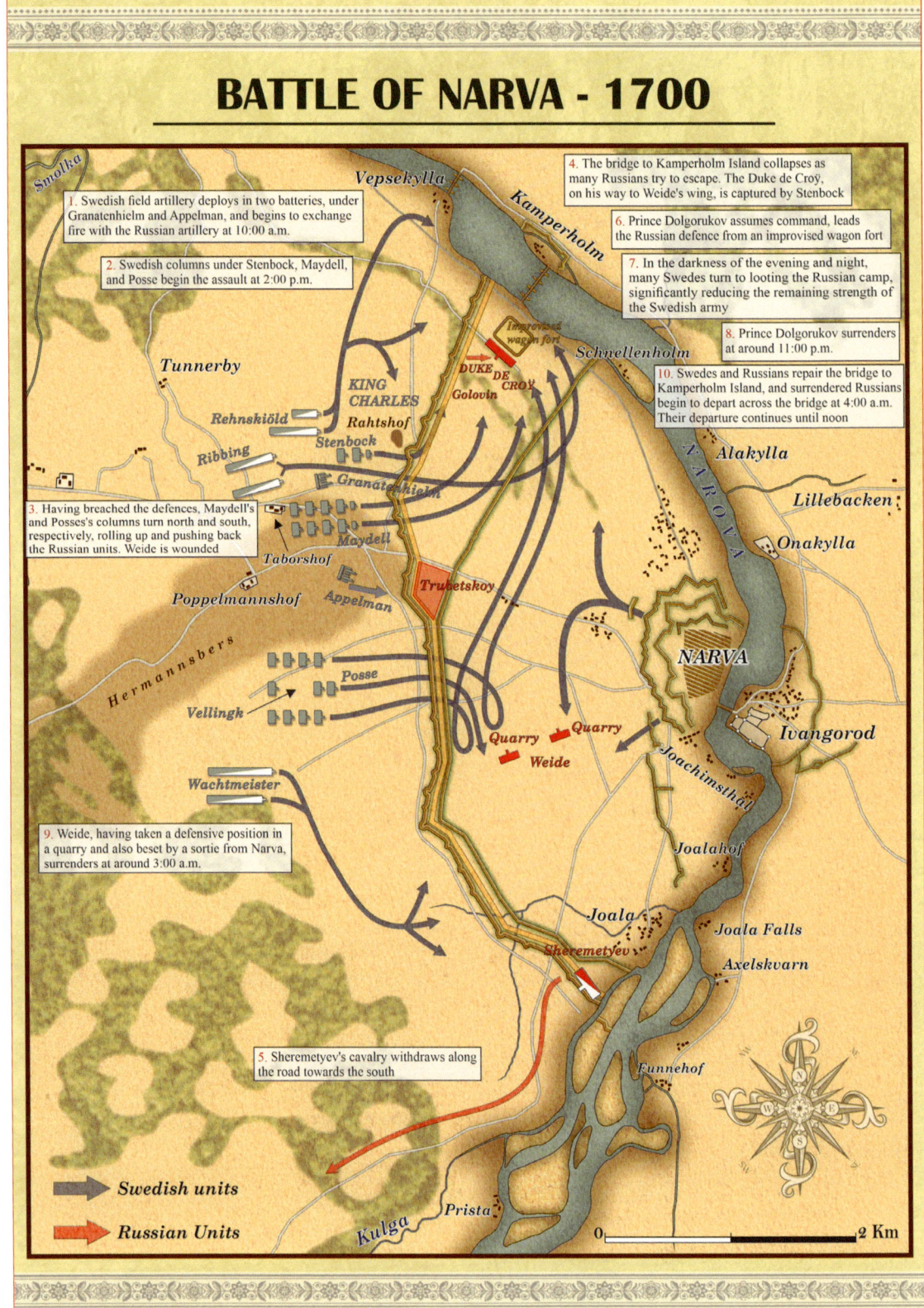

The Battle of Narva, 30 November 1700

that the enemy could see nothing of us at a distance of 40 paces, and therefore we suffered no damage from the Russian artillery and can say that we lost only few if any men before we were within range and this took only a moment.[3]

Major Carl von Numers of the Life Guard, who led the first line, agreed, commenting:

> …during our approach the enemy fired horribly with his cannons, but just when he would make his largest defensive [effort], God allowed such a snowfall from heaven that we could not see them or they us, until we approached him [the enemy] at a distance of 30 paces, when on both sides a fierce fire broke out, during which we with great fortune and without great loss advanced across his defensive line in such good order as if we had marched with our regiment [along a road].[4]

The blizzard and the assault shook the Russians badly. Panicked Russians shot blindly with muskets and cannons while the Swedish grenadiers with good visibility fired their muskets at close range, causing heavy casualties in the Russian ranks. With pikes and muskets the Swedes then made their way past the ditch by filling it with fascines, tore down the *chevaux-de-frise*, climbed up the exterior slope of the rampart, and attacked the Russians behind the breastwork. Several Swedes were hit by Russian fire, but the column nonetheless broke through and cut down the defenders. The Life Guard Captain Olof Stiernhöök later wrote in his diary:

> They shot strongly both with muskets and cannons but this did not result in much, and everything went over [our heads]. When we reached 30 paces, we fired our salvoes, which, glory to God, caused better effect, because they fell like grass. Then we ran towards them, sword in hand, and tore down their *chevaux-de-frise*…[5]

Another captain of the Life Guard, Carl Magnus Posse, later wrote to his brother:

> I can say that it was a hot thing; you cannot believe how fast they aimed their cannons, and how far they shot with their muskets, because their gunpowder is much stronger than ours. This was our good fortune, because God made their shot go too high. And then we broke in; their defensive line was more than three ells high with broad moats in front so deep that the water reached a man to the waist. There were *chevaux-de-frise* along the entire line. God helped us breach it with small loss of men. You can believe that we ran on, killing Russians like one destroys insects in the pigsty at [the farming estate] Stora Säby…[6]

---

[3] Carl Cronstedt to Jacob Troilius, 6 December 1700 (S.S.), p.403. There is a writing error in the letter ('we cannot say that we lost only few if any men') but Cronstedt's intention is clear: they suffered few if any losses before they penetrated the enemy lines.
[4] Numers, cited in Generalstaben, *Karl XII På Slagfältet* 2, p.343.
[5] Olof Stiernhöök, 'Drabanten Och Kaptenen vid Lifgardet Olof Stiernhööks Journal 1700–1703,' *Karolinska Förbundets Årsbok* 1912, pp.315–408, on p.366.
[6] Carl Magnus Posse to his brother Nils Posse, 9 December 1700 (S.S.), p.87.

What presumably happened was the kind of combat envisaged in the Swedish infantry instruction issued in 1701, which concluded:

> when a battalion advances against the enemy in the field, eight grenadiers, with bayonets on their muskets, advance ahead of the commanding officer in two lines, and when battle commences, they should march on both sides of him, both to protect the colours and from time to time to do their best to shoot at the enemy officers, but otherwise conserve their munitions until the [battalion's] pikemen charge into [the enemy line]; but the colours should enter into the middle of the file when they charge, and all music then should remain behind the battalion.[7]

According to the instructions of King Charles XI, the men should spend as little time as possible firing at an enemy behind the breastwork of a fortified position or, preferably, fire only one salvo before storming it, so as to remove the enemy's advantage as soon as possible. Unsurprisingly, this is what happened at Narva, since both opportunity (distance, weather, and height of the fortifications) and the already-practised tactics encouraged this course of action.

The Swedes fired one salvo at 30 paces, according to instructions, and then charged with pike, bayonet, and sword.

The blizzard had lasted for about 15 minutes. The wind and snowfall ceased just as the Swedes penetrated the Russian defences. It is not a wonder that Cronstedt later wrote that the blizzard was a gift from God. When the strong winds and heavy snowfall ceased, the Swedish units easily reformed their ranks within the Russian defensive area.

Since the defensive line was so long, the Russians could not take advantage of their numerical superiority, and were locally outnumbered by the Swedish columns. Moreover, the Russians had clumsy plug bayonets, few or no pikes, and apparently mostly also lacked swords or sabres. This put them at a disadvantage, in particular against the Swedish Life Guard, which combined a high level of training and experience with having recently been issued efficient socket bayonets in addition to their traditional pikes.

On the Swedish right wing, Major General Knut Posse led the Life Guard in the assault. His almost 3,000 men attacked a sector of the fortified line that stretched out for about 600m, and was primarily manned by the First Selected Moscow Regiment, also known as Weide's Regiment, and whatever other soldiers were nearby.[8] Posse's troops faced less than 2,000 Russians. While the weather conditions certainly helped to minimise Swedish losses,

---

7 Förordning Och Reglemente För Infanteriet, Lais den 7 mars 1701 (Reval, 1701). The Swedish Infantry Instruction issued in 1701.

8 A Swedish battalion had an establishment strength of 600 men, typically divided into four ranks each of 150 men with a front of about 185 metres. Following the instruction of 1694, the battalion adopted a close-order formation during the assault, which resulted in front of an estimated 110 metres. The distance between the advancing close-order battalions was a little more than a battalion front. The total front of the right column was accordingly 3 x 110 + 2 x 120 = 570 metres, which corresponds to the surviving battle sketches. Generalstaben, *Karl XII på slagfältet* 2, p.342.

Posse's superiority in numbers and the better training of the Swedish soldiers ensured the outcome and the Swedes broke through.

The result of the assault was that the Swedes breached the Russian line at two points: between the bastion 200m south of Prince Trubetskoy's camp, and at another point 600m south of the camp. This separated the Russian left wing from the rest of the Tsar's army. The Swedish right wing had reached its first objective without significant losses.

On the Swedish left wing, the Swedes attacked the defensive line between a point 200m north of Trubetskoy's camp and the Rathshof Redoubt. The left infantry column under Colonel Stenbock attacked the Rathshof Redoubt itself. Stenbock's column was deployed slightly forward of Major General Maydell's group, and there is a credible tradition that Stenbock and his Dalecarlians were the first to climb over the Russian fortifications.[9]

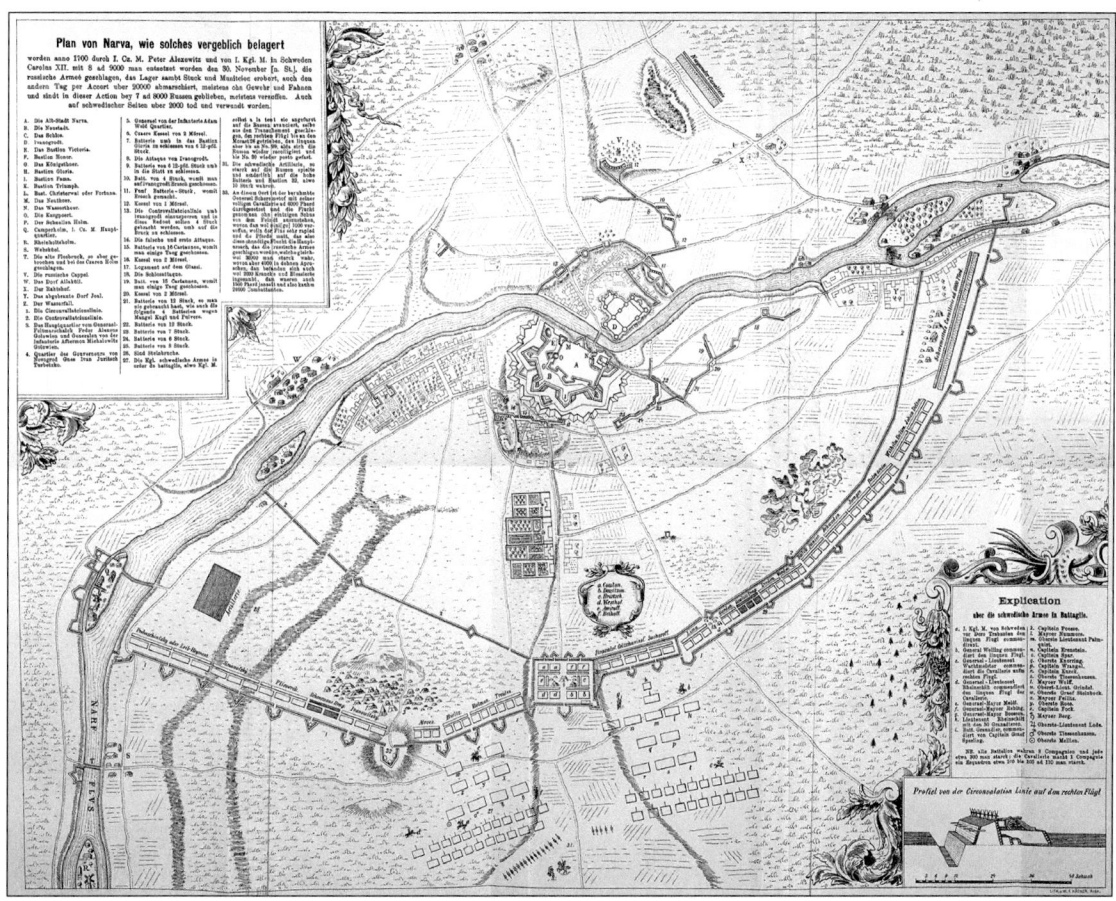

Nineteenth century map based on Hallart's notes and sketches, published together with his diary. The map, although not contemporary, gives a detailed and generally reliable overview of the battle and the fortifications erected during the siege. It also illustrates Narva's destroyed suburbs, the quarry (left, inside the fortified lines), the ravines near the bridge to Kamperholm Island, the Joala Falls (right), and even the rural road leading south on the left bank of the River Narova. However, it is misleading with regard to the disposition of, in particular, the Russian regiments and in some cases even their identification. Hallart presumably used already-dated information on the Russian deployment when he compiled his notes. (Author's collection)

---

9   Pihlström, *Kungl. Dalregementets Historia* 3, p.92.

Regimental 3-pdr. The rope wound around the barrel was used by the crew for pulling the gun into place when no horse(s) was available. Johan Möllerheim, 1720 (Author's collection)

Soon afterwards, Maydell's column, on an approximately 250m front, advanced against the Russian line from a point around 200m north of Trubetskoy's camp to the corner bastion 250m further north-west. The distance between the two infantry columns was about 300m. Here, the concentrated Swedish assault force may not have outnumbered the Russians, but they were close: almost 2,900 Swedes attacked perhaps 3,500 Russians from Mewes's, Bieltz's, and Pohlmann's Regiments. Within less than 30 minutes, the Swedes breached the Russian front in two locations. The Russian front was thus split into three separate parts.

Company colour of the Life Guard of Foot, with battle damage. This colour, flown by the Life Company, was carried in the Battle of Narva. The colour shows the Swedish lion and crowns on a white base. All colours within the Life Guard were white. The reverse side is reconstructed in the colour artwork section, in the paining depicting the Life Guard assaulting the Russian circumvallation line. Infantry colours were about 210cm x 190cm in size. (Army Museum, Stockholm; AM.091586)

C1

12

Battle Between the Lines

On the Swedish right wing, Posse's column turned south immediately after the breach. On the left wing, meanwhile, Maydell's column in the same manner turned north, for the time being ignoring Prince Trubetskoy's camp. The Russians fled before them, in the words of Lieutenant General Hallart 'chased from one cover into another'.[1] Many attempted to cross the defensive line, so as to escape towards the bridge at Vepsekylla. However, Rehnskiöld's cavalry set out to intercept them on the direct order of King Charles, together with Hastfehr's Finnish battalion from Stenbock's infantry group. This pushed the fleeing Russians back across the defensive line, which further increased the chaos inside the Russian lines caused by Maydell's advance towards the north.

King Charles at the Battle of Narva. Issued immediately after the battle in celebration of the victory, this is perhaps the best illustration of the Swedish King's actual dress and appearance at the time. On this medal, by Carl Gustav Hartman, he is depicted still wearing a wig, an item that he very soon would discard. Other portraits suggest that King Charles's hair was fairly long under the wig, and combed back and upwards (in the words of the propagandistic poet Anders Odel in 1739, 'like a crown around his head'). The King wears a breastplate for protection, and a blue coat lined with lynx fur against the cold. He wears yellow leather breeches and black riding boots with spurs. The King has wound a black taffeta cravat several times around the neck, and he wears a hat of otter fur. Although not visible in this depiction, King Charles also wore gloves of stag leather with large cuffs of tough elk leather. He is armed with the customary sword and a pair of pistols. The stilted Latin text SUPERANT SUPERATA FIDEM refers to the King and his soldiers. It translates as 'Conquerors Overcome Probability', which suggests a triumphant feeling that in modern vernacular might be better rendered as 'we are the champions'. (Public Domain)

---

1 Hallart, *Tagebuch*, p.57.

PETER THE GREAT'S DISASTROUS DEFEAT

Another depiction of King Charles at the Battle of Narva, with a wig and the same kind of winter garments. Portrait attributed to David von Krafft. Private Collection (Public Domain)

Yet another depiction of King Charles in the Battle of Narva, with the same kind of dress but this time without the wig, by David von Krafft. It remains unknown whether the King wore a wig at Narva. The earliest portrait that depicts King Charles without a wig was painted by Johann Heinrich Wedekind at around this time, but we do not know whether he painted it during the King's visit to Reval in November 1700 before the battle or in Lais (modern-day Laiuse) the following year. What is clear is that King Charles discarded the wig at around this time. Although less detailed than the previous, this equestrian portrait depicts the blue winter coat lined with lynx fur in better detail. This painting also suggests that the winter coat has a pale blue base colour, not the dark blue more common in Swedish uniforms at the time and depicted in virtually all later portraits of King Charles. Private Collection (Public Domain)

The Swedes were not in a forgiving mood, and the civilian administrator Ingel Biörndahl, who came to Narva a few days after the battle, described in a letter how:

> As soon that the [Swedish] soldiers saw the Russian camp they could not be held back, but all desired and demanded with one mouth to attack the enemy immediately, regardless of the fact that for four days they had marched along deep and muddy roads. The Dalecarlians, who had done good service, demanded in the name of God to be allowed to close with the Russians, who had caused us to march such a long and difficult road. The officers had a hard time keeping their infantry in order when the action mowed down the enemy like reaping grass. I could barely get across the dead when I rode through the fortified area. When the Russians saw such a downfall, many of them threw themselves on the ground like dead and [our] soldiers marched over them, but afterwards they [the Russians] stood up again. When the men of the Guard saw that these dead disappeared thus, they paid no more attention to their falling but, when they found them on the ground, woke them up with their bayonets so that they remained on the ground for real.[2]

Portrait of King Charles at Narva or soon afterwards, wearing his characteristic blue coat lined with lynx fur over a breastplate, but without a wig under his hat. Portrait by David von Krafft, possibly based on a 1701 painting by Axel Sparre. Private Collection (Public Domain)

Yet, Russian resistance increased as soon as the first panic had subsided. Schnewentz's Dragoon Regiment was well-trained and, fighting dismounted, stubbornly resisted the Swedish advance. Meanwhile, the Preobrazhenskiy and Semyonovskiy Guard Regiments, originally deployed closest to the bridge to Kamperholm Island, formed up in a new line against Stenbock's and Maydell's columns.

It was probably this resistance that the Life Guard Captain Olof Stiernhöök had in mind when he added a laconic sentence as an afterthought in his aforementioned diary:

> Then we …. went in and massacred everything that got in our way. And it was an overly terrible massacre. They shot strongly at us again and shot a lot of good people dead.[3]

The already routed Russian regiments could not be stopped, however. They fled towards the bridge to Kamperholm Island, and the numerous non-combatants in the camp joined in the flight. As a result, the panic and confusion continued, and with the throng of people who attempted to cross the single bridge, it collapsed. Hundreds of Russians fell into the stream and drowned, while being fired upon by Swedish musketeers.

It seems that Rehnskiöld by then had already gained control over the second bridge, at Vepsekylla. If the Swedish commanders hoped to trap the

---

2   Biörndahl's relation, UUB, F 102; cited in Generalstaben, *Karl XII på slagfältet* 2, p.344.
3   Stiernhöök, 'Drabanten och kaptenen vid Lifgardet Olof Stiernhööks journal 1700–1703,' p.366.

Russian army on the western side of the River Narova, by design and good luck, this had largely been accomplished.

Then the cavalry reserve under Major General Johan Ribbing rode into the fortified area. As noted, the north-western part of the fortified area contained areas of broken ground. Described as natural trenches or ravines, in some places more than 10m deep, they became the focal point of the Russian resistance. When the Swedes reached the deepest ravines, they found themselves unable to cross as long as Russian soldiers defended the other side. Yet, the broken ground gave the Russians only a limited reprieve. The panic engendered by the swift Swedish advance dissolved Russian morale. Many soldiers ceased following orders, and the story goes that in some units, the soldiers mutinied against their foreign officers. Hallart makes a point of telling the readers of his diary that he and Croÿ saw 'with our own eyes many Germans, both males and females, massacred by the Russians.'[4] It was certainly true that, for the better part of a century, the Russian Orthodox Church had preached hatred to all foreigners, a situation caused by the foreign invasions, religious wars, and weak tsars of the early years of the seventeenth century in the Time of Troubles.[5] Tsar Peter had begun to reverse this process, but he had not yet been able to rid army and society of Church propaganda.

Murders certainly took place within the Russian camp, and almost certainly by mutinous Russian soldiers. Hallart supplies a list of those foreigners who were 'massacred by Russians'. Since he knew most or all of them personally, it is certain that their loss made an impact on him. However, none of the officers listed served in the Russian Army. Every identified victim belonged to Croÿ's or Hallart's personal suites. We do not know when they were murdered, but neither did Hallart or Croÿ, since their dependents and servants did not accompany them in battle but remained in camp. The list of victims of the massacre include one of Hallart's engineers (Carl Trummer from Vienna), his aide (Carl von Imhoff from Nuremberg), two other unknown officers, the anonymous wives of two German officers at least one of whom belonged to the Saxon contingent, and most people from Croÿ's suite, including his secretary, chef, and several servants.[6] The massacre was an ugly episode of the battle, and it must have taken place in Prince Trubetskoy's camp at some point when the battle seemed lost. However, this massacre cannot be taken as evidence for the wholesale slaughter of officers of foreign origin within the Russian line regiments. Besides, we have seen that most officers of ultimately foreign origin in the Russian Army at this time were in reality second-generation immigrants born in Russia, who certainly spoke Russian and would not necessarily have been regarded as 'heathen foreigners' by their men.

---

4 Hallart, *Tagebuch*, p.59.
5 For further details and the reasons thereof, see Michael Fredholm von Essen, *Sweden's War in Muscovy, 1609–1617: The Relief of Moscow and Conquest of Novgorod* (Warwick: Helion & Co., 2024), pp.354–5.
6 Hallart, *Tagebuch*, p.64.

Yet, the lack of control within the Russian units was real. Hallart relates how

> …the confusion was so great that everyone ran into each other like a herd of sheep, the regiments melded so that no one any longer could be recognised by its distinctly coloured uniform, not a single officer was there commanding, or listened to…[7]

Croÿ was on the Russian right wing at the time, together with the other senior Saxon officers – Baron von Langen and Hallart – and about seven others. They surrendered to Stenbock around 5:00 p.m. By then, Stenbock was already slightly wounded from a shot in the foot, although this apparently did not prevent him from retaining command. The traditional interpretation of events is that, witnessing the mutinies and murders, the Saxon officers abandoned the already lost right wing, instead hoping to save themselves by surrendering to the Swedes. A more likely explanation is given by the Swedish field chancellery secretary, Josias Cederhielm. He noted that while Croÿ, Hallart, Langen, and their followers certainly abandoned the hopeless situation in the northern sector of the battlefield, they attempted to relocate to Weide's left wing, which was still intact and, in the most part, not yet engaged in the battle. Croÿ's plan, according to Cederhielm, was to march out with the '11,000 strong' (according to the well-informed Cederhielm) Russian left wing and after a flank march attack the by then thoroughly disorganised Swedes in the rear. However, during this attempt to regroup, Croÿ, Hallart, Langen, and their followers encountered a small group of Swedish soldiers. Croÿ's group claimed to be burghers of the besieged town of Narva, and refused to surrender either their weapons or themselves. The Swedes did not believe them, not least because of Croÿ's luxurious red coat. The impasse seems to have been resolved only when Colonel Stenbock appeared on the scene, at which point Croÿ, Hallart, and Langen finally surrendered. Cederhielm relates that the story that Croÿ and his associates had set out in fear of their lives with the sole intention of surrendering to the Swedes was no more than an attempt to ingratiate themselves with their captors.[8] Hallart merely notes that they surrendered to Stenbock, whom he knew from Imperial service, and then spent the night by a fire on the field, where they stayed until late the following morning, when a Swedish unit escorted them into Narva.

---

7   Hallart, *Tagebuch*, p.58.
8   Josias Cederhielm to his brother Germund Cederhielm, 27 November 1700 (S.S.). 4 January 1701 (S.S.), *Karolinska krigares dagböcker* 8, 163, 165–6. What speaks in favour of Cederhielm's interpretation of events is that, (1) he was in the party and Hallart formally surrendered to him, (2) in the weeks after the battle he was in a position to learn more about what took place, and (3) upon his release Hallart immediately again went into Russian service, without any noticeable fear of being murdered by unruly soldiers. Cederhielm, a civilian, subsequently retained the sword and pair of pistols that Hallart had surrendered to him.

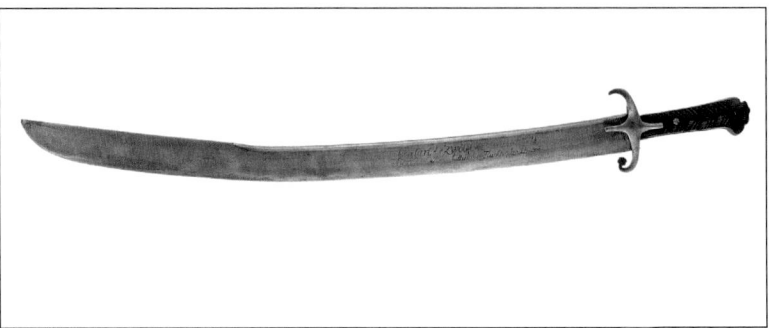

The sabre that Tsar Peter gave the Duke de Croÿ, who ultimately surrendered it to Stenbock. The sabre is of Polish *karabela* type, with a hilt probably of walnut wood stylised as the head of a bird and a blade possibly made in Germany. Total length 90.7cm, blade length 76.2cm, blade width 4.6cm, weight 1.25kg. (Royal Armoury, Stockholm. Photo: Helena Bonnevier)

Prince Dolgorukov, the next in the Russian chain of command, took over the defences in the northern sector when Croÿ relocated in search of Weide's wing. Dolgorukov gathered the remnants of the Russian right wing including the Guard regiments next to the collapsed Kamperholm Bridge. Using materials from barracks and wagons, the Russians built a wagon fort, a traditional defensive measure much used in Russia although also in Sweden. They moved nine cannon from the redoubts to the wagon fort. Using this as an improvised defensive line, Dolgorukov and his men offered a bitter resistance when attacked by the Swedes. Hallart later related that their plan was to fight on with those units that still functioned, or, if the tide could not be turned, at least attempt to achieve reasonable terms of surrender.[9] If correct, this indeed supports Cederhielm's report that Croÿ and Hallart had coordinated their plans with the Russian generals, and that they still hoped to disrupt, and ultimately defeat, the Swedish advance. The defensive characteristics of the broken ground were in their favour, and the Preobrazhenskiy and Semyonovskiy Guard Regiments still remained largely intact. The Guard units were joined by remnants of other units, as well as non-combatants, and together they formed up in the wagon fort. Taking advantage of the broken ground and the wagon fort, the Russians prepared to sell their lives dearly.

Meanwhile, the Swedes faced other difficulties as well. The fortified area was full of improvised barracks, tents, huts, and dugouts. Many of them came with breastworks built of fascines and earth, and even the dugouts functioned as improvised trenches and strongpoints. The Swedes had to capture them one at a time, since they were manned by Russians who would not surrender. By now, the Swedes were also out of ammunition. Cronstedt relates how:

---

9   Hallart, *Tagebuch*, p.58.

> …in the end we lacked gunpowder and shot so that the soldiers must scrounge for whatever munitions they could find in the Russian tents, until it got dark and our men were disordered and the damned Finns and other soldiers began looting and drinking…[10]

Combat was intense, and led to serious casualties on both sides. Cronstedt, who described the desperate struggle, noted that having finally beaten them, in some of the huts they found up to 20 dead Russians.[11] This stubborn but largely improvised resistance continued well into the night.

Many Swedish battalions lost cohesion during this struggle. After storming a fortified defensive line in column, they had made a ninety-degree turn, merely to assault a series of additional strongpoints, along the first defensive line as well as scattered throughout the camp. This broke up formations, and many clearly succumbed to the temptation to loot the Russian camp, where they found large supplies of mead and vodka which they promptly consumed. There was indeed so much vodka that Captain Posse of the Life Guard later drew the overly suspicious conclusion that the Russians had left it there on purpose, as a stratagem, so as to make the Swedes drunk and easier to defeat, in case they breached the defensive line.[12]

Darkness fell early, with sunset at 3:16 p.m. and looting continued for hours. After nightfall, in their drunken state, some Swedish units took each other for enemies and opened fire, which led to needless additional casualties. Without absolving the soldiers from the Swedish core territories, both Cronstedt and Hallart particularly blamed the Finnish units for these excesses.[13] This might be correct, since most Finnish infantry entered battle as ad hoc units and, in some cases, apparently without their regular officers. Moreover, many Finnish units were newly raised and accordingly less trained, and less accustomed to discipline, than most others. The breakdown in discipline was such, Hallart related, that had the Russians been able to assemble 1,000 men, they could easily have defeated the dispersed Swedish army.[14] For this reason, as well for the losses suffered in the struggle, the strength of several battalions fell rapidly. Hallart saw Swedish battalions consisting of no more than 20 to 30 pikemen and 40 to 50 musketeers, and most Swedish officers were wounded. Besides, he noted, the chaos was such that the generals no longer knew the location of their units, and the confusion was total.[15]

Despite the breakdown in discipline and the Russian resistance in the north, King Charles had reason to be satisfied in this sector. The remaining Russians were cut off from supplies and compatriots, and also lacked means of escape. Sooner or later, they were likely to surrender, if the Swedes could only maintain pressure on them.

---

10 Carl Cronstedt to Jacob Troilius, 6 December 1700 (S.S.), p.402.
11 Carl Cronstedt to Jacob Troilius, 6 December 1700 (S.S.), p.402.
12 Carl Magnus Posse to his brother Nils Posse, 9 December 1700 (S.S.), p.88.
13 Carl Cronstedt to Jacob Troilius, 6 December 1700 (S.S.), 404; Hallart, *Tagebuch*, p.59.
14 Hallart, *Tagebuch*, p.59.
15 Hallart, *Tagebuch*, p.60.

In fact, Swedish infantry reinforcements from the right wing were already on their way. The Swedish right wing, too, had breached the Russian defensive line, in their case south of Prince Trubetskoy's camp. It has been mentioned that Major General Knut Posse led the Life Guard in the assault, quickly breaking through the First Selected Moscow Regiment. The result of the assault was that the Russian line was broken between the bastion 200m south of Trubetskoy's camp and a point another 600m south of the camp. This separated the Russian left wing from the rest of the Tsar's army. Immediately after the breach, Posse's column turned south, followed by Vellingk and the rest of the Swedish right wing.

Weide's Russian units were rolled up and pushed back, just as happened to the north of Trubetskoy's camp. They could not break out towards the west, because there Wachtmeister's Swedish cavalry prevented any such attempts.

However, although some Russian regiments seem to have broken during Major General Posse's assault, the First Selected Moscow Regiment, which consisted of better-trained soldiers, soon reformed, and continued to resist the Swedes. Moreover, there were quarries east of the defensive line, and some of the broken Russian regiments took refuge there, where they established a new defensive position. Having regrouped, the Russians again advanced towards the abandoned defensive line. Weide ordered a full-scale counter-attack and the Russians succeeded in retaking one or more lost redoubts, at least one with functioning cannon which they turned against the Swedes, but then Weide was wounded and the counter-attack petered out.

The successful Swedish assault created great consternation among Sheremetyev's cavalry. They probably feared being caught within the confined space of the defensive lines. The cavalrymen may also have remembered their previous, unsuccessful encounter with the Swedes at Pühajõgi Pass on 27 November. As a result, the Russian cavalry retreated from the battlefield. The traditional interpretation is that they panicked, fled, and attempted to swim across the River Narova at Joala. If so, this was a great mistake, because in this sector the river was very rapid, and the story goes that Sheremetyev managed to escape, but about 1,000 of his horsemen were caught in the strong current, and both men and horses drowned in the rapids at Joala Falls.[16] At Joala, the River Narova rapidly descended through several ravines, which culminated in the Joala Falls, which fell eight metres before the river again slowed down somewhat at the approach to Narva and Ivangorod.

However, this traditional interpretation is certainly wrong. Based on documents from Sheremetyev, later discovered in the Austrian State Archives, his cavalry in reality rode south on the left bank of the River Narova all the way to Wask-Narva (modern-day Vasknarva; Russian: Syrensk) on Lake Peipus, a journey of more than 50km, where they crossed the bridge towards Gdov and by this way continued to Pskov.[17] Can this be reconciled with the traditional interpretation of the Russian cavalry in a panic flight across the River Narova? Notably, neither Hallart nor Tsar Peter, both of whom

---

16 Hallart believed in this story, which apparently also reached Tsar Peter. Hallart, *Tagebuch*, 58; Tsar Peter's diary, i.e., *Zhurnal ili Podennaya zapiska*, 18.
17 Velikanov, 'K voprosu ob organizatsii i chislennosti russkoy armii v Narvskom pokhode,' 133.

disseminated the story, was in a position to actually observe Sheremetyev's retreat; they only heard about it later. Most of Sheremetyev's men must have known that there was a waterfall less than a kilometre downstream of their present position, and any horseman who entered the water would immediately note the rapid water flow. Possibly, one or two of the less disciplined units, or individual members from them, took the plunge and perished in the water. Or, perhaps more likely, the memories of those who perished when the bridge collapsed also gave rise to the story of the drowning cavalry. Either way, this would explain the well-known but incorrect story of Russian cavalrymen drowning in the rapids. Yet, we can expect that the majority, quite possibly all, of Sheremetyev's men definitely preferred to follow the small road away from Narva on the left bank of the river, just as Sheremetyev later wrote. Intelligence that some Russian units were at Wask-Narva reached the Swedes at Narva on 13 December, which seems to confirm Sheremetyev's story.[18] Alexander Gordon of Auchintoul confirms the story, too, noting that

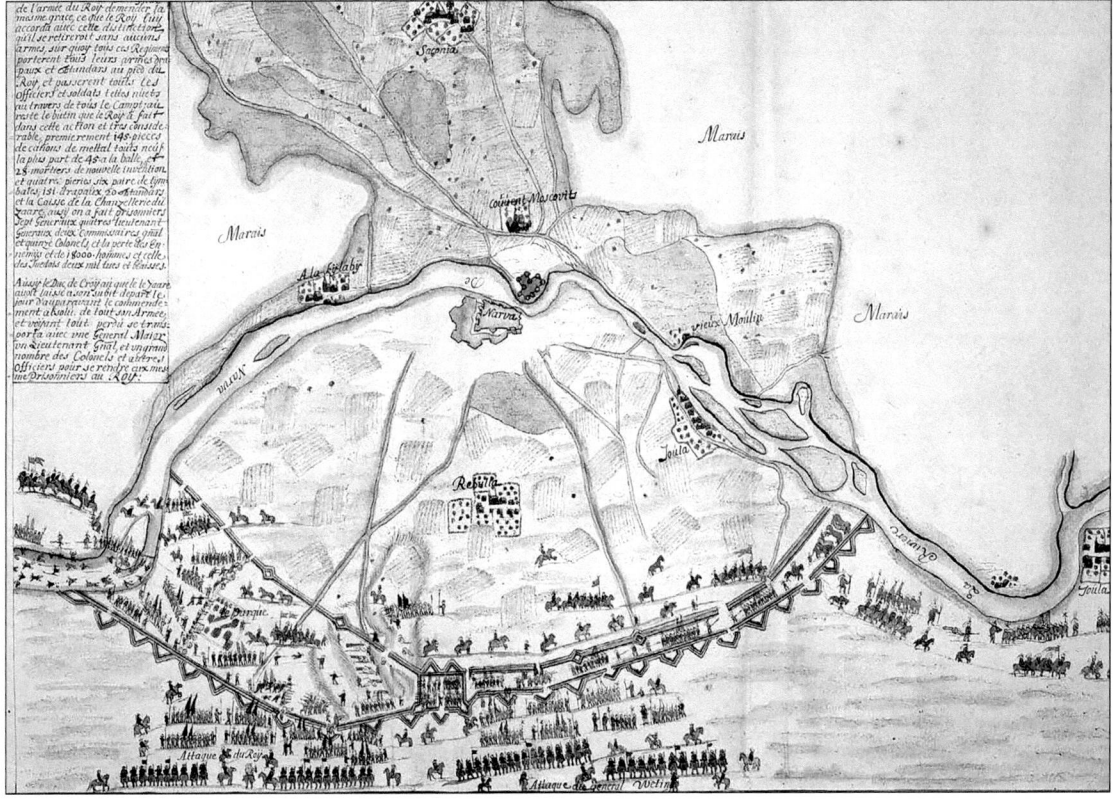

The Swedish assault at Narva. Left: The collapse of the Kamperholm Bridge causes many Russians to perish in the water. Right: Sheremetyev's cavalry withdraws in an orderly fashion along the road on the left bank of the River Narova. (Austrian National Library. Public Domain)

---

18 Hallart, *Tagebuch*, 67.

4,000 of the Novgorod and Pskov cavalry, 'knowing the country, crossed the river, some leagues above the town' and reached Pskov safely.[19] The old style cavalryman who served under Sheremetyev confirmed that they rode to Wask-Narva on their way to Gdov and Pskov, and complained that 'many men were fatigued and many horses died.'[20] A strenuous 50km ride, for sure, but not a fatal flight. Later, the Swedes found that Russian units had looted and burnt the settlement at Wask-Narva, which gives further credibility to Sheremetyev's explanation.

The retreat of Sheremetyev's cavalry did much to assure Swedish success in the sector. It almost certainly enabled Wachtmeister's cavalry to cross the defensive line without resistance. Hallart later wrote that the retreat of the cavalry was the 'absolutely biggest reason' for the Russian defeat.[21] Tsar Peter did not share in Hallart's assessment; he preferred to blame the streltsy and their 'ignorance' of modern warfare.[22] We have seen that there is no evidence to support the Tsar's assignation of blame.

---

19 Alexander Gordon of Auchintoul, *The History of Peter the Great, Emperor of Russia: To Which is Prefixed, A Short General History of the Country, From the Rise of That Monarchy; and an Account of the Author's Life* 1 (Aberdeen: F. Douglass and W. Murray, 1755), p.154.
20 Anon., 'Letopisets 1700 goda,' p.152.
21 Hallart, *Tagebuch*, p.58.
22 Tsar Peter's diary, i.e., *Zhurnal ili Podennaya zapiska, blazhennyya i vechnodostoynyya pamyati gosudarya imperatora Petra Velikago s 1698 goda dazhe do zaklyucheniya neyshtatskago mira* 1 (St. Petersburg: Imperatorskaya akademiya nauk, 1770), p.18.

13

The Russians Regroup

Yet, the Russian centre remained undefeated in Prince Trubetskoy's camp on the eastern slope of the Hermannsberg. Moreover, the Russian resistance in the northern sector seemed invulnerable to the means available to the Swedish units there. While Sheremetyev's cavalry had fled, Weide's infantry and dragoons remained and were numerically superior to the Swedes in the southern sector. It was imperative for the Swedish commanders to gather their strength in one sector only, or they would be slowly overwhelmed.

Learning of the successful breach in the southern sector, King Charles ordered Vellingk to leave a suitable force to hold the Russian left wing under Weide, so that they were unable to join forces with Prince Trubetskoy's men, or the Russian right wing under Dolgorukov. Then, Vellingk was to advance along the countervallation line towards the Kamperholm Bridge.

Vellingk set out towards the north. He definitely brought the Life Guard of Foot, and probably also most of his other units. Vellingk also led some of the cavalry to the northern sector of the battlefield. He left Major Gotthard Wilhelm von Wulffen with the Hälsinge Regiment in the southern sector, but possibly no other units. Cronstedt noted that while '9,000 Russians' remained in the left wing (that is, with Weide), Wulffen, despite being badly wounded, kept them pinned down with only his 400 men (one battalion) until evening without receiving any support from other units.[1]

Vellingk and the men from the Swedish right wing arrived in the northern sector about 5:00 p.m., after a march of more than three kilometres. It was already dark, but they immediately attacked the improvised Russian wagon fort. However, the Russians stubbornly defended themselves. Major Carl von Numers related that, 'This dispute about the wagon fort lasted a considerable time, and until darkness began to fall so that finally our own did not recognise each other.'[2] In the darkness, the soldiers were no longer able to maintain formations. We have already seen that many Swedish soldiers, in particular those from Finland, sneaked off to loot the abandoned Russian camp. Vellingk's units seem to have been sent into battle piecemeal, each as soon as it arrived. This was insufficient to break the Russian resistance.

---

1   Carl Cronstedt to Jacob Troilius, 6 December 1700 (S.S.), p.403.
2   Numers; cited in Generalstaben, *Karl XII på slagfältet* 2, p.347.

In the darkness of the night, the weary and starving Swedish soldiers from the right wing also began to plunder the rich Russian supplies in the camp, which as noted included large quantities of mead and vodka. Many of the soldiers became heavily intoxicated. In this drunken state, the Swedish units each took the other for enemies and began to fire upon one another. Major Carl von Numers, who arrived with Vellingk, related how his Life Guard battalion encountered the already present Dalecarlian and Västmanland battalions (from the other wing but now in the same part of the battlefield). Not recognising each other in the darkness, the two sides began to exchange fire, something which Numers finally managed to stop by ordering his drummers to play a Swedish march. Then, the Dalecarlians and Västmanlanders finally recognised their fellow countrymen, responded with the same march tune, and the friendly fire ceased.[3] It has been suggested that one reason for the friendly fire was that some Swedish battalions were carrying captured Russian colours.[4] This seems unlikely; while it is correct that they were carrying such trophies, these colours would have been no more visible in the darkness than the regular issue Swedish colours.

King Charles had hitherto remained outside the fortified area together with Rehnskiöld, the Drabant Corps, and the Life Dragoons. Accompanied by his Chamberlain, Axel Hård, he now entered through one of the breaches and rode through the abandoned Russian camp towards the left wing, where the situation seemed most critical.[5] King Charles and the Drabant Corps followed in the wake of Stenbock and his men towards the contested wagon fort. In the darkness, the King accidentally slid down into one of the muddy ravines or ditches behind which the Russians earlier had taken refuge. King Charles fell under his horse but he was saved by Hård and two Finnish soldiers, although in the darkness he lost his sword and one of his boots – with the stocking still inside! Yet, this mishap did not discourage him. The King took a sword from one of the Drabant troopers and borrowed Hård's boots. We do not know how the unfaltering Hård managed without them in the cold but somehow, he made do.[6] The King's sword was recovered the following day. The Finns also managed to pull up the King's horse.[7] Soon, King Charles, with boots but still lacking a stocking, reached the eastern side of the wagon fort, which the Swedes were then in the process of attacking. Having arrived, King Charles took personal command of the tired Swedish units. He formed them up in a line, and led the men against the wagon fort in a desperate charge. The King's horse was killed under him by artillery fire, but he continued to exhort his men against the wagon fort. After the battle, a spent musket ball was found lodged in King Charles's black taffeta cravat. In the excitement of battle, he seems to have been unaware that he was hit.

---

3   Numers; cited in Generalstaben, *Karl XII på slagfältet* 2, p.348.
4   Wrangel, 'Några anteckningar,' p.149.
5   Axel Hård af Segerstad was a distant relative of Colonel Carl Hård af Segerstad, whom Croÿ in 1678 had duped with the forged letters into surrendering Helsingborg.
6   Until four years later, when the stalwart Hård was accidentally shot by King Charles, the wound that ultimately caused his death.
7   Carl Magnus Posse to his brother Nils Posse, 9 December 1700 (S.S.), 88.

Fortunately for the King, the ball had lost much of its velocity before it hit him, and it caused no damage.

The assault was greatly facilitated by the fact that Chief of Artillery Siöblad had by then managed to move a few cannon from Granatenhielm's battery through the breach, and even more impressively in the darkness, across the broken ground and ravines that shielded the Russian flank. Yet, the Russians had nine cannon of their own, and the operation developed into an artillery duel simultaneous with the repeated Swedish assaults. It took several hours of combat in the dark before the Russians showed signs of weakening. We do not know exactly when; Cronstedt noted that the battle continued into the darkest night.[8]

The lead musket ball found lodged in King Charles's black taffeta cravat, together with the golden casket which subsequently was made to safeguard it. Over the centuries, the musket ball has corroded and even lost its deformed shape. The casket measures: length 30mm, height 18mm, width 24mm. (Royal Armoury, Stockholm. Photo: Helena Bonnevier)

While the battle for the wagon fort continued unabated, the Swedes also stormed Prince Trubetskoy's fortified camp. With the Swedish right wing significantly weakened (we have seen that it now probably consisted only of Wulffen with a battalion of the Hälsinge Regiment) and obliged to pin down Weide's entire wing, it was dangerous to leave Prince Trubetskoy in their rear. Late in the day, possibly at the same time that he learnt of Vellingk's success in the southern sector, King Charles ordered Siöblad, Major General Maydell, and Colonel Stenbock to form a new battle group for this purpose. So far, Trubetskoy's camp had been under artillery fire from Appelman's battery, and possibly those cannon from Granatenhielm's battery that had been unable to enter through the breach.

For this reason, and because of the successful Swedish breaches of the defensive line both north and south of the camp, quite a few of Trubetskoy's men, as well as Prince Trubetskoy himself, abandoned the fortified camp when they saw the Swedes breaking through on both sides. Trubetskoy himself was later found in the wagon fort, and it is likely that many soldiers of the centre withdrew there, together with their commander. As a result, the Swedish assault on the camp was resolved quickly and successfully: the entire centre of the Russian line fell into Swedish hands.

Then, finally, possibly at around 8:00 p.m., resistance in the surrounded Russian right wing began to falter. They had suffered significant casualties. The Semyonovskiy Guard Regiment alone had lost 17 officers and 477 under-officers and common soldiers dead or wounded.[9] The Russian generals sent two men, a Prince of the Kozlovskiy family and an otherwise unknown Major Piel, to negotiate terms for surrender, but Prince Kozlovskiy was shot while

---

8   Carl Cronstedt to Jacob Troilius, 6 December 1700 (S.S.), 403.
9   Petrov, *Gorod Narva*, p.232.

crossing in the darkness and Piel then returned.[10] Finally, Major General Ivan Buturlin, the deputy commander of the right wing, managed to contact the Swedes to commence negotiations. Buturlin and two of his officers offered themselves as hostages. The Russians wanted terms for free departure with weapons, standards, and artillery. However, King Charles was unwilling to accept these terms. As to the demand to march off the field with all cannon, the King merely answered that 'your artillery is already behind our back, there is no more to say about this.'[11] King Charles also threatened to recommence combat, and order his artillery to resume fire on the wagon fort. It seems likely that in the darkness, the Russian commanders still believed that they faced a Swedish army of a size comparable to their own. They did not know that the Swedes were out of ammunition and supplies and that no more reinforcements were available. At this point, the Russian commanders – Prince Dolgorukov, Avtonom Golovin, Ivan Buturlin, and Prince Alexander – agreed to surrender at around 11:00 p.m.[12]

The Russian units surrendered their colours and standards, but were allowed to retain their weapons as they crossed the river and departed from the battlefield.[13] Beyond this, there is some uncertainty about the exact terms negotiated for the surrender. What is clear is that the Swedes had no means to keep the surrendered Russians in captivity – the Swedes had neither men nor supplies for such an option. When Major General Posse approached the wagon fort and the Kamperholm Bridge with his two Life

Major General Ivan Buturlin, deputy commander under General Golovin, depicted while in Swedish captivity; by Elias Brenner, early 1700s (Author's photo)

10   Neither Prince nor Major can be conclusively identified. In Russian, the Major's name was spelled Pil' or, in one unreliable source, Spil'. The name may possibly have been Swedish Pihl, German or Dutch Piel, or English Peel. After the battle, Piel ended up in Swedish captivity.
11   Tsar Peter's diary, i.e., *Zhurnal ili Podennaya Zapiska*, pp.19–20; Maykova, *Gistoriya* 1, p.207.
12   Generalstaben, *Karl XII på slagfältet* 2, p.240.
13   Later, a Russian tradition arose according to which the Guard regiments were permitted to retain their colours. However, not only were these listed as Swedish trophies in contemporary records but they still remain in the Army Museum, Stockholm, so this story can be discounted as fiction. Moreover, the Guard regiments were issued new colours after the battle. Teodor J. Petrelli and Axel Lagrelius, *Tillägg till Narvatroféer i Statens trofésamling* (Uppsala: Almqvist & Wiksell, 1907), pp.30 & 32–4. Contra: Bertil Wennerholm, 'Russian Banners as Swedish Trophies from Narva 1700: A New Attempt at Identification,' Karin Tetteris (ed.), *In Hoc Signo Vinces: The Vexillological Seminar, Stockholm 2011 & 2013* (Stockholm: Armémuseum, 2016), pp.31–7. The author wishes to thank Arne Danielsson (1921–2013), Keeper of Trophies, who in 1979 invited him to assist in the documentation and preservation of the State Trophy Collection as a student trainee, which offered excellent opportunities to study the Russian trophies from Narva.

THE RUSSIANS REGROUP

Guard battalions, he found that the Russians there far outnumbered his own men, and all still carried their weapons.[14] Moreover, his men had hardly any ammunition left. King Charles sent Vellingk to bring more from Narva, but so late in the evening, new supplies were unlikely to arrive soon.

The same problem with numerous surrendered, but still armed, Russians repeated itself elsewhere as well, and even on the day after the battle (1 December), when King Charles sent one of his Drabant troopers, Patrik Thomson, to stop the persistent looting that still continued. Thomson set out alone. Suddenly, he encountered a formed unit of men, with muskets at shoulder arms, and realised that they were Russian soldiers who had not yet surrendered:

> And in the same moment that we saw each other, both they and I stopped; and when I noticed that they appeared just as shocked, I got hold of myself and signed to them with my carbine, that they should remove the musket from the shoulder [from the slope], which their captain soon commanded. Finding that I had won the game, I signed to them that they should place the butt on the ground [order arms], and then, lay down the musket on the ground [ground arms]. And when this was accomplished, I signed with my sword and bandolier that each should take them off and put them on the musket, as they stood in files and ranks. Then I allowed them to take their bandoliers and each put his sword and musket on top of it. And when this was done, I removed my hat and put it under my arm. Each of them, both officers and men, did the same, at which point I signed to them to walk towards the place where His Excellency [Captain Lieutenant Arvid Horn] was with the Drabant Corps...[15]

Having singlehandedly accomplished the surrender of a whole unit of soldiers, Thomson no doubt understood the dilemma that the army commanders now faced. The best outcome for everybody was to allow the Russian units free departure as soon as possible. Swedish sappers together with Russian soldiers began repairing the damaged Kamperholm Bridge. The bridge at Vepsekylla seems not to have been used for the Russians to leave the field. It was likely deemed too far away, and the Swedes lacked the men to guard both bridges. Swedes and Russians shared the goal of enabling the Russian units to depart as soon as possible.

We have seen that General Vellingk ordered Major von Wulffen with a battalion of the Hälsinge Regiment to hold the line against Weide's Russians so as to prevent them from advancing against the Swedes in the northern sector, and that Weide, probably because of his wounds, failed to break out. When Dolgorukov surrendered in the northern sector of the battlefield, the wounded Weide and the Russian left wing still held out in the southern sector. By then, he faced a threat from the Swedish artillery and the now Swedish-manned captured guns in Prince Trubetskoy's camp. Moreover, Weide lacked the means to move his men across the River Narova. Neither

---
14 Wrangel, 'Några anteckningar,' p.151.
15 Patrik Thomson's diary; cited in Carl Grimberg, *Svenska folkets underbara öden 4: Karl XI:s och Karl XII:s tid t.o.m. år 1709* (Stockholm: Norstedt & Söner, 1922), p.542.

he nor his men, mostly from Moscow and the east, had the local knowledge that had enabled Sheremetyev's cavalry to find a safe way out. Finally, the Swedes in Narva also sallied out: Major Carl Philip von Funcken with what remained of both the Estonian cavalry companies and the Ingrian Retinue of Nobles together with 400 infantry.[16] The Russians who manned the siegeworks facing the fortress either had already abandoned them, or did so now, some moving north towards the wagon fort while others, the majority, joined Weide's wing. Funcken's men accordingly seized the siegeworks. But he did not remain there, he soon established contact with Wulffen and his battalion. While the sortie from Narva posed no real threat Weide's men, their presence made it yet more difficult for the Russians to advance in support of Dolgorukov's men to the north – since this would leave Funcken and his men in the Russian rear.

At this point, Weide learnt that Dolgorukov had surrendered. Weide's units were still in good order and in a position to attack the Swedes, but a courier from Prince Dolgorukov urged Weide to surrender. As noted, Dolgorukov was then the senior Russian officer in command. It was likely Major General Buturlin who informed Weide about the surrender, and if so, facilitated by the Swedes in whose interest it certainly was to persuade Weide to surrender, too.

At 2:00 a.m. on 1 December, Weide sent a letter to the Swedes which read:

> Despite being cut off from the army, we still want to defend ourselves to the last drop of blood; but if you offer us an accord that is reasonable to both sides, I will, if it is generous, accept it.[17]

When Weide's emissary arrived, King Charles was likely asleep on the ground next to a camp fire and with only his coat to protect against the cold. Like his men, the Swedish King cannot have had any sleep for at least 22 hours. Unfortunately for Weide, the surrender of the Russians in the wagon fort meant that King Charles, when awakened, felt able to insist upon harsher terms with regard to the remaining Russians. The terms that the dog-tired King offered were far from generous. Ultimately, Weide had to accept King Charles's demand that his men march out without their weapons, and only with whatever personal items they could carry. They were also ordered not further to ravage any Swedish lands. It is uncertain how many Russians were included under these terms. Hallart noted that they were from 10,000 to 12,000 men, mostly from the original Russian left wing but also including those soldiers who had manned the siegeworks and the non-combatants who had been caught south of Prince Trubetskoy's camp.[18]

The repair of the Kamperholm Bridge was completed at 4:00 a.m., which enabled the Russians in the northern sector to evacuate. The sun only rose at 8:38 a.m., but by then, Weide's men were already marching northwards towards the bridge. On the way they passed under the eyes of King Charles

---

16   Generalstaben, *Karl XII på slagfältet* 2, p.351.
17   Jöran Nordberg, *Konung Carl den XII:tes historia*1 (Stockholm: Peter Momma, 1740), p.133.
18   Hallart, *Tagebuch*, p.60.

who, from a hill east of the Rathshof Redoubt, watched the defeated Russians march by in a long procession, with their heads uncovered, surrendering their weapons and standards. They were guarded by Swedish troops lined up as a long avenue through which the Russian soldiers had to march.[19]

The Russians were so numerous that the last left only just before noon. The departure could not be accomplished without incidents. When the last Russians were about to cross the bridge, gangs of drunken Swedish and Finnish soldiers suddenly turned on the last marching Russians, killing them and stealing their belongings.[20]

When the sun set at 3:15 p.m., the Swedes were again in undisputed control of Narva and Ivangorod.

---

19   Adlerfeld, *Military History of Charles XII*, pp.55–56.
20   Hallart, *Tagebuch*, p.60.

14

Dead and Wounded

Of the entire Russian army, it was only Sheremetyev's cavalry and the unknown number of mostly non-combatants who crossed the Kamperholm Bridge before it collapsed who avoided falling into captivity. Many of the wounded froze to death during the cold night. Soon after the battle, the Russian units on the eastern side of the River Narova which had laid siege to Ivangorod, surrendered too, under terms similar to those of the rest of the army.

The Russian surrender and ultimate free departure mean that it is difficult to estimate Russian battle casualties.

Hallart estimated 7,000 to 8,000 dead, of whom he concluded that 3,000 to 4,000 drowned in the river which as discussed must have been an exaggeration.[1] Alexander Gordon estimated up to 12,000 dead.[2] Swedish sources claimed a far higher number of dead, exemplified by the estimate of 'at least 18,000' in official and semi-official accounts.[3]

Yet more soldiers, by Russian official accounts estimated at between 5,800 and 6,000, died of cold and hunger during the hard march back to Russia.[4] Others, in particular those who had been forced to hand over their weapons, were murdered by angry peasants along the road, who were eager to take revenge for previous depredations. In December, Prince Repnin reported the arrival in Novgorod of most of the defeated Russian army. Russian official accounts subsequently concluded that a total of 22,967 Russian soldiers from the Battle at Narva assembled in Novgorod.[5] This seemingly supports Alexander Gordon's estimate of up to 12,000 dead if understood as total losses during the campaign. The question remains, however, whether all of the cavalry survivors joined the contingent that assembled at Novgorod, some cavalry may instead have returned home. A modern survey shows 18,422

---

1 Hallart, *Tagebuch*, 60.
2 Alexander Gordon of Auchintoul, *History of Peter the Great* 1, 154.
3 Nordberg, *Konung Carl den XII: tes historia* 1, 134; Adlerfeld, *Military History of Charles XII*, 56.
4 Tsar Peter's diary, i.e., *Zhurnal ili Podennaya zapiska*, 25; Maykova, *Gistoriya*, 210.
5 Tsar Peter's diary, i.e., *Zhurnal ili Podennaya zapiska*, 25; Maykova, *Gistoriya*, 209; Tat'yana Anatol'yevna Bazarova, '"Chinit' Otpor bodro bezo vsyakiye robosti": Zapisnaya kniga ukazov novgorodskogo gubernatora A. I. Repnina 1700–1701gg.', *Novgorodskiy Istoricheskiy Sbornik* 16 (26) (2016), pp.377–415, on p.377 n.5.

survivors from the army at Narva, with the important caveat that there are no surviving records of survivors from the Guard, Pskov, Smolensk, and a few other regiments including all the cavalry.[6]

Russian regimental rolls from 12 January 1701 show that the total loss of personnel was about 25 percent (including deserters).[7] Total losses in men were at least 7,000, but in reality, significantly higher, since records are missing for many units. Colomb's, Bruce's, and Zakhariy Vestov's regiments of Prince Trubetskoy's Novgorod Division were particularly depleted, with losses of 68, 57, and 56 percent respectively. In Golovin's Division (excluding the two Guard regiments) only 250 of 356 officers remained. Weide's Division fared somewhat better, which can be explained by the comparatively less combat his units engaged in (Table 7 below).

Table 7. Known Russian casualties in the Battle of Narva based on roll calls, specified as officers and others (under-officers and common soldiers), respectively[8]

Regiment	Officers Lost	Others lost	Total Lost	Percentage
Avtonom Golovin's Division				
Preobrazhenskiy Guard Regt.				unknown
Semyonovskiy Guard Regt				unknown
Schnewentz's Dragoons	6	275	281	27.0%
Matvey Fliwerk	16	380	396	32.5%
Carl Gustav Ivanitskiy	10	449	459	34.1%
Ivan Mewes	15	349	364	28.9%
Il'ya Bieltz	21	230	251	25.3%
Astafiy Pohlmann	16	170	186	14.9%
Ivan Treyden	7	193	200	14.9%
Matvey Treyden	8	191	199	14.6%
Carl Peter Devson	7	379	386	29.1%
Adam Weide's Division				
First Selected Moscow Regt	3	-	-	unknown
Gulitz's Dragoons	-	133	133	16.0%
Alexander Gordon	6	167	173	16.0%

---

6   Velikanov, ' K voprosu o sostoyanii russkoy armii posle Narvskogo porazheniya,' pp.30–33.
7   Velikanov, 'K voprosu o sostoyanii russkoy armii posle Narvskogo porazheniya,' p.36.
8   Velikanov, 'K voprosu o sostoyanii russkoy armii posle Narvskogo porazheniya,' 30–33. Percentages calculated by Velikanov based on available rolls from August 1700 and January 1701.

Erich von Werden	7	427	434	36.7%
Nikolay Balck	1	154	155	13.1%
Wilhelm von Schweiden	-	396	396	30.3%
Tomas Junger	-	248	248	20.9%
Fyodor Balck	8	234	242	23.9%
Vilim von Del'den	6	381	387	32.5%
Ivan von Del'den	1	315	316	26.3%
Novgorod Division				
Roman Bruce	-	457	457	57.1%
Ivan Colomb	-	542	542	67.8%
Miron Bayishev	-	-	365	36.1%
Zakhariy Vestov	-	-	566	55.9%
Yuriy Vestov				unknown
Vasiliy Kozodavlev				unknown
Belgorod Contingent				
Martem'yan Sukharev	-	-	274	41.6%
Vasiliy Yelchaninov	-	-	251	35.0%
Stepan Strekalov	-	-	141	37.1%
Venedikt Baturin				unknown
Cavalry				
All units				unknown
Artillery				
All units				unknown

The Russians also suffered heavy losses in armaments, as the Swedes captured at least 4,050 muskets and all 173 cannon, including 64 siege guns. Soon thereafter, the Swedes took an additional 22 mortars from a baggage train near Jama, still on its way to Narva.[9]

---

[9] Velikanov and Lobin, 'Russkaya Artilleriya v Narvskom pokhode, 1700,' pp.3–10. For the official report of the captured cannons, see Elis Decker, 'Specification på de Ryske Trophéer, som äro tagne wid Narva d. 20 November 1700 och efter Hans Excell. Hr General-Feldtygmästaren Siöblads Ordres af Lieutenanten Elis Delcker efter Svensk Måttstock visiterade,' *Handlingar hörande til Konung Carl XII:s historia* 4 (Stockholm: Zacharias Hæggström, 1826), pp.214–15; and the numerous drawings of the captured cannons by Philip Jacob Thelott, Army Museum, Stockholm.

The Swedes captured 151 infantry colours and 20 cavalry standards ('except those torn in the battle, lost in the darkness, or dropped in the river, each of which later recovered from the water'), six pairs of kettledrums, and the Tsar's war chest containing 60,000 Dutch and German thaler silver coins.[10] Known as *efimki* in Russia, these coins were imported as bullion through Arkhangel'sk to be melted down and recoined into kopeks. King Charles's accountant somewhat incorrectly assessed them as the equivalent of 32,000 roubles.[11] The Swedes also obtained large quantities of ammunition, food supplies, tents, and horse fodder.

Contrary to what had been agreed in the negotiations, the Swedes retained a number of Russian officers as prisoners of war. They did so under various pretexts, claiming that the Russians had hidden colours and other war booty that should have been surrendered to the victors. Hallart, seemingly correctly, noted that the real reason was that the Swedish commanders wanted the officers as hostages.[12] The total number of prisoners who were retained was apparently 132, but this figure includes their servants.[13] King Charles and his commanders probably found it advisable to retain the officers as prisoners of war since they had to release all of the common soldiers. Allowing the officers to leave as well would have enabled Tsar Peter to rebuild his army before the Swedes had time to consolidate their gains.

The prisoners of war included all of the senior commanders: Field Marshal Duke de Croÿ, Prince Yakov Dolgorukov, Prince Alexander of Imeretia, General Avtonom Golovin, General Adam Weide, Governor Prince Ivan Trubetskoy of Novgorod, Lieutenant General von Hallart, Major General Ivan Buturlin, and the Saxon envoy Major General Baron Johann Ernst von Langen.

However, the Swedes retained a number of lower-ranking officers as prisoners, too. Among them were Colonels Johann Ernst von Blomberg, head of the Preobrazhenskiy Guard Regiment; Vilim von Del'den (wounded); Alexander Gordon of Achintoul (wounded); Alferiy Schnewentz; Yuriy

---

10   Hallart, *Tagebuch*, 61; Wisocki-Hochmuth, p.122; Nordberg, *Konung Carl den XII:tes historia* 1, p.133; Adlerfeld, *Military History of Charles XII*, p.56. See also Petrelli and Lagrelius, *Tillägg till Narvatroféer i Statens trofésamling*, pp.32–34, which reprints the official report of Lieutenant Sperling of the Life Guard, who was tasked to compile a list of the captured standards. See also Sperling, pp.22–3. Silver coins: *Magnus Stenbock och Eva Oxenstierna* 1, p.149; L. G. Beskrovnyy (ed.), *Severnaya voyna 1700–1721 gg. - Sbornik dokumentov 1: 1700–1709* (Moscow: MVD RF/ Kuchkovo pole, 2009), p.73.
11   The rouble had depreciated in the seventeenth century, so the official exchange rate since 1681 was set at 55 kopeks per thaler (1 thaler = 0.55 rouble). This would make the bullion the equivalent of 33,000 roubles. However, Tsar Peter in 1698 debased the silver content of the rouble further, from 40g to 28g (70 per cent), which possibly confused the Swedish accountant. Since this was bullion, the Tsar's further debasement should not effect the value.
12   Hallart, *Tagebuch*, p.60.
13   An approximate list is provided in Sperling, pp.23–5.

Vestov; Carl Gustav Ivanitskiy; Joachim Gulitz; Jacob Pindegrass; Pierre Lefort, and Jacob Gordon.[14] Others were lieutenant colonels and majors.[15]

The Swedes also retained a few under-officers, artillerymen, and fireworks specialists as prisoners of war. Most were likely of foreign origin or descent. Some of the foreign officers may have been naturalised Russians, while others were born in Russia to foreign fathers.[16] The prisoners of war were brought into Narva on 2 December. Ultimately, most were transported to Stockholm in Sweden, from where they were dispersed. Many attempted to escape from captivity, alone or in small groups. Apparently the first successful escape took place already in 1702.[17] The most spectacular escape, however, was that of Prince Yakov Dolgorukov, the Commissary General. In June 1711, Dolgorukov and other prisoners of war were shipped across the Baltic Sea from Finland to Umeå in Sweden. Finding that there were only 20 Swedes for 44 Russian prisoners, Dolgorukov led a revolt during which he and his comrades disarmed the Swedes and in two weeks of sailing reached Reval, which was then in Russian hands.[18] The rest of the prisoners

Prince Andrey Khilkov, diplomat and Russian resident in Stockholm, shown while in Swedish captivity by Elias Brenner, early 1700s. Although interned when the Tsar declared war, Khilkov nonetheless ran a successful intelligence collection organisation in Sweden. (Author's photo)

14 Hallart, *Tagebuch*, 62; Nordberg, *Konung Carl den XII:tes historia*1, 133–4. Little is known of Pindegrass. Hallart reports that a Colonel Jacob Gordon went into captivity with the others. By some accounts, this was Patrick Gordon's son Jacob, but he was Colonel of the Butyrsk Regiment which did not participate in the battle. The possibility remains that another, otherwise unknown officer named Jacob Gordon, was captured at Narva, where several Gordons are known to have fought. An example of this is another captive, Lieutenant Colonel Andrey Aleksandrovich Gordon of Fyodor Balck's Regiment. What speaks in favour of Hallart's reference to a Colonel Jacob Gordon is that in captivity, he became acquainted with both Colonel and Lieutenant Colonel Gordon, as well as a major and a captain likewise named Gordon. All were captured at Narva or thereabouts. Hallart, *Tagebuch*, p.74. Some claim that Vasiliy Kozodavlev too was retained in captivity, but a letter from Sheremetyev dated 14 February 1701 (O.S.) shows that he was not. Beskrovnyy, *Severnaya voyna 1700–1721 gg. - Sbornik dokumentov* 1, 96. However, Kozodavlev must then again have fallen into Swedish captivity at a later date, since a letter cited in Ustryalov, *Istoriya tsarstvovaniya Petra Velikago* 4: 1, p.68, suggests that Kozodavlev was among those who escaped with Prince Dolgorukov's group (on which see below).

15 Such as Lieutenant Colonel Ivan Ivanovich Balsyr of Mewe's Regiment, but also several others.

16 Ustryalov, *Istoriya Tsarstvovaniya Petra Velikago* 4:2, pp.469–71, lists casualties and also identifies those officers who were not Russian nationals. Based on this list, which may or may not be complete, foreign nationals constituted a clear minority.

17 The successful escape made the Swedes temporarily introduce harsher terms of internment also for Prince Andrey Khilkov, diplomat and Russian resident in Stockholm. Yet, this did not prevent Khilkov from setting up and running a successful intelligence collection organisation in Sweden, an accomplishment described in approving terms by one of his later successors, the KGB veteran Boris Grigor'yev (who was stationed in Sweden for similar tasks between 1977 and 1982), in Tore Forsberg and Boris Grigorjev, *Spioner emellan* (Saltsjö-Duvnäs: Efron& Dotter, 2006), pp.98–101.

18 Among the escapees was Kozodavlev and Joachim Gulitz. Before the escape, Gulitz's wife had acquired permission to visit her husband in Sweden, where she arrived only days after the Russian officers escaped. The annoyed Swedish government then retained her as a hostage,

of war were ultimately released in prisoner exchanges with captured Swedish officers and officials, or died in captivity of natural causes, such as Prince Alexander of Imeretia. The Duke de Croÿ remained in captivity at Reval.

Fallen Russian officers included Colonels Vasiliy Yelchaninov (wounded and captured at Ivangorod, died soon afterwards in Narva); Martem'yan Sukharev (fell at Ivangorod), Carl Peter Devson, Astafiy Pohlmann, Tomas Junger, Matvey Fliwerk, Ivan Colomb, Erich von Werden, and Casimir von Krage, the Chief of Artillery (who probably soon died from his wounds in captivity). Lieutenant Colonel Pavel Cunningham, the commander of the Semyonovskiy Guard Regiment, fell in the battle as well.[19]

Swedish losses were lower, but no less serious. According to rolls and similar reports, the outcome for the Swedes in the battle was that 30 officers and 648 soldiers died, and 67 officers and 1,181 soldiers were wounded (Table 8).[20] This makes a total of 1,926 casualties, dead and wounded, which corresponds to 18 percent of King Charles's army.[21] The infantry suffered the highest casualties: 53 percent of the Västmanland Regiment, 42 percent of the Närke-Värmland Regiment, 28 percent of the Dalecarlia Regiment, and 23 percent of the Hälsinge Regiment. In comparison, the Life Guard of Foot managed to go through the battle with losses of only 19 per cent, which possibly shows their superior training and experience. Around 30 to 40 percent of the wounded might be expected to later die from their injuries, or from the infections they contracted by being placed alongside those who were sick.[22] Among the senior officers, Ribbing fell in the battle, while Rehnskiöld, Maydell, and Stenbock were wounded. Colonel Hans Henrik Rehbinder of the Karelian (Viborg and Nyslott County) Cavalry Regiment fell in the battle. His brother Colonel Bernhard Rehbinder of the Åbo and Björneborg County Cavalry Regiment suffered a bad wound, which together with his old age caused him to retire from the army. Captain Klijssendorff of the Dalecarlia Regiment was killed at the head

Prince Alexander of Imeretia, after a few years in Swedish captivity, by Martin Mijtens the Elder (Gripsholm Castle)

---

hoping that this would persuade Gulitz to return to captivity. Ustryalov, *Istoriya tsarstvovaniya Petra Velikago* 4: 1, p.68.

19 See, e.g., Hallart, *Tagebuch*, 62.
20 Contra: Martin Hårdstedt, 'Narva 1700,' Lars Ericson, Martin Hårdstedt, Per Iko, Ingvar Sjöblom, and Gunnar Åselius, *Svenska slagfält* (np: Wahlström & Widstrand, 2003), pp.254–61, on p.254, p.259, accepts the number of wounded but estimates the Swedish dead as 900.
21 The figure corresponds well with the '2,000 dead and wounded' reported by Wisocki-Hochmuth, 122.
22 Laidre, *Segern vid Narva*, 175.

of his grenadier platoon in the very first assault.[23] The same fate befell Captain Carl Eriksson Sparre of the Life Guard, as well as many other officers.

King Charles lost three of his six Drabant aides: Knut Leijonhufvud, Fabian Reinhold Wrangel, and Per von Günthersberch, who died after some time from the 13 wounds he sustained in the battle. This can be taken as evidence that King Charles and his aides were at the forefront of combat. As a whole, the Drabant Corps suffered only 24 per cent casualties. It is perhaps telling that of the King's aides who survived, Berndt Otto Stackelberg and Carl Gustav Dücker would both ultimately be promoted to the rank of field marshal.[24]

The Russian surrender freed several Swedish prisoners of war. Among them was Major Patkul, who had been captured at Varja and provided exaggerated information on King Charles's approaching army, and Ensign Barohn, the envoy who had suffered torture at Tsar Peter's hands.

Since Narva was too small to host even the Swedish survivors, most had to go into the barracks abandoned by the Russians. The effect was as devastating as it was predictable. By the eighth day after the battle, the first cases of dysentery and other diseases that had previously plagued the Russians, had already broken out among the Swedish soldiers. Many died from the epidemics.

Table 8. Swedish casualties in the Battle of Narva, specified as officers and others (under-officers and common soldiers), respectively. The figures are primarily based on roll calls but estimates have been used for some units.[25]

Regiment	Dead		Wounded		
	Officers	Others	Officers	Others	Percentage
Life Drabant Corps	12	-	26	-	24.1%
Life Guard of Foot	6	132	15	170	19.0%
Life Dragoon Regt	-	45	9	93	28.6%
Dalecarlia Regiment	3	55	7	121	28.2%
Hälsinge Regiment	2	24	2	100	22.6%
Västmanland Regiment	1	92	4	197	52.9%
Närke-Värmland Regt	3	100	3	200	41.8%
Other units	3	200	1	300	-
Total	30	648	67	1,181	

---

23 Pihlström, *Kungl. Dalregementets historia* 3, p.93. Among the fallen of the Dalecarlia Regiment was Captain Benjamin von Essen (1664–1700), who died from wounds sustained during the battle.

24 The third survivor of King Charles's aides at Narva, Gotthard Henrik von Lantingshausen, died in the 1704 Battle of Punitz (Poniec).

25 Generalstaben, *Karl XII på slagfältet* 2, 353; Wernstedt, *Kungl. Svea livgardes historia* 4, 377. Two Life Guard officers ultimately died of their wounds.

15

Aftermath

By now, we have seen that the term 'Battle of Narva' in reality is a misnomer. The battle was essentially an assault upon a fortified position. A better designation would be the 'assault on the circumvallation line at Narva.' It only remained for King Charles to take possession of his conquest, which of course was the town of Narva which he successfully had relieved.

On 2 December, King Charles rode into Narva, where the victory was celebrated with a salute from the fortress and a special service in the town's church. He promoted the town's able defender, Horn, to major general. The King also promoted Magnus Stenbock, colonel of the Dalecarlia Regiment, to major general for his achievements in the battle (and Stenbock would go on to become one of Sweden's most distinguished field marshals). Yet, it had been a very hard-fought battle. Stenbock was a veteran of the Nine Years' War, during which he participated on the losing side in the bloody Battle at Fleurus, and had subsequently led a regiment in Imperial service. Yet, the Battle of Narva was an experience of quite another character and magnitude. Stenbock wrote to his wife, Eva Magdalena Oxenstierna, that 'I now see war being waged wholly differently from what I learnt.'[1]

The Swedish victory at Narva had the immediate effect of Tsar Peter evacuating his remaining regular units from Ingria (but not his irregular raiders who remained a serious threat to communication lines). This removed the immediate threat to the Swedish core territories. Tsar Peter also had to rebuild his military forces. It took a year for Russia to replace the lost artillery. Additionally, since the Russian commanders who took part in the battle were captured almost to a man, Tsar Peter had to rebuild his officer corps from scratch. Later historians have often argued that for this reason King Charles should have pressed on into Russia, to conclude the war then and there. Yet, Tsar Peter had other, undefeated armies at his disposal. Although not as modern as the one he had lost, they were certainly able to fight. Moreover, logistics precluded a continuation of operations against Russia. Estonia, Livonia, and Ingria had suffered greatly, and moreover, had still not recovered from the devastating famine of 1696–1697. The Swedish

---

1   Lars Rosander, *Sveriges Fältmarskalkar: Svenska Fältherrar från Vasa till Bernadotte* (Lund: Historiska Media, 2003), 282.

army went into winter quarters around the Estonian town of Dorpat, but food supplies remained scarce.

In addition to logistics, King Charles and his commanders had to consider the strategic implications of this year's campaigns. Russia was not the only, nor the most dangerous enemy. Having forced the Danes out of the war, pushed back King Augustus, and destroyed Tsar Peter's main army, an offensive against the Polish-Lithuanian Commonwealth and Saxony was the logical next step. The Swedish commanders accordingly began to plan for an offensive against King Augustus. Or, rather continued these plans. Already on 22 November, at Wesenberg, King Charles had issued orders to Governor-General Dahlbergh in Riga to gather supplies for the Swedish army's march through Livonia towards King Augustus, after the threat to Narva had been dealt with, 'which we from the Almighty surely can expect', as the confident King Charles put it.[2] King Augustus was still regarded as the more dangerous adversary of the hostile triple alliance against Sweden.

The Swedish victory at Narva resonated widely across Europe. The French envoy, Count Louis de Guiscard, who was in Reval, wrote that he found it 'unbelievable how this action ended, and never before since the beginning of the world was ever heard of such a miracle by a King earlier or later.'[3] Colonel Axel Sparre of the Västmanland Regiment, who because of logistical problems did not reach Narva in time to participate in the battle, commented that Count Guiscard was 'so surprised by this affair that he for several days could not speak.'[4] Sparre's comment probably contained a grain of truth, although likely was somewhat exaggerated. The Swedish Colonel, a veteran of Dutch service, may have had personal reasons to dislike the French envoy.

In Paris, people nonetheless cheered in the streets. The Ottoman Sultan, Mustafa II, sent couriers with congratulations to King Charles. Mustafa expressed his admiration for the 'incomparable heroism' with which King Charles had repulsed his 'faithless neighbours', and wished the Swedish King continued success. The Sultan assured that it would always give him a great pleasure 'to further hear what such a young lord with God's help might accomplish.'[5]

Drawing of King Charles in breastplate. (Johan David Schwartz, c. 1708–1710; Royal Library, Stockholm)

---

2   National Archives, Riksregistraturet, SE/RA/1112.1/B/619 (1700), pp.313–17, 12 November 1700 (S.S.); Generalstaben, *Karl XII på slagfältet* 2, 355.

3   Letter from Reval, 26 November 1700 (S.S.?), UUB, f.102; cited in Generalstaben, *Karl XII på slagfältet* 2, 354.

4   Axel Sparre to Fabian Wrede, Lais, 26 December 1700 (S.S.), De la Gardie Archive 13; cited in Generalstaben, *Karl XII på slagfältet* 2, 354. Colonel Axel Axelsson Sparre would ultimately be promoted to field marshal.

5   Grimberg, *Svenska Folkets Underbara Öden* 4, 542.

AFTERMATH

On 15 February 1701, a general thanksgiving day was celebrated in churches all over Sweden. On Brunkeberg Square in Stockholm, the court artist and architect, Nicodemus Tessin, built a 25 metre high wooden pyramid that was lit up by 2,500 whale-oil lamps. On 28 August, the captured banners, cannon, and kettledrums were paraded through Stockholm. The Russian prisoners of war were not forced to attend, and most refused even to look out through the windows while the parade passed through. Celebrations, and the accompanying propaganda, soon eradicated any understanding of how hard-fought the battle really had been. Perhaps this was inevitable, since only a few of those Swedes who fought in the battle had by then returned to Stockholm, where the desperate struggle was turned into a preordained triumph that for all times would symbolise Sweden's invincible military might against Russia.

Weide's Division surrenders to King Charles, as depicted in a romanticised 1905 painting by the Swedish artist Gustaf Cederström. Purchased in 1906 for the National Museum, Stockholm, by a group led by His Majesty's Marshal of the Realm, Baron Fredrik von Essen, as a means to raise the population's willingness to defend the country, the painting exerted a strong influence on the general public and early twentieth century historians. Cederström used items from the Army Museum as props to present a, for its time, reasonably realistic image of King Charles's army. However, he painted the defeated Russians as archetypal Asiatics mostly armed with already-obsolete weapons and armour so as to emphasise their backwardness. (National Museum, Stockholm)

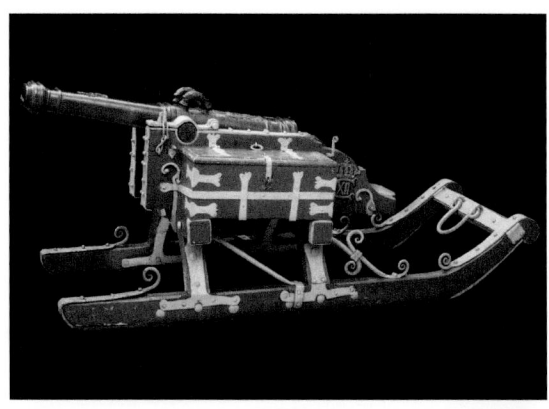

Artillery sledge carriage, early 1700s. Blue painted wood with yellow painted iron reinforcements. Although this carriage is fitted with a three-barrelled gun of unknown provenience, it is typical of those employed for regimental 3-pdr cannons in the eastern campaigns from 1700 to 1710. Length including barrel 2.20m, length excluding barrel 2.12m, width 88.0cm, height 83.0cm. (Army Museum, Stockholm; AM.049723)

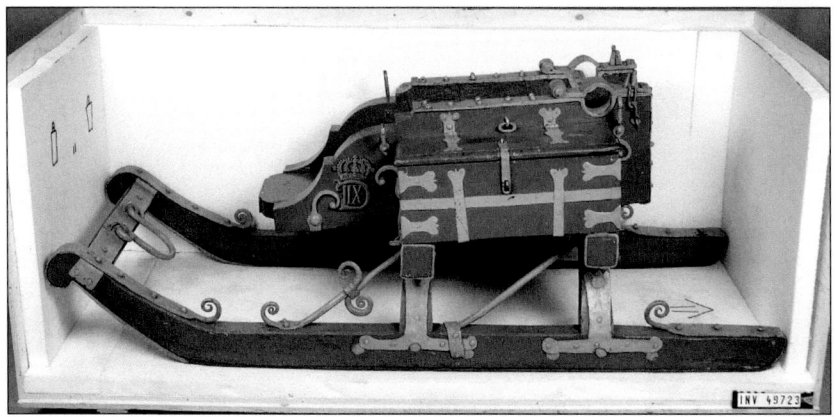

When the other prisoners of war were sent to Sweden, the Duke de Croÿ asked for, and received, permission to remain in Reval. King Charles sent him 1,500 Reichsthalers to cover his expenses. These funds did not last long. Lacking money, Croÿ wrote to Tsar Peter, who granted him 6,000 roubles. The Duke liked a lavish lifestyle and had a good time in Reval. By all accounts, he thoroughly enjoyed his period in captivity. When Croÿ died of natural causes in the spring of 1702, he was heavily in debt. The Tsar promised to pay off the creditors, but no money arrived. An old law in Reval stated that anybody who lacked funds to pay his debts would not receive a burial before his relatives had paid what was due. The corpse was accordingly laid in a coffin in an old crypt in St Nicholas's Church in Reval, awaiting payment and burial, and was ultimately forgotten for the better part of a century. In 1800 or thereabouts, Croÿ's corpse was accidentally rediscovered, and it was found to have mummified. In 1819, the Duke's earthly remains, together with his wig and uniform, were accordingly placed on a catafalque and covered with a glass coffin, so that Croÿ's mummy could be exhibited to the curious. Tourists paid a small fee to see the mummified field marshal.

This state of affairs lasted until 1870, when the Governor General of Estonia, Prince Mikhail Shakhovskoy, decided to put an end to the undignified display of a dead field marshal of the Russian Army. Emperor Alexander II ordered a quiet burial. It still took until 15 January 1897 before what remained of the mummy was placed in a new coffin and lowered into a grave built in the crypt of the same church.

AFTERMATH

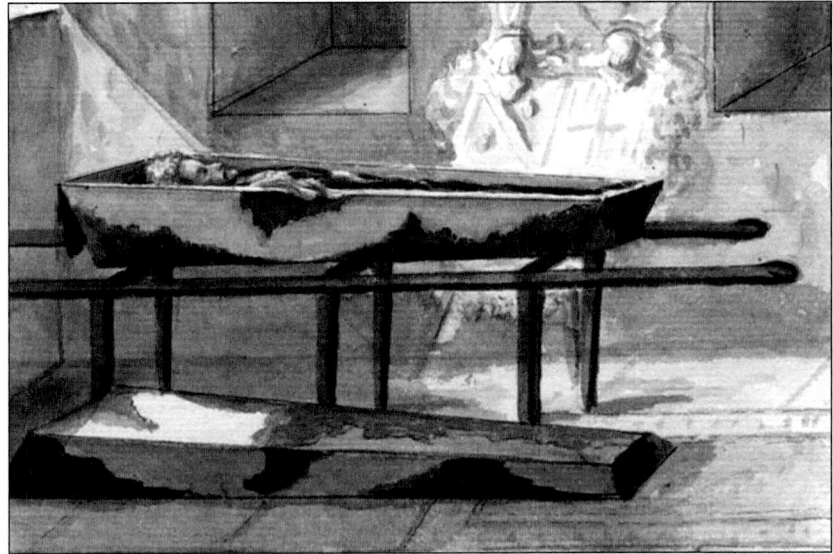

The mummy of Charles Eugène de Croÿ, as it was in the years around 1800. (Johann Christoph Brotze)

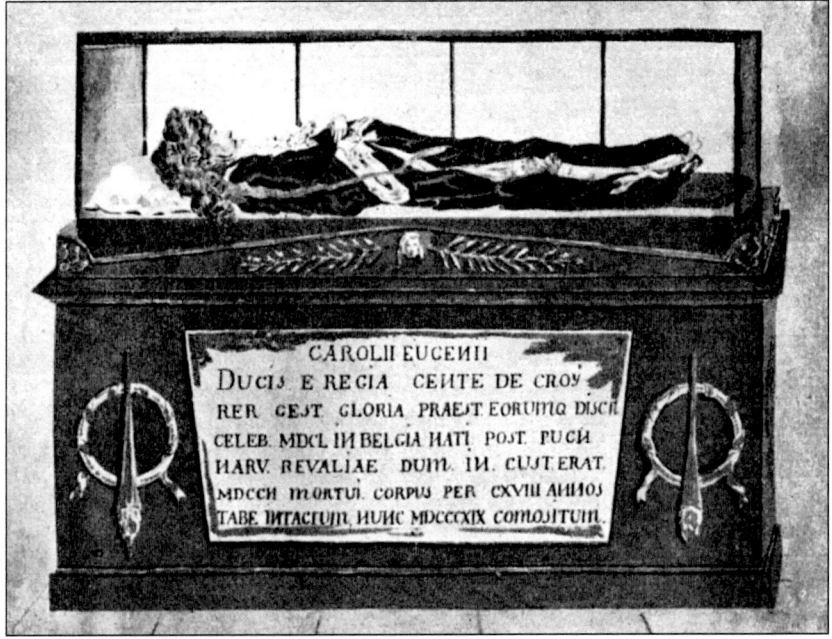

The mummy of Charles Eugène de Croÿ, as put on display in 1819.

The mummy of Charles Eugène de Croÿ, photograph taken in 1896 before burial.

It is difficult to assess King Charles's leadership during the Battle of Narva. The victory had not been as clear-cut as later propaganda alleged. Had Weide not been wounded, would he have pushed back against the Swedes, whom we have seen were then badly disorganised and out of ammunition? Had Croÿ not been captured, would he have assumed command of Weide's wing and used it more decisively? Had Tsar Peter stayed with the army, would his Guard units have surrendered or dug in to fight a second day? Could Sheremetyev's cavalry have played a more active role? An historian cannot answer these questions, but there was nothing predetermined about the Swedish victory. The Battle of Narva displays the important role that chance and individual agency play in war. There is no doubt that King Charles displayed personal bravery, led his men from the front, and by pure luck avoided being killed by enemy fire at least twice during the assault on the wagon fort. We also know that King Charles personally directed at least the formation of the assault columns, so he certainly played a command role. But to what extent did he actually command his men, as opposed to merely taking the lead to inspire them? It would be churlish to claim that King Charles only followed the lead of other, more experienced officers. Yet, we do not know to what extent the battle plan originated with the experienced and trusted Rehnskiöld, or to what extent the inexperienced young King was its author. While Rehnskiöld likely drew up at least the broad outline of the plan of assault, it would have been out of character for King Charles not to add his own views.

It is also hard to assess how the battle formed King Charles's character and to what extent it came to guide his future choice of tactics and strategy. The Battle of Narva was a formative experience. We have seen that the King henceforth kept the memory of the battle alive by withdrawing into solitude and personal prayer during each anniversary of the battle.[6] But to what extent, if any, did the Battle of Narva influence his future actions? After the battle, King Charles was overheard saying that it was 'no real sport fighting Russians, since they do not stand fast.'[7] Was this a spur-of-the-moment joke caused by youthful exuberance, or was this the young King's personal reflection on the combat value of the Russian Army? Many later observers concluded, based on this statement, that King Charles henceforth looked down on the combat ability of Russian soldiers, and that this made him unnecessarily reckless when fighting Russians, which ultimately, the logic goes, explained his subsequent defeat at the hands of Peter the Great at Poltava in 1709. Yet, we have seen that in reality, most Russian units put up a hard fight, and it was certainly no preordained fate that the Swedish army would win. Ultimately, as with so much else relating to King Charles's personality, we do not really know what he thought during and after the Battle of Narva.

---

6   Yet, we do not know whether the young King did so for personal reasons, or because he wished to follow in the footsteps of his father Charles XI who never forgot the desperate 1676 Battle of Lund and for the rest of his life respected its anniversary, not with celebration but with prayer and solitude.

7   Swedish: *ryssar är intet lust att slåss med, emedan de intet stå som andra*. Colonel Axel Sparre; cited in Liljegren, *Karl XII: En Biografi*, 95.

AFTERMATH

For Tsar Peter, the Battle of Narva was indeed a disastrous defeat. Not only had Russia lost thousands of soldiers and almost all its experienced commanders, but the Tsar's decision to abandon the army just before battle was widely interpreted as caused by fear of the Swedes, or possibly even cowardice. Tsar Peter explained his departure by the urgent need to speed up the arrival of reinforcements (an army of some 10,800 regulars under Prince Anikita Repnin and another of between 8,000 and 12,000 Ukrainian Cossacks under Hetman Ivan Obidovskiy), address supply issues, confer with his important ally, King Augustus, and receive a so far imagined (but possibly expected) embassy from the Ottoman Empire.[8] Possibly, Tsar Peter also expected King Charles to dig in outside Narva, build up strength, and allow his army some rest instead of ordering an immediate assault – all of which would have enabled the Tsar to bring in Repnin's and Obidovskiy's reinforcements. Perhaps Tsar Peter actually thought that his confidant Hummert had revealed his army's weaknesses to the Swedes, and this was the real reason why King Charles marched against him at such speed with an army of allegedly 24,000 to 25,000 men, which if true, would have necessitated Repnin's and Obidovskiy's reinforcements for any hope of a Russian victory. After the battle, Swedish propagandists quickly distributed the story that Tsar Peter was a coward who had abandoned his army because he was afraid to meet King Charles. Russian propagandists countered by blaming Hummert's treachery, which in their view gave Sweden an easy victory. Later historians, at first primarily in Russia but later elsewhere as well, noted the propagandistic content of the Swedish pamphlets and mostly give Tsar Peter at least the benefit of the doubt. After all, he showed personal bravery on other occasions. One could argue that bailing out before disaster struck was the prudent course of action for a monarch. By doing so, he gambled his army on the outcome of the ensuing battle, but he did not risk his crown.

Yet, there was something unseemly in the Tsar's haste to dump full responsibility on a subordinate and then bail out before dawn that speaks in favour of the interpretation that nervousness played a role in the decision. He was still only Peter, not Peter the Great. Tsar Peter was still learning the art of war, and in time he certainly would find the confidence to face King Charles. He also realised the need to intensify the modernisation of the Russian Army. Besides, four years after Tsar Peter's disastrous defeat at Narva, at a time when King Charles and the Swedish main army were engaged in a campaign far away from the Gulf of Finland, the Tsar returned to Narva with another army, and this time with considerably more success.[9]

---

8 Hallart, *Tagebuch*, 51.
9 On this action, see Boris Megorsky, *Peter the Great's Revenge: The Russian Siege of Narva in 1704* (Warwick: Helion, 2018).

Colour Plate Commentaries

A. The Swedish Life Guard Assaults the Russian Circumvallation Line at Narva
Carried forward by the sudden blizzard in their back, the Life Guard's pikemen and musketeers tear down the *chevaux-de-frise*, climb up the exterior slope of the rampart, and attack the Russians behind the breastwork with bayonet, pike, and sword. Although recently rearmed with flintlock muskets with bayonets, the men still wear either the traditional brimmed hat or a *karpus* cap instead of the tricorne that several years later came to define the Carolean uniform.
(Artist: Steve Noon)

B. King Charles at the Battle of Narva
This equestrian portrait depicts King Charles in the blue winter coat lined with lynx fur that he wore at Narva. Additionally, he wears a breastplate for protection (barely hinted at in the portrait), yellow leather breeches, and black riding boots with spurs. The King has wound a black taffeta cravat several times around the neck, and wears a brimmed hat of otter fur in place of the tricorne worn later. This portrait suggests that the winter coat has a pale blue base colour, not the dark blue more common in Swedish uniforms at the time and depicted in virtually all later portraits of King Charles. The pale blue colour in this painting corresponds to the uniform of the Drabant Corps in 1700, which seems appropriate since the King was its captain. It remains unknown whether King Charles wore a wig at Narva. It is clear that King Charles discarded the wig at around this time. (Detail from a painting by David von Krafft)

C. Musketeer, Life Guard of Foot
The Life Guard of Foot was an enlisted unit, so many of its soldiers had some previous experience of battle. Otherwise, it functioned as an ordinary infantry regiment. This musketeer carries a modern flintlock musket with bayonet together with an old infantry sword, model 1685. Russian accounts speak of the Swedish manner of hand-to-hand combat, in which the musketeer first made a one-handed attack with the musket and bayonet, and then, when his opponent attempted to parry the bayonet, thrust him through with the sword. This guardsman seems experienced in this style of fighting. Although it is hard to say how widespread the method was, the relatively low rate of casualties suffered by the Life Guard during the assault (19 per cent,

the lowest among the Swedish infantry units), even though they fought in the vanguard, shows the experience of the unit and how lethal they really might be on the battlefield. Both sword and bayonet are worn on the waist and sword belt. The guardsman carries the standard cartridge box with the royal cypher used by all musketeers, as well as the customary priming horn. He wears an infantry coat issued in 1695 generally (although not wholly) based on model 1687, buttoned all the way down but without collar. The Life Guard wore blue coats with yellow lining, blue breeches, and yellow stockings. Under-officers wore blue stockings. This guardsman has attached a whisk of straw to his black hat, bound with galloon, in the customary Swedish manner as a field sign to distinguish friend from foe. The use of this field sign was mandatory, so we can assume that most, if not all, used it. Many Carolean soldiers kept the hair in order with a hair bag, in the style employed by this musketeer.

D. Grenadier, Dalecarlia Regiment

Grenadiers wore distinctive caps, which supposedly enabled the soldier to throw grenades without accidentally hitting the brim of his own hat. Probably far more importantly, the grenadier cap also made the grenadier look taller and thus more impressive. This was likely the real reason for the new style of cap, since otherwise a *karpus* cap would suffice. Grenadiers in any case tended to be physically impressive, since it was only the tallest and strongest men who were selected as grenadiers. Grenades were heavy, up to 1kg in weight, and few could throw them longer than some 30 paces, even if they wanted to. A grenadier carried a leather bag with grenades into battle. Otherwise, a grenadier was armed similarly to a musketeer, except that he was issued a sling with his musket so that he could sling it across the shoulder when handling grenades. The musket is a modern flintlock with bayonet. Both sword and bayonet are worn on the belt. The smaller pouch with the royal cypher is the standard box for cartridges and was also carried by musketeers. This grenadier wears an infantry coat based on model 1687, buttoned all the way down but without collar. The Dalecarlia Regiment wore blue coats with yellow lining, yellow leather breeches, and yellow stockings,

E. Trooper, Åbo and Björneborg County Cavalry Regiment

The Finnish cavalry regiments wore grey uniforms, although at least according to regulations, with lining in the provincial colour. Both the Nyland and Tavastehus County Cavalry Regiment (since 1696) and the Åbo and Björneborg County Cavalry Regiment (since 1690) were ordered to issue grey coats with red lining in the years before war broke out. However, a letter to the King dated 19 November 1701 (S.S.) makes clear that both regiments, despite regulations, by then wore light grey coats with grey lining (Höglund and Sallnäs, *Stora Nordiska Kriget*, p.12). This cavalryman's coat follows the old style, buttoned all the way down. The *karpus* cap remained common within the Finnish cavalry. Naturally, he wears riding boots with spurs. This cavalryman is armed with a modern flintlock carbine, hooked to a bandolier, and an old cavalry sword with a thumb ring similar in style to the infantry model 1685. He has clearly not yet been issued with the modern

Carolean cavalry sword. This is unsurprising, since equipment and uniforms were generally not discarded before they wore out. For the same reason, it is difficult to say which cavalry regiments still retained breastplates. They were certainly used within some Swedish cavalry units in the early years of the Great Northern War. Based on the available information, this cavalryman can for these reasons be said to represent both the Nyland and Tavastehus County and the Åbo and Björneborg County Cavalry Regiments in the Narva campaign.

F. Artilleryman

This artilleryman wears a grey coat with blue lining, based on model 1687 and accordingly buttoned all the way down but without collar. In addition, he wears yellow leather breeches (not visible), blue stockings, and a *karpus* cap with blue lining of a similar hue to the coat. Both artillery officers and common artillerymen carried the model 1675 artillery hanger or hunting sword (Swedish: *hirschfängare*; from German: *hirschfänger*, 'deer hunter') as a sidearm, since a long sword would interfere with their work.

G. Musketeer, Preobrazhenskiy Guard Regiment

The Preobrazhenskiy Regiment wore dark green uniforms since the 1690s. This reconstruction shows a musketeer issued with a new Hungarian style uniform coat, in the already traditional dark green colour of the regiment, with red cuffs. This musketeer also wears a red, fur-trimmed cap inspired by Polish styles, since its top is less tall than the corresponding traditional Russian caps. Caps of this new style were likely issued to all new regiments in Tsar Peter's army. In addition, this soldier wears high red leather boots in the new style inspired by the West. The soldier's primary weapon is a flintlock musket. This comes with a cartridge box and the customary priming horn. Little is known about the other weapons of the Preobrazhenskiy Guard Regiment. This soldier carries a sidearm and almost certainly (although invisible in this reconstruction) a plug bayonet.

H. Musketeer, Semyonovskiy Guard Regiment

The Semyonovskiy regiment wore blue uniforms with red since the 1690s. This musketeer has been issued the new Hungarian style uniform coat, together with a new style red, fur-trimmed cap, red stockings, and Western European shoes. Like his counterpart from the Preobrazhenskiy Guard Regiment, he has been issued a flintlock musket, cartridge box, and priming horn. This soldier probably carries a plug bayonet (invisible in this reconstruction) on his left side, and possibly also a sidearm of some kind. He brings food supplies and perhaps a few personal belongings in a knapsack.

I. Musketeer, Yuriy Vestov's Pskov Streltsy regiment

The streltsy were old style, hereditary musketeers. They received their arms and equipment from the state, so were uniformly armed and clothed. A streltsy regiment would present a uniform appearance. As daily dress, the streltsy wore long caftans with wide sleeves that narrowed at the wrist. Caps, trimmed with fur, remained traditional, which meant a fairly tall top in comparison to the lower but similar modern cap issued to the new regiments. The streltsy also wore traditional Russian boots. Streltsy units wore coloured coats of various shades, but supposedly switched them for plain grey coats while on campaign.

In addition to his musket, this old style strelets from Pskov carries a sabre and, following in the footsteps of his ancestors, a *berdysh*, a pole-axe with a 40 to 100cm long head mounted on a shaft. In the past, the berdyshis are said to have been used as a musket rest as well as for hand-to-hand combat in particular against horsemen. The berdysh remained in common use throughout the seventeenth century but was found to be less utilitarian against modern continental-style infantry. Although accordingly not as frequently carried as in the past, some berdyshes probably appeared at Narva, at least within the ranks of provincial streltsy units. When not in use, the weapon was carried slung in a shoulder-loop.

This old style strelets carries a traditional matchlock musket. By the time of the Narva campaign, most streltsy had already rearmed with flintlock muskets. Most were gradually turning themselves into modern musketeers. But not this strelets, who instead has protected the musket lock with a traditional cloth lock cover. Many streltsy used dedicated cloth lock covers decorated in appliqué, with patterns chiefly consisting of stylised flowers, plants, and animal heads. Their dimensions were about 25cm x 37cm and they were made of fulled woollen fabric. Several were taken as trophies by the Swedish army and have been preserved in the Army Museum, Stockholm.

J. Dragoon, Joachim Gulitz's 'Preobrazhenskiy' Dragoon Regiment

Hereditary servicemen who enlisted in Gulitz's Dragoon Regiment received money to purchase dark green coats, red caps, and red sashes. Being hereditary servicemen, they were responsible for their own clothing, hence the regiment did not issue uniforms as such. However, regulations specified which colours to be used for important items of clothing, so the regiment nonetheless must have presented a reasonably uniform appearance. This dragoon has acquired high red leather boots in the new style inspired by the west.

Dragoons carried flintlock muskets that were shorter than ordinary ones. The Russian dragoon musket could be slung from a bandolier worn over the left shoulder, in similarity to a carbine in the Swedish army. The dragoon musket had an iron sling bar and ring on the left side so that the dragoon could attach his gun to the corresponding hook on the bandolier. The musket comes with a cartridge box and priming horn. The dragoon has either been issued or privately purchased (or inherited) a sabre as sidearm.

K. Old Style Cavalryman, Sovereign's Division

The old style cavalry was not uniformed but turned out in civilian dress. The traditional clothes worn by Russians at the time were of Inner Asian origin, ranging from the caftan to the high, soft boots associated with equestrian nomads. Tsar Peter hated these traditional garments, which he believed impaired the modernisation effort, and ultimately forbad them. This old style cavalryman belongs to the Sovereign's Division from Moscow, so can afford an affluent lifestyle and good clothes. He has probably also brought a serving man or two, armed and equipped in similar fashion to himself. This cavalryman is not a senior noble or boyar, however. Since service in the old style cavalry was hereditary, he has merely followed in the footsteps of his father. Armed with a sabre and a pair of pistols, he has discarded the armour worn up to the time of his father's generation. This hereditary serviceman has also given up the composite bow carried until late in the seventeenth century. Instead, he might bring a carbine or musket in addition to the pistols. He carries a round powder flask and a flat sabretache container for ammunition or personal belongings. The Polish style sabretache reminds us that affluent Russians, especially in the western parts of the country, had adopted a number of Polish practices. The old style cavalry who fought in the Narva campaign came from Moscow and prosperous cities in north-Western Russia such as Novgorod, Pskov, and Smolensk. Hereditary servicemen lived in other parts of Russia as well, and many of them were impoverished. The vast majority of hereditary servicemen could not afford either musket or carbine, and by this time many did not even own a horse. Essentially, they were peasants but technically of a higher social status. Some served with a spear and axe instead of firearms which meant that they were quite unable to play any real role on a modern battlefield.

L. Charles Eugène Duke de Croÿ
The Duke de Croÿ, reconstructed wearing the spectacular, Western-style red coat which he favoured. Field marshals dressed as they wished, especially when the Tsar was not around. Turned out like this, it is perhaps unsurprising that the Swedish soldiers who encountered the Duke on the battlefield did not believe his explanation that he was a mere burgher out of Narva. Sadly, the coat did not survive the battle unharmed. It was badly torn by a near hit from the Swedish artillery. The Duke himself was not harmed.

COLOUR PLATE COMMENTARIES

Colour illustrations (standards)

M. Nyland and Tavastehus County Cavalry Regiment
Swedish cavalry standards were 60cm x 60cm. The design based on the provincial coat of arms was traditional, but this standard was known as model 1686, since new regulations for colours and standards were introduced in that year. Henceforth, a cavalry standard had the provincial coat of arms on one side, and the royal cypher on the other. The life company, unlike the others, flew a white standard, although it was decorated in the same manner.

N.
Karelian (Viborg and Nyslott) Cavalry Regiment
Another cavalry standard based on model 1686. The Karelian design was belligerent, illustrating the seemingly eternal struggle between the straight Finnish sword and the curved Russian sabre.

Tiesenhausen's Enlisted Estonian Cavalry Regiment
This cavalry standard, based on the coat of arms of Estonia, depicts three yellow lions, with the year 1700 and the Latin text PRO DEO ET PATRIA ('For God and Country'). (Swedish National Archives)

Note each flag from Plate O to Plate V depicts the flags as an original eighteenth century painting and a photo of its current state.

O. Preobrazhenskiy Guard Regiment, 15th Company
This Colour was probably made in Moscow in 1700 of black Chinese silk damask for the 15th Company of the Preobrazhenskiy Guard Regiment. The colour comes with an intarsia and painted motif in the form of a sword reaching down from a grey cloud, surrounded by a painted gold chain from which is suspended a medallion with an image of the crucified apostle 'St Andrew the First-Called', that is, the Order of St Andrew. At the time, there was only one known knight of the order, Tsar Peter's friend and confidant, General and Admiral Fyodor Golovin. Henceforth, however, the usage of the new and hitherto seldom-used symbol grew increasingly common in military regalia, and the Order of St Andrew became the highest award of the Russian Empire. The main motif of this colour is surrounded by palm leaves in straw coloured silk damask. The number of golden stars, 15, identify the company, in this case the 15th. The colour of a Guard regiment has a number of details that differ from the corresponding design features of the colours of line regiments. These include the cross inside a cloud in a canton in the upper hoist, the sunburst with the all-seeing eye above the sword instead of a hand (which is found in the colours of line regiments), and the fact that there are six palm leaves on each side instead of four (most or all new line regiments) or five (the old Selected Regiments, although it can only be confirmed for the First). In addition, in the colours of the Preobrazhenskiy Guard Regiment only, the gold chain was surmounted by a crown. Size: 230 x 208cm. (Army Museum, Stockholm; ST 22:146)

P. Semyonovskiy Guard Regiment, Colonel's Life Company

Colour likely made in Moscow in 1700 of white Chinese silk damask for the Life Company of the Semyonovskiy Guard Regiment. The colour of a colonel's life company was, in the infantry according to the regulations issued in 1700, always white and carried the image of a double-headed eagle, which symbolises Russia's imperial power. As noted, the colour of a Guard regiment has a number of details that differ from the corresponding design features of the colours of line regiments. These include the cross inside a cloud in a canton at the upper hoist, the sunburst with the all-seeing eye, and the fact that there are six palm leaves instead of four (for line regiments) or five (the old Selected Regiments). Size: 228cm x 204cm. (Army Museum, Stockholm; ST 22:148)

Q. Semyonovskiy Guard Regiment, 3rd Company

Colour likely made in Moscow in 1700 of blue Chinese silk damask for the 3rd Company of the Semyonovskiy Guard Regiment. The colour comes with an intarsia and painted motif in the form of a sword reaching down from a grey cloud, surrounded by the painted gold chain of the Order of St Andrew. The main motif is surrounded by palm leaves in straw-coloured silk damask. Three golden stars identify the company as the 3rd. As noted, the colour of a Guard regiment has a number of details that differ from the corresponding design features of the colours of line regiments. These include the cross inside a cloud in canton on the upper hoist, the sunburst with the all-seeing eye above the sword instead of a hand, and the fact that there are six palm leaves instead of four (for line regiments) or five (the old Selected Regiments). Finally, the known colours of the Semyonovskiy Guard Regiment differ from those of the Preobrazhenskiy Guard Regiment in that they lack the crown above the gold chain, which are on the colour of the latter. Size: 229cm x 212cm. Stave length: 250cm. (Army Museum, Stockholm; ST 22:149)

R. First Selected Moscow Regiment, also known as Lefortovo Regiment, Colonel's Life Company

Colour made in Moscow in 1700 of white Chinese silk damask, attributed to the Life Company of the First Selected Moscow Regiment. The double-headed eagle carries a medallion on its breast which depicts Tsar Peter on horseback. Established in 1656–1657, the First Selected Moscow Regiment was the oldest new style regiment still in service. Formerly commanded by Tsar Peter's friend and drinking buddy François Lefort, the regiment as well as its quarters were gradually becoming known as Lefortovo, after its colonel. Adam Weide assumed command of the First Selected Regiment after the 1699 death of Lefort. We have seen that at Narva, the regiment was commanded by Weide's deputy regimental commander, Giorgio or Yuriy Lima, a naturalised naval officer of Venetian origin. He went on to assume full command of the regiment after Weide's fall into Swedish captivity. Lima still commanded the regiment when he fell in the 1702 battle of Hummelshof against the Swedes. Wilhelm von Schweiden then assumed command of the regiment. Size: 211x216cm. (Army Museum, Stockholm; ST 22:128)

COLOUR PLATE COMMENTARIES

S. First Selected Moscow Regiment, also known as Lefortovo Regiment
Colour made in Moscow in the second half of 1700 of yellow Chinese silk damask, attributed to the First Selected Moscow Regiment. Colours made according to Tsar Peter's decree of 30 June 1700 (O.S.) were somewhat plainer than those manufactured in the first half of the year. The sword is painted, not sewn, and the Order of St Andrew is of a plainer design. However, this infantry colour, although following the same style of other infantry colours manufactured in 1700, is distinguished by an additional dark green laurel wreath and coiling ribbons. The manufacture of these added details is believed to have pushed up the cost of the colour to more than twice that of the other, plainer ones of same general type. The additions are believed to celebrate the First Selected Regiment's distinguished record in the second Azov campaign of 1696. Size: 205cm x 205cm. Stave length: 240cm. (Army Museum, Stockholm; ST 22:193.4)

T. Alferiy Schnewentz's 'Preobrazhenskiy' Dragoon Regiment
Made in 1700 in Moscow of black Chinese silk overshot, with intarsia and painted motif consisting of a yellow cross of Constantine surrounded by seven palm leaves of each side. A scroll with Russian text translates 'With this I shall conquer my enemies.' Size: 137cm x 103cm. Stave length: 290cm. (Army Museum, Stockholm; ST 22:221.4)

U. Joachim Gulitz's 'Preobrazhenskiy' Dragoon Regiment, 8th Company
Made of green silk damask, with intarsia and painted motif in gold and silver paint. The banner depicts a probably white cross of Constantine surrounded by five palm leaves on each side (that is, fewer than for Schnewentz's Dragoon Regiment), with a scroll with Russian text that translates 'With this sign I shall conquer.' Tsar Peter ordered Grigoriy Timofeyev in Moscow to manufacture the 12 banners of Gulitz's 'Preobrazhenskiy' Dragoon Regiment on 24 July 1700 (O.S.). The eight stars denote the 8th Company. Size: 144cm x 107cm. (Army Museum, Stockholm; ST 22:217.5)

V. Matvey Fliwerk's Regiment
This infantry colour can with a reasonable degree of certainty be attributed to Fliwerk's Regiment, since the regiment as far as is known flew green colours and lost them at Narva. Moreover, the motif of the colour corresponds to those of the other new infantry regiments that Tsar Peter formed in Moscow in the first half of 1700. The colour is made of green Chinese silk damask with a chrysanthemum pattern, with intarsia and painted motif in the form of a hand holding a sword reaching down from a grey cloud, surrounded by the painted gold chain of the Order of St Andrew. The main motif is surrounded by palm leaves in straw coloured silk damask. As noted, colours made in the first half of 1700 were more elaborate, and accordingly more expensive, than those manufactured during the second half of the year. Size: 200cm x 200cm. (Army Museum, Stockholm; ST 22-164.1)

W.

Wilhelm von Schweiden's Regiment, Colonel's Pennant
By tradition, officers in the old style cavalry often flew pennants of this style. Made of Chinese silk damask with a painted motif in the form of two swords and presumably the owner's coat of arms, depicting a cluster of grapes, this pennant also carries the painted initials of the owner. Little is known about Wilhelm von Schweiden, who was either born or, more likely, naturalised in Russia. His use of the Latin alphabet for initials suggests that he was naturalised, while flowing a personal pennant in traditional Russian design when he served as the colonel of a new infantry regiment may indicate that he wished to emphasise his place of belonging in the Russian service nobility. Size: 239.5cm x 54.1cm. (Army Museum, Stockholm; ST 23-254)

Boris Sheremetyev's Old style Cavalry, Company Banner
The religious motif is typical of late seventeenth century Russian banners. Made in Moscow in 1697 of silk damask with a motif painted in gold, except the steps and lance tip which are painted in silver. The principal motif consists of the Holy Cross flanked by the lance and sponge, placed on a postament of stairs. The Russian texts translate as 'The King of Glory, Jesus Christ Will Prevail'. Old style cavalry units often did not follow any particular organisation model, but the six stars may at this time suggest that this banner belonged to the 6th company of a certain regiment. Colours have faded, but the centre was originally orange, with white borders. The stave was painted red, with flowering vines, and fitted with an apple-shaped bulb over the grip. Size: 140cm x 137cm. Stave length: 252cm. (Army Museum, Stockholm; ST 21:69)

X.

Ivan Kokoshkin's Pskov Streltsy Regiment, Colonel's Company
This colour was not flown at Narva, because it was captured with other supplies when Wolmar Anton von Schlippenbach took six Russian transports on Lake Peipus while they were en route to Narva. Ivan Kokoshkin was then no longer the colonel of the regiment, since he commanded a cavalry regiment at Narva. Nonetheless, the colour is typical of late seventeenth century Russian infantry colours. Made in 1693 in Moscow of Chinese silk damask, with motif painted in gold and silver paint, the colour shows the Russian double-headed eagle and was for this reason probably intended as the colour of the colonel's company. Why was the colour shipped to Tsar Peter's army at Narva? Did the transports also carry reinforcements, and if so, from which regiment? We simply do not know. Our knowledge of the provincial Russian regiments at Narva is imperfect. Size: 299cm x 328cm. (Army Museum, Stockholm; ST 21:37)

15. Prince Ivan Trubetskoy's Personal Standard
Standard made of silk taffeta with a unicorn motif, with the Russian letters at the corners commonly interpreted as the initials of Prince Yuriy Petrovich Trubetskoy. The writing of the initials in this order was common in Poland,

where Prince Trubetskoy grew up. However, the unicorn was a princely symbol in Russia that would not be used by 'mere' noblemen. Prince Trubetskoy passed his personal standard down to his son Prince Ivan Trubetskoy, who likewise used it as a personal standard, including at Narva where it fell into Swedish hands. Size: 72cm x 72cm. (Army Museum, Stockholm; ST 21:213)

16. Drum Cover
Drum cover made of fabric for a so-called colonel's or lieutenant colonel's drum, captured at Saladen, 1703. Made of fulled woollen fabric and decorated in appliqué in a pattern of stylised flowers, animal heads, and plants. Such appliqué decorations were traditional in Russia and were used in lock covers and *chekhols* as well. This drum cover has a lining of linen. Height: 48.0cm. Diameter: 53.0cm. (Army Museum, Stockholm; AM.084618)

Further Reading

Although many books that include brief descriptions of the Battle of Narva have been published in Swedish and Russian, the best modern, for want of a better word, military history of King Charles's wars remains the four-volume work *Karl XII På slagfältet* by the Swedish General Staff, published in 1918–1919. Mostly written by the renowned military historian Carl Bennedich (1880–1939), a large number of historians and military officers participated in the project.

The General Staff history is based on the archive documents relating to the Swedish army under King Charles that can be found in Swedish archives and is reliable in its use of official records including orders of battle, casualty lists, and logistical inventories. However, its more general conclusions on strategy and tactics cannot always be taken at face value because of a bias in favour of King Charles and the Swedish army. The General Staff historians were greatly influenced by the early nineteenth century military theorist Carl von Clausewitz, and possibly yet more by their contemporary, the prominent military historian Hans Delbrück. A major thread in Delbrück's work was the choice between strategies of attrition and annihilation, which he argued stand in opposition to one another.[1] Since prevalent Swedish military thinking held that the strategy of annihilation was superior, the General Staff historians wanted to show that King Charles must have followed, or possibly even introduced, such a strategy.[2] With regard to Narva, they had to go to great lengths to show that even though King Charles let the Russians go, possibly encouraged thereto by Rehnskiöld, they argued that it was only the unquestionable Swedish lack of men and munitions that

---

1 Strategy of attrition: The general decides from moment to moment whether to achieve his goals by battle or manoeuvre. Strategy of annihilation: The general sets out directly to attack the enemy, destroy his armed forces, and thereby impose the will of the victor on the conquered until the defeated side accepts his conditions. Attrition and annihilation are here used for Delbrück's terms *Ermattungsstrategie* (strategy of exhaustion, that is, with limited objectives) and *Niederwerfungsstrategie* (strategy of overthrow, that is, with the objective of disabling the opponent's military capacity) despite not being literal translations, since this is how his work ultimately was translated into English.
2 It is telling that when the next generation of General Staff historians set out to describe the wars and military reforms of the early seventeenth century Swedish King Gustavus Adolphus, they instead argued, equally incorrectly, that he too was a keen supporter of the strategy of annihilation, and possibly introduced it. Fredholm von Essen, *Lion from the North* 1, 266.

made the King consent to anything but the total annihilation of the enemy.[3] Indeed, the General Staff historians argued that for King Charles, anything else was a 'totally alien' idea.[4] They also argued, with a hyperbole that must have sounded excessive even as they wrote, that King Charles's choice and command of tactics at Narva was 'the highest ever achieved by a general.' They even argued that the Battle of Narva was the first real battle of annihilation since the Roman victory at Cannae in 216 BC, and the direct descendant thereof, even though quite different in character. Indeed, the Battle of Narva was not only one Cannae, they judged, but two – one against the Russian remnants in the wagon fort and another against Weide's wing.[5] Based on this conclusion alone, it will not come as a surprise to learn that Carl Bennedich was known to indulge in a certain degree of hero-worship with regard to King Charles, who is unlikely to have pondered Cannae during the desperate night combat at Narva.

Incidentally, the General Staff historians also displayed a conspicuously negative view of Russian soldiers, whom they constantly described as primitive and utterly incapable of performing well. Although this was a commonplace assessment in Western armies at the time of their research, it had more to do with the early twentieth century military defeats of Russian armies against Japan and in the First World War, and Western propaganda, than the situation in the year 1700. As we have seen, King Charles's commanders at Narva knew full well, after penetrating the Russian defences, that the battle was not yet won, and that the Russians still constituted a dangerous enemy.

Another important modern Swedish reference work is volume four of *Kungl. Svea livgardes historia* (1954), which describes the history of the Swedish Royal Life Guard. Initiated by Bertil C: son Barkman and written by Folke Wernstedt, this work covers a longer period of time than that of King Charles and, since it focuses on the Life Guard, does not cover every incident of the war. Yet, it updates and often provides a better reading of the sources than the General Staff work. Publication of the multi-volume work started in 1937 and was not concluded until 1983.

Among other Swedish regimental histories, the most useful is Hans Ulfhielm's *Kungl. Artilleriet: Karl XI:s och Karl XII: s tid* (1993), which forms part of the multi-volume *Kungl. Artilleriet* which describes the history of the Royal Artillery. It gives a detailed overview of in particular artillery equipment, organisation, and operations during the war, and serves as an important corrective to Bennedich's traditional view that the artillery played a relatively unimportant role in the Carolean army.

---

[3] Rehnskiöld reportedly suggested building 'a golden bridge' for the defeated enemy to flee by, a concept known from ancient history and famously linked to Scipio Africanus since 'trapped men draw extra courage from desperation' (Vegetius Renatus, *Epitoma Rei Militaris* 3.21). Petrov, *Gorod Narva*, 234 n.4. Such a suggestion would both be prudent and correspond to previous military practices, and the works of the ancient military theorists were much read by Swedish commanders. There is thus nothing inherently implausible in Rehnskiöld, and likely King Charles as well, considering this option, which they ultimately also, quite literally, adopted.

[4] Generalstaben, *Karl XII på Slagfältet* 2, 350.

[5] Generalstaben, *Karl XII på Slagfältet* 2, 354.

In comparison, more recent *general* works in Swedish on the wars under King Charles are most often derivative and contain little new analysis, although particular aspects have been the subject of often excellent articles and monographs. Many can be found in John B. Hattendorf's edited volume *Charles XII: Warrior King* (2018), which gives probably the best overview in English on the life and character of King Charles.

Modern Russian historians have published outstanding new research on the Petrine army and the Narva campaign. References will be found in footnotes, since most is available only in Russian. Yet, the works of Boris Megorsky (also available in English) and Vladimir Velikanov must be singled out as particularly important.

Primary sources to the Battle of Narva include, first and foremost, Ludwig Nicolaus von Hallart's *Tagebuch* or diary, which he originally wrote during the siege. Hallart reworked his notes several times, so while the dates mentioned in the diary would appear reliable sources of information, other data may have been added later. In particular Hallart's notes on the Russian Army seem, unfortunately, not to be reconcilable with what is known from Russian sources. In all probability, Hallart's information on Russian units and numbers, despite its appearance of credibility, derived from later data on the Russian order of battle, in particular the maps of the battle that were later compiled and published in Sweden and the Netherlands. Many of the battle maps eventually published are unreliable with regard to the Russian dispositions, since few Russian documents survived the battle. Already Aleksey Vasil'yevich Makarov (1674 or 1675 to 1740), Tsar Peter's cabinet secretary, noted the disappearance of most documentation of the September-November 1700 campaign that culminated, and ended, with the Battle of Narva. The published edition of Hallart's work, too, provides a beautiful and quite detailed map of the battle, but again it is uncertain to what extent the Russian dispositions are correctly given. As with the diary, we do not really know when and how Hallart compiled the background data for it. In addition to these documents, Hallart wrote a report, on 6 December 1700, about the Battle of Narva addressed to King Augustus.

We also have a number of primary sources in the form of reports, journals, and letters produced immediately after the battle, but these also need to be read with caution. Many of the Swedish journals and letters were penned only after their authors had read the intentionally propagandistic reports produced by the Swedish field chancellery for public consumption, whether at home, among foreign diplomats, or within the exhausted army. Most who wrote home after the battle merged descriptions of what they had seen with their own eyes with what they afterwards had read in the public reports. They could hardly do otherwise, since each soldier only witnessed a small part of the battlefield, yet was expected to give a good account of the battle to friends and family.

Keeping this precaution in mind, we still have important contemporary descriptions of the battle. The Swedish Drabant Corps officer, Carl Gustav Wrangel, contributed a report on the Narva campaign (published in *Karolinska Förbundets Årsbok* 1910). It gives a good overview of the campaign and Battle of Narva and adds numerous details that Wrangel must have seen with his own eyes or heard immediately after they took place to what was already mentioned in the official, propagandistic reports.

A Swedish fortification lieutenant, Ludwig Wisocki-Hochmuth, gives a good description of the battle in his journal (published in *Karolinska Krigares dagböcker* 2, 190). Some of his notes probably derive from official reports. Yet, on occasion Wisocki-Hochmuth adds important details which occasionally can be confirmed by the results of modern scholarship based on archival sources unavailable to him, which makes the fortification officer an important eyewitness.

Important, but shorter, Swedish primary sources that describe the battle include the lively, albeit somewhat incoherent, letter that Captain Carl Magnus Posse of the Life Guard wrote to his brother Nils Posse (published in *Historisk Tidskrift* 2, 1882). Another captain of the Life Guard, Olof Stiernhöök, wrote a diary or journal which briefly describes the march to and the Battle of Narva (published in *Karolinska Förbundets Årsbok* 1912). A young officer named C. H. P. Sperling, probably of the Life Guard, wrote a journal in which he also incorporated what seems to be his official reports on captured standards and prisoners of war (published in *Karolinska Krigares dagböcker* 3, 1907; his first initials probably stand for Carl Henrik). Finally, the artillery officer Carl Cronstedt described the battle in a letter to Jacob Troilius (published in *Handlingar rörande Skandinaviens Historia* 19, 1834). The battle is mentioned in several other letters and journals as well, although often in passing, such as the journal by regimental quartermaster Anders Koskull of the Västmanland Regiment who disposed of the Battle in Narva in one sentence, mentioning that he suffered serious wounds in the legs in the battle and accordingly had to be left behind when the army marched out again (*Karolinska krigares dagböcker* 6, 1912, p.303). Colonel Magnus Stenbock's letter to his wife about the campaign and battle is reprinted in *En brefväxling* (1913–1914).

Several letters from Russian soldiers who fought at Narva have survived into the present. An anonymous but scholarly old style cavalryman in Sheremetyev's contingent wrote a chronicle ('Letopisets 1700 goda') that adds to our knowledge of how some Russian soldiers viewed the campaign. A firm believer in the intolerant preaching of the clergy, this cavalryman was convinced that the defeat at Narva was God's punishment for Tsar Peter's incomprehensible refusal to slaughter or enslave the entire heathen foreign population in proper Old Testament style (pp.140–41). Facing such beliefs, it was perhaps no wonder that Tsar Peter thought it a duty to drag his country into the Age of Enlightenment! Less erudite but perhaps more poignant letters by ordinary soldiers have recently been published by Sergey A. Kozlov ('Okopnyye pis'ma russkikh soldat 1700 g.', 2008).

Alexander Gordon of Auchintoul, who fought in the battle on the Russian side, eventually published his reminiscences in *The History of Peter the Great* (1755). Written long after the events, it unfortunately adds but little to our knowledge of the battle itself.

After the Great Northern War was over, Tsar Peter's cabinet secretary, the aforementioned Aleksey Makarov, headed a team that prepared the official Russian history of the war. Commonly known as *Gistoriya Sveyskoy voyny*

('History of the Swedish War'), it was first published as *Zhurnal ili Podennaya zapiska . . . Petra Velikago* (1770–1772) and is for this reason also known as Peter the Great's Journal. A French edition, *Journal de Pierre le Grand*, appeared in 1772.

Other near-contemporary narrative sources to the battle are primarily those histories of the life of King Charles that, based on remaining documents and eyewitnesses, were published after his death. The first was the well-known writer Voltaire's *Histoire de Charles XII* (1731). Somewhat obsessed with the Swedish King, Voltaire began work in 1727, corresponded with those who had known the King, continually added materials, and frequently rewrote his observations, with revised editions published in 1732, 1748, and 1751.

In part because he was dissatisfied with Voltaire's biography, King Charles's court priest Jöran Nordberg published his biography of the King, *Konung Carl den XII:tes historia* (1740). Nordberg knew both the King and his campaigns well, because he served in the army headquarters from 1703 to 1709. Nordberg's biography was translated into French and German.

Another Swedish near-contemporary historian was Carl Adlerfeld (1706–1747), the son of the Swedish officer Gustavus Adlerfeld (1671–1709) who fell at Poltava. The elder Adlerfeld wrote an anonymous treatise of the deeds of King Charles before he fell. Extracts were published in German as *Warhaffter Entwurff der Krieges-Thaten Carls XII* (1707). The original notes, when finally recovered after the war, provided the inspiration for the younger Adlerfeld to continue, and rewrite, his father's notes as a full biography. Published in French as *Histoire Militaire de Charles XII. Roi de Suede* by Gustavus Adlerfeld(1740), it was translated into German and also English, as *The Military History of Charles XII, King of Sweden* 1 (1740).[6] Incidentally, Adlerfeld the elder, who only joined the King's army after the Battle of Narva, heard the rumours about the number of Russians and, based on these, mistakenly claimed that 8,000 Swedes defeated 80,000 Russians at Narva, which caused the story to spread that the Swedes had been outnumbered 10 to 1.[7]

---

6   On the works of the two Adlerfelds, see Carl J. H. Hallendorff, 'Anmärkningar öfver G. Adlerfelts Histoire Militaire de Charles XII,' *Historisk tidskrift* 19 (1899), pp.177–98. Later research tends to give higher credence to the suggestion that the younger Adlerfelt only lightly edited his father's work.

7   Adlerfeld, *Military History of Charles XII*, pp.49 & 56.

Select Bibliography

Printed Contemporary Sources and Compilations

Anon. *Kårt dock sanfärdig berättelse om den glorieuse och i mannaminne oförlijklige seger hwarmed den aldrahögsta Gud den 20 november hafwer behagat wälsigna Kungl: Maij:tz af Swerige rättmätige vapn emot dess trolöse fiende Czaren af Muscow, Narva den 28 novemb. 1700*. The official and quite propagandistic Swedish report of the Battle of Narva

Anonymous, 'Wahrer Verlauf dessen, wass beij dem entsatz vor Narva passiret, wie solches ein Muscovitischer Captain von der Garde des Obristen Blumbergs Regiment Hr Theodorus Soltikov, welcher, an S. Königl. Maij:st in Pohlen abgeschicket, umständlich berichtet.' n.d. (December 1700). *Historisk Tidskrift* 21 (1901): 328–30. The official and, if possible, even more propagandistic Russian response to the official Swedish report, republished by Edvard Beckman

Anonymous, 'Letopisets 1700 goda.' *Letopis' zanyatiy Arkheograficheskoy kommissii, 1865–1866*, Vol. 4: 3. St Petersburg: Arkheograficheskaya kommissiya, 1868: 131–57

Anonymous *Utförlig Berättelse huruledes Kongl. Mayttz trogne Province Ingermanland .... blifwit medh ett orättmätigt Krijgh anfallen; Enkannerl:n Fästningarne Narven och Ivangorod, medh en Starck Fientelig Hähr omkringrände, och utj egen Persohn belägrade; Uthaff Hans Kongl. Mayttz Trolöse Fiende Zahren af Muscou: Med allt hwad som derwid utifrån Begynnelsen till ändan förelupit. Journal-wijs Författad och Sammandragen*. January 1701. Report based on journal notes compiled under the leadership of the commandant of Narva, Henning Rudolph Horn

Anonymous (Gustavus Adlerfeld). *Warhaffter Entwurff der Krieges-Thaten Carls XII. Königes von Schweden. Worin was Merckwürdiges in diesem Kriege vorgelauffen und passiret, biss an den Alt-Ranstädtischen Frieden beschrieben ist. Aus einem in diesem Kriege gehaltenen Journal extrahirt und ausgezogen* (Np [Hamburg?], 1707)

Anonymous, *Zhurnal ili Podennaya zapiska, blazhennyya i vechnodostoynyya pamyati gosudarya imperatora Petra Velikago s 1698 goda dazhe do zaklyucheniya neyshtatskago mira*, 2 volumes (St Petersburg:

Imperatorskaya akademiya nauk, 1770–1772). First printed edition of the above

Anonymous, *Journal de Pierre le Grand depuis l'année 1698, jusqu'à la conclusion de la paix de Nystadt*, 2 volumes (London: 1772), First printed edition of the above in French

Adlerfeld, M. Gustave, *Histoire Militaire de Charles XII. Roi de Suede: Depuis l'an 1700 jusqu'à la Bataille de Pultowa en 1709, écrite par ordre exprès de Sa Majesté*. (Amsterdam: Wettstein & Smith, 1740)

Adlerfeld, Gustavus, *The Military History of Charles XII, King of Sweden*, 3 volumes (London: J. and P. Knapton, 1740)

Barohn, Simon Daniel. *Karolinska krigares dagböcker jämte andra samtida skrifter* 12. Lund: Gleerup, 1918: pp.371–8. Cf. Quennerstedt, August, for the entire series of Carolean diaries

Beskrovnyy, L. G. (ed.). *Severnaya voyna 1700–1721 gg. - Sbornik dokumentov 1: 1700–1709* (Moscow: Ministerstvo Vnutrennikh Del (MVD) RF/Kuchkovo pole, 2009)

Cederhielm, Josias. *Karolinska Krigares Dagböcker Jämte Andra Samtida Skrifter* 8 (Lund: Gleerup,1913), pp.137–257

Cederhielm, Josias (Folke Wernstedt, ed.) 'Josias Cederhielms dagboksanteckningar 1700–1706 (1709)'. *Karolinska Förbundets Årsbok* 1925: 53-177

Cotossichin [Kotoshikhin], Grigori Carpofsson. *Beskrifning om muschofsche Rijkets Staat* (Stockholm: Ljus, 1908)

Cronstedt, Carl. Bref ... *Handlingar rörande Skandinaviens Historia* 19 (Stockholm: A. Wiborg, 1834) 401–4

Decker, Elis. 'Specification på de Ryske Trophéer, som äro tagne wid Narva d. 20 November 1700 och efter Hans Excell. Hr General-Feldtygmästaren Siöblads Ordres af Lieutenanten Elis Delcker efter Svensk Måttstock visiterade.' *Handlingar rörande til Konung Carl XII: s historia* 4 (Stockholm: Zacharias Hæggström, 1826), 214–15

Gordon, Alexander, of Auchintoul, *The History of Peter the Great, Emperor of Russia: To Which is Prefixed, A Short General History of the Country, From the Rise of That Monarchy; and an Account of the Author's Life*, 2 volumes (Aberdeen: F. Douglas and W. Murray, 1755)

Hallart, Ludwig Nicolaus von, *Das Tagebuch des Generals von Hallart über die Belagerung und Schlacht von Narva 1700* (Reval: Franz Kluge, 1894). Published by Friedrich Bienemann.

Hallendorff, Carl (ed.), *Karl XII i Ukraina: En karolins berättelse* (Stockholm: Bröderna Lagerström, 1915). A journal attributed to Captain Peter Schönström

Nordberg, Jöran Andersson, *Konung Carl den XII: tes Historia*, 2 volumes (Stockholm: Peter Momma, 1740)

Kelch, Christian, *Liefländische Historia 2: Continuation 1690 bis 1706*. (Dorpat: Verlag von Schnakenburg, 1875)

Koskull, Anders, *Karolinska krigares dagböcker jämte andra samtida skrifter* 6 (Lund: Gleerup, 1912), 299–338

Kozlov, Sergey Aleksandrovich, 'Okopnyye pis'ma russkikh soldat 1700 g.' *Istoriya Rossii do XX veka: Novyye podkhody k izucheniyu* (St Petersburg: Istoricheskaya illyustratsiya, 2008), 201–13

Maykova, Tat'yana Sergeyevna (ed.), *Sveyskoy voyny (Podennaya zapiska Petra Velikogo)*, 2 volumes (Moscow: Krug, 2004)

Palmquist, Erik, *Några observationer angående Ryssland, sammanfattade av Erik Palmquist år 1674* (Moscow: Lomonosov, 2012)

Posse, Carl Magnus (Emil Hildebrand ed.), 'Ur frih. Carl Magnus Posses korrespondens.' *Historisk Tidskrift* 2 (1882): 81–94.

Quennerstedt, August (ed.), *Karolinska krigares dagböcker jämte andra samtida skrifter*. (Lund: Gleerup, 12 vols., 1901–1921)

Sperling, C. H. P. *Karolinska krigares dagböcker jämte andra samtida skrifter* 3. (Lund: Gleerup, 1907), 1–59

Stenbock, Magnus. (Carl Magnus Stenbock, ed.) *Magnus Stenbock och Eva Oxenstierna: En brefväxling* (Stockholm: P. A. Norstedt & Söner, 2 vols., 1913–1914)

Stiernhöök, Olof (Samuel E. Bring, ed.), 'Drabanten och kaptenen vid Lifgardet Olof Stiernhööks journal 1700–1703' (Lund: Karolinska Förbundets Årsbok, 1912) 315–408

Troupitzen, Lorentz von, *Kriegs Kunst: Nach Königlicher Schwedischer Manier eine Compagny zurichten, in Regiment, Zug- vnd Schlacht-Ordnung zubringen, zum Ernst Anzuführen, Zugebrauchen, vnd in Essewürcklich, Zuunterhalten* (Frankfurt-am-Main: Matthaeus Merian, 1633)

Weide, Adam, *Voinskiy ustav, sostavlennyy i posvyashchennyy Petru Velikomu Generalom Weide, v 1698 godu* (St Petersburg: Voyennaya Tipografiya, 1841). Weide's instruction for the Russian infantry, written in 1698

Wisocki-Hochmuth, Ludwig, *Karolinska Krigares Dagböcker Jämte Andra Samtida Skrifter* 2 (Lund: Gleerup, 1903), 101–214

Wrangel, Carl Gustav (Samuel E. Bring, ed.), 'Några anteckningar om och af generalmajoren och kaptenlöjtnanten vid drabanterna Karl Wrangel,' *Karolinska Förbundets Årsbok* 1910: 112–53

Later Studies

Åberg, Alf, and Göte Göransson. *Karoliner* (Stockholm: Trevi, 1976.)

Alm, Josef, *Eldhandvapen 1: Från deras tidigaste förekomst till slaglåsets allmänna införande* (Stockholm: Rediviva, 1976)

Alm, Josef, *Arméns eldhandvapen förr och nu.* (Stockholm: Kungl. Armémuseum, 1953)

Armémuseum. *Segerns pris / The Prize of Victory: Narva 1700.* (Stockholm: Armémuseum, n.d. (2018))

Artéus, Gunnar. *Karolinsk och Europeisk Stridstaktik 1700–1712.* (Lidköping: Exlibria, 1972)

Bazarova, Tat'yana Anatol'yevna. '"Chinit' otpor bodro bezo vsyakiye robosti": Zapisnaya kniga ukazov novgorodskogo gubernatora A. I. Repnina 1700–1701 gg.' *Novgorodskiy istoricheskiy sbornik* 16 (26) (2016): 377–415

Beckman, Edvard. 'Några anteckningar om slaget vid Narva,' *Historisk Tidskrift* 21 (1901): 317–32

Bengtsson, Frans G., *Karl XII:s levnad* (Stockholm: Norstedt/Månpocket, 1992)

Chirkin, Sergey Aleksandrovich, 'Military Actions at Narva in 1700 According to the Memoirs of Swedish Warriors' *RUDN Journal of Russian History* 21: 3 (August 2022): 384–93

Ericson Wolke, Lars. *The Swedish Army in the Great Northern War 1700–21: Organisation, Equipment, Campaigns and Uniforms* (Warwick: Helion & Co., 2018)

Fredholm von Essen, Michael. *Muscovy's Soldiers: The Emergence of the Russian Army 1462–1689* (Warwick: Helion & Co., 2018)

Fredholm von Essen, Michael, *Charles XI's War: The Scanian War between Sweden and Denmark, 1675–1679* (Warwick: Helion & Co., 2019)

Fredholm von Essen, Michael, *Lion from the North*, 2 volumes (Warwick: Helion & Co., 2020)

Fredholm von Essen, Michael, *Charles X's Wars*, 3 volumes (Warwick: Helion & Co., 2021–2023)

Fredholm von Essen, Michael, *Sweden's War in Muscovy, 1609–1617: The Relief of Moscow and Conquest of Novgorod* (Warwick: Helion & Co., 2024)

Generalstaben. *Karl XII på slagfältet: Karolinsk slagledning sedd mot bakgrunden av taktikens utveckling från äldsta tider*, 4 vol. (Stockholm: P. A. Norstedt & Söner, 1918–1919)

Golovanova, Marina, 'Flags Dating Back to 1700 in the Documents From the Russian State Archive of Ancient Acts,' Karin Tetteris (ed.). *In Hoc Signo Vinces: The Vexillological Seminar, Stockholm 2011 & 2013* (Stockholm: Armémuseum, 2016), 15–19

Grimberg, Carl, *Svenska folkets underbara öden 4: Karl XI:s och Karl XII:s tid t.o.m. år 1709* (Stockholm: Norstedt & Söner, 1922)

Hårdstedt, Martin. 'Narva 1700.' Lars Ericson, Martin Hårdstedt, Per Iko, Ingvar Sjöblom, and Gunnar Åselius. *Svenska slagfält*. (np: Wahlström & Widstrand, 2003), 254–61

Hattendorf, John B. et al. (eds), *Charles XII: Warrior King* (np: Karwansaray, 2018)

Höglund, Lars-Eric, *Den Karolinska Arméns Uniformer under Stora Nordiska Kriget*, 2nd Edn (Karlstad: Acedia Press, 1996)

Höglund, Lars-Eric; and Åke Sallnäs, *Stora Nordiska Kriget 1700–1721: Fanor och uniformer* (Karlstad: Acedia Press, 2000)

Isberg, Alvin, 'Propaganda och fakta om slaget vid Narva,' Karolinska förbundets årsbok 1963: 111–40

Jonasson, Gustaf (ed.), *Historia kring Karl XII* (Stockholm: Wahlström & Widstrand, 1964)

Knarrström, Bo, *Slagfältet: Om bataljen vid Landskrona 1677 och fynden från den första arkeologiska undersökningen av ett svenskt slagfält* (Saltsjö-Duvnäs: Efron& Dotter, 2006)

Knarrström, Bo; Patrik Nilsson; Ulf Sundberg; and Bo Sunnefeldt. *De fruktade ingen förutom Gud: Karolinska armén*. np: SMB, 2023

SELECT BIBLIOGRAPHY

Laidre, Margus. *Segern vid Narva: Början till en stormakts fall* (Stockholm: Naturoch Kultur, 1996). With editions also published in Estonian and Russian

Larsson, Anders. *Karolinska uniformer och munderingar åren 1700 till 1721: Samt vissa handgrepp och exercise* (Östersund: Jengel, 2022)

Lewenhaupt, Adam. *Karl XII:s officerare: Biografiska anteckningar*. Stockholm. P. A. Norstedt & Söner, 1920–1921

Liljegren, Bengt. *Karl XII: En biografi* (Lund: Historiska Media, 2000)

Manoylenko, Yuriy Yevgen'yevich. '"V nachale slavnykh del": Podgotovitel'nyy etap petrovskikh reform artillerii.' *Russkiy 'bog voyny': Issledovaniya i istochniki po istorii otechestvennoy artillerii* (St Petersburg: Istoriyavoyennogodela, 2017), 398–417

Megorsky, Boris, *The Russian Army in the Great Northern War 1700–21: Organisation, Materiel, Training and Combat Experience, Uniforms* (Warwick: Helion & Co., 2018)

Megorsky, Boris, *Peter the Great's Revenge: The Russian Siege of Narva in 1704.* (Warwick: Helion & Co., 2018)

Nilsson, J. P., *Karl XII på slagfältet: Från Narva till Poltava och Fredriksten* (np: SMB, 2018)

Petrelli, Teodor Johannes, and Axel Lagrelius, *Narvatroféer i Statens trofésamling: Några blad vid Nordiska Museets Öppnande* (Uppsala: Almqvist & Wiksell, 1907)

Petrelli, Teodor Johannes, and Axel Lagrelius. *Tillägg till Narvatroféer i Statens trofésamling* (Uppsala: Almqvist & Wiksell, 1907)

Petri, Gustaf, *Kungl. Första livgrenadjärregementets historia 3:Östgöta infanteriregemente under Karl XI och Karl XII* (Stockholm: Norstedt& Söner, 1958)

Petrov, Aleksandr Vasil'yevich, 'Narvskaya operatsiya.' *Voyennyy sbornik* 7 (1872): 5–38

Petrov, Aleksandr Vasil'yevich, *Gorod Narva, yego proshloye i dostoprimechatel'nosti v svyazi s istoriyey uprocheniya russkago gospodstva na Baltiyskom poberezh'ye, 1223–1900* (St Petersburg: Ministerstvo Vnutrennikh Del (MVD), 1901)

Pihlström, Anton, *Kungl. Dalregementets historia*, 6 vols (Stockholm: P. A. Norstedt & Söner, 1902–1938)

Rabinovich, Moisey Davydovich, *Polki Petrovskoy Armii, 1698–1725: Kratkiy spravochnik.* (Moscow: Sovetskaya Rossiya, 1977)

Schorr, Daniel A., and Lars-Eric Höglund. *Swedish Colors and Standards of the Great Northern War 1700–1721*, 2nd edn, (Karlstad: Acedia Press, 1994)

Seitz, Heribert, *Svärdet och värjan som armévapen* (Stockholm: Kungl. Armémuseum, 1955)

Seitz, Heribert, 'Den karolinska värjans taktiska betydelse för kavalleriet.' *Ny Militär Tidskrift* 8 (1944): 1–12

Shamenkov, Sergey, *Charles XII's Karoliners 1: The Swedish Infantry and Artillery of the Great Northern War, 1700–1721* (Warwick: Helion & Co., 2022)

Shamenkov, Sergey, *Charles XII's Karoliners 2: The Swedish Cavalry of the Great Northern War, 1700–1721* (Warwick: Helion & Co., 2023)

Shamenkov, Sergey I, 'Vengerskoye Plat'ye Pekhotnykh Polkov Armii Petra Velikogo, 1699-1703,' *Istoriya voyennogo dela: Issledovaniya i istochniki* 1 (2012): 421–63

Shamenkov, Sergey I, 'Vengerskoye Plat'ye Pekhotnykh Polkov Armii Petra Velikogo, 1699–1703.' *Istoriya voyennogo dela: Issledovaniya i istochniki* 3 (2013): 466–90

Svensson, Alex (ed.), *Karl XII som fältherre*. (Stockholm: SMB, 2001) An anthology of old and new that gives readers who understand Swedish an excellent overview of the conflicting interpretations of King Charles over time

Törnquist, Leif. *Infanteriets fanor m/1686* (Stockholm: Svenska vapenhistoriska sällskapet, Nya serien 30, 2015)

Törnquist, Leif, *Kavalleriets standar och dragonfanor m/1686*. (Stockholm: Svenska vapenhistoriska sällskapet, Nya serien 32, 2017)

Ulfhielm, Hans (ed.), *Kungl. artilleriet: Karl XI:s och Karl XII:s tid* (Stockholm: Militärhistoriska förlaget 1993)

Ustryalov, Nikolay Gerasimovich, *Istoriya Tsarstvovaniya Petra Velikago* (St. Petersburg: Tipografiya II otdeleniya sobstvennoy Ye. I. V. Kantselyarii, 6 vols., 1858–1863)

Villius, Hans (ed.), *Karl XII: Ögonvittnen* (Stockholm: Wahlström & Widstrand, 1960, 1995)

Velikanov, Vladimir S, 'K voprosu ob organizatsii i chislennosti russkoy armii v Narvskom pokhode 1700 goda.' *Voyna i oruzhiye* 2:1 : *Novyye issledovaniya i materialy*. (St Petersburg: VIMAIViVS, 2011), 130–43

Velikanov, Vladimir S, 'Reorganizatsiya ratnykh lyudey novgorodskogo razryada v 1700–1707 godakh.' *Voyna i oruzhiye* 3:1 : *Novyye issledovaniya i materialy* (St Petersburg: VIMAIViVS, 2012) 216–30

Velikanov, Vladimir S, 'K voprosu o sostoyanii russkoy armii posle Narvskogo porazheniya (zima 1700–1701 godov)'. *Voyna i oruzhiye* 7:2 : *Novyye issledovaniya i materialy* (St Petersburg: VIMAIViVS, 2016) 26–42

Velikanov, Vladimir S.; and Aleksey N. Lobin, 'Russkaya Artilleriya v Narvskom pokhode, 1700.' *Staryy Zeughaus* 48 (4, 2012): 3–10

Wennerholm, Bertil, 'Russian Banners as Swedish Trophies from Narva 1700: A New Attempt at Identification.' Karin Tetteris (ed.). *In Hoc Signo Vinces: The Vexillological Seminar, Stockholm 2011 & 2013* (Stockholm: Armémuseum, 2016), 31–37

Wernstedt, Folke, *Kungl. Svea livgardes Historia 4: 1660–1718* (Stockholm: Stiftelsen för Svea livgardes historia, 1954)

Biographical Databases

Murdoch, Steve; and Alexia Grosjean. *The Scotland, Scandinavia and Northern European Biographical Database* (SSNE). Website: www.st-andrews.ac.uk/history/ssne/

Riksarkivet (Swedish National Archives). *Svenskt biografiskt lexikon* (SBL). Website: sok.riksarkivet.se/SBL/

About the Author

Professor Michael Fredholm von Essen is an historian and former military analyst who has published extensively on the history of Eurasia and has lectured around the world, both at conferences and as a visiting professor. He has published a large number of books, including *The Goths* 1–2 (Society of Ancients, 2021–2022); *Afghanistan Beyond the Fog of War* (NIAS Press, 2018); *Transnational Organized Crime and Jihadist Terrorism: Russian-Speaking Networks in Western Europe* (Routledge, 2017); numerous articles in *Slingshot*, the journal of the Society of Ancients, and *Arquebusier*, the journal of the Pike and Shot Society; and many books for Helion & Company.

About the Artist

Sergey Shamenkov graduated from the Academy of Arts in Lviv. He is a sculptor, author, and illustrator specializing in uniformology, military history, and costume history. His principal area of interest is the study of the Swedish army of Charles XII. When not painting, he is involved in reenactments, depicting Ukrainian and Swedish units of the 17th and 18th centuries. Sergey has illustrated many Helion titles.

Other titles in the Century of the Soldier series

No 28 **Muscovy's Soldiers:** *The Emergence of the Russian Army 1462–1689*

No 29 **Home and Away:** *The British Experience of War 1618–1721*

No 30 **From Solebay to the Texel:** *The Third Anglo-Dutch War, 1672–1674*

No 31 **The Battle of Killiecrankie:** *The First Jacobite Campaign, 1689–1691*

No 32 **The Most Heavy Stroke:** *The Battle of Roundway Down 1643*

No 33 **The Cretan War (1645–1671):** *The Venetian-Ottoman Struggle in the Mediterranean*

No 34 **Peter the Great's Revenge:** *The Russian Siege of Narva in 1704*

No 35 **The Battle Of Glenshiel:** *The Jacobite Rising in 1719*

No 36 **Armies And Enemies Of Louis XIV:** *Volume 1 - Western Europe 1688–1714: France, Britain, Holland*

No 37 **William III's Italian Ally:** *Piedmont and the War of the League of Augsburg 1683–1697*

No 38 **Wars and Soldiers in the Early Reign of Louis XIV:** *Volume 1 - The Army of the United Provinces of the Netherlands, 1660–1687*

No 39 **In The Emperor's Service:** *Wallenstein's Army, 1625–1634*

No 40 **Charles XI's War:** *The Scanian War Between Sweden and Denmark, 1675–1679*

No 41 **The Armies and Wars of The Sun King 1643-1715:** *Volume 1: The Guard of Louis XIV*

No 42 **The Armies Of Philip IV Of Spain 1621–1665:** *The Fight For European Supremacy*

No 43 **Marlborough's Other Army:** *The British Army and the Campaigns of the First Peninsular War, 1702–1712*

No 44 **The Last Spanish Armada:** *Britain And The War Of The Quadruple Alliance, 1718–1720*

No 45 **Essential Agony:** *The Battle of Dunbar 1650*

No 46 **The Campaigns of Sir William Waller**

No 47 **Wars and Soldiers in the Early Reign of Louis XIV:** *Volume 2 - The Imperial Army, 1660–1689*

No 48 **The Saxon Mars and His Force:** *The Saxon Army During The Reign Of John George III 1680–1691*

No 49 **The King's Irish:** *The Royalist Anglo-Irish Foot of the English Civil War*

No 50 **The Armies and Wars of the Sun King 1643-1715:** *Volume 2: The Infantry of Louis XIV*

No 51 **More Like Lions Than Men:** *Sir William Brereton and the Cheshire Army of Parliament, 1642–46*

No 52 **I Am Minded to Rise:** *The Clothing, Weapons and Accoutrements of the Jacobites from 1689 to 1719*

No 53 **The Perfection of Military Discipline:** *The Plug Bayonet and the English Army 1660–1705*

No 54 **The Lion From the North:** *The Swedish Army During the Thirty Years War: Volume 1, 1618–1632*

No 55 **Wars and Soldiers in the Early Reign of Louis XIV:** *Volume 3 - The Armies of the Ottoman Empire 1645–1718*

No 56 **St. Ruth's Fatal Gamble:** *The Battle of Aughrim 1691 and the Fall Of Jacobite Ireland*

No 57 **Fighting for Liberty:** *Argyll & Monmouth's Military Campaigns against the Government of King James, 1685*

No 58 **The Armies and Wars of the Sun King 1643-1715:** *Volume 3: The Cavalry of Louis XIV*

No 59 **The Lion From the North:** *The Swedish Army During the Thirty Years War: Volume 2, 1632–1648*

No 60 **By Defeating My Enemies:** *Charles XII of Sweden and the Great Northern War 1682–1721*

No 61 **Despite Destruction, Misery and Privations...:** *The Polish Army in Prussia during the war against Sweden 1626–1629*

No 62 **The Armies of Sir Ralph Hopton:** *The Royalist Armies of the West 1642–46*

No 63 **Italy, Piedmont, and the War of the Spanish Succession 1701–1712**

No 64 **'Cannon played from the great fort':** *Sieges in the Severn Valley during the English Civil War 1642–1646*

No 65 **Carl Gustav Armfelt and the Struggle for Finland During the Great Northern War**

No 66 **In the Midst of the Kingdom:** *The Royalist War Effort in the North Midlands 1642–1646*

No 67 **The Anglo-Spanish War 1655–1660:** *Volume 1: The War in the West Indies*

No 68 **For a Parliament Freely Chosen:** *The Rebellion of Sir George Booth, 1659*

No 69 **The Bavarian Army During the Thirty Years War 1618–1648:** *The Backbone of the Catholic League (revised second edition)*

No 70 **The Armies and Wars of the Sun King 1643–1715:** *Volume 4: The War of the Spanish Succession, Artillery, Engineers and Militias*

No 71 **No Armour But Courage:** *Colonel Sir George Lisle, 1615–1648 (Paperback reprint)*

No 72 **The New Knights:** *The Development of Cavalry in Western Europe, 1562–1700*

No 73 **Cavalier Capital:** *Oxford in the English Civil War 1642–1646 (Paperback reprint)*

No 74 **The Anglo-Spanish War 1655–1660:** *Volume 2: War in Jamaica*

No 75 **The Perfect Militia:** *The Stuart Trained Bands of England and Wales 1603–1642*

No 76 **Wars and Soldiers in the Early Reign of Louis XIV:** *Volume 4 - The Armies of Spain 1659–1688*

No 77 **The Battle of Nördlingen 1634:** *The Bloody Fight Between Tercios and Brigades*

No 78 **Wars and Soldiers in the Early Reign of Louis XIV:** *Volume 5 - The Portuguese Army 1659–1690*

No 79 **We Came, We Saw, God Conquered:** *The Polish-Lithuanian Commonwealth's military effort in the relief of Vienna, 1683*

No 80 **Charles X's Wars:** *Volume 1 - Armies of the Swedish Deluge, 1655–1660*

No 81 **Cromwell's Buffoon:** *The Life and Career of the Regicide, Thomas Pride (Paperback reprint)*

No 82 **The Colonial Ironsides:** *English Expeditions under the Commonwealth and Protectorate, 1650–1660*

No 83 **The English Garrison of Tangier:** *Charles II's Colonial Venture in the Mediterranean, 1661–1684*

No 84 **The Second Battle of Preston, 1715:** *The Last Battle on English Soil*

No 85 **To Settle the Crown:** *Waging Civil War in Shropshire, 1642–1648 (Paperback reprint)*

No 86 **A Very Gallant Gentleman:** *Colonel Francis Thornhagh (1617–1648) and the Nottinghamshire Horse*

No 87 **Charles X's Wars:** *Volume 2 - The Wars in the East, 1655–1657*

No 88 **The Shōgun's Soldiers:** *The Daily Life of Samurai and Soldiers in Edo Period Japan, 1603–1721 Volume 1*

No 89 **Campaigns of the Eastern Association:** *The Rise of Oliver Cromwell, 1642–1645*

No 90 **The Army of Occupation in Ireland 1603–42:** *Defending the Protestant Hegemony*

No 91 **The Armies and Wars of the Sun King 1643–1715:** *Volume 5: Buccaneers and Soldiers in the Americas*

No 92 **New Worlds, Old Wars:** *The Anglo-American Indian Wars 1607–1678*

No 93 **Against the Deluge:** *Polish and Lithuanian Armies During the War Against Sweden 1655–1660*

No 94 **The Battle of Rocroi:** *The Battle, the Myth and the Success of Propaganda*

No 95 **The Shōgun's Soldiers:** *The Daily Life of Samurai and Soldiers in Edo Period Japan, 1603–1721 Volume 2*

No 96 **Science of Arms: the Art of War in the Century of the Soldier 1672–1699:** *Volume 1: Preparation for War and the Infantry*

No 97 **Charles X's Wars:** *Volume 3 - The Danish Wars 1657–1660*

No 98 **Wars and Soldiers in the Early Reign of Louis XIV:** *Volume 6 - Armies of the Italian States 1660–1690 Part 1*

No 99 **Dragoons and Dragoon Operations in the British Civil Wars, 1638–1653**

No 100 **Wars and Soldiers in the Early Reign of Louis XIV:** *Volume 6 - Armies of the Italian States 1660–1690 Part 2*

No 101 **1648 and All That:** *The Scottish Invasions of England, 1648 and 1651: Proceedings of the 2022 Helion and Company 'Century of the Soldier' Conference*

No 102 **John Hampden and the Battle of Chalgrove:** *The Political and Military Life of Hampden and his Legacy*

No 103 **The City Horse:** *London's militia cavalry during the English Civil War, 1642–1660*

No 104 **The Battle of Lützen 1632:** *A Reassessment*

No 105 **Monmouth's First Rebellion:** *The Later Covenanter Risings, 1660–1685*

No 106 **Raw Generals and Green Soldiers:** *Catholic Armies in Ireland 1641–1643*

No 107 **Polish, Lithuanian and Cossack armies versus the might of the Ottoman Empire**

No 108 **Soldiers and Civilians, Transport and Provisions:** *Early Modern Military Logistics and Supply Systems During the British Civil Wars, 1638-1653*

No 109 **Batter their walls, gates and Forts:** *The Proceedings of the 2022 English Civil War Fortress Symposium*

No 110 **The Town Well Fortified:** *The Fortresses of the Civil Wars in Britain, 1639-1660*

No 111 **Crucible of the Jacobite '15:** *The Battle of Sheriffmuir 1715*

No 112 **Charles XII's Karoliners Volume 2** - *The Swedish Cavalry of the Great Northern War 1700-1721*

No 113 **Wars and Soldiers in the Early Reign of Louis XIV:** *Volume 7 - Armies of the German States 1655–1690 Part 1*

No 114 **The First British Army 1624–1628:** *The Army of the Duke of Buckingham (Revised Edition)*

No 115 **The Army of Transylvania (1613–1690):** *War and military organization from the 'golden age' of the Principality to the Habsburg conquest*

No 116 **The Army of the Manchu Empire:** *The Conquest Army and the Imperial Army of Qing China, 1600–1727*

No 117 **French Armies of The Thirty Years' War 1618–48**

No 118 **Soldiers' Clothing of the Early 17th Century:** *Britain and Western Europe 1618–1660*

No 119 **Novelty and Change:** *Proceedings of the 2023 Helion and ompany 'Century of the Soldier' Conference*

No 120 **Peter The Great's Disastrous Defeat:** *The Swedish Victory at Narva, 1700*

SERIES SPECIALS:

No 1 **Charles XII's Karoliners:** *Volume 1: The Swedish Infantry & Artillery of the Great Northern War 1700–1721*